D1797354

A.S. Bhalla is a special professor at the School of Contemporary Chinese Studies, University of Nottingham and was formerly Fellow of Sidney Sussex College, Cambridge and Special Adviser to the President of International Development Research Centre (IDRC), Ottawa. Earlier he had a distinguished career in the United Nations Civil Service. He has held academic positions at Cambridge, Oxford, Yale and Manchester. He is the author of *Poverty and Exclusion of Minorities in China and India*, *Royal Tombs of India* and *Poverty among Immigrant Children in Europe* among other publications.

MONUMENTS, POWER AND POVERTY IN INDIA

From Ashoka to the Raj

A.S. Bhalla

BLOOMSBURY ACADEMIC
LONDON • NEW YORK • OXFORD • NEW DELHI • SYDNEY

BLOOMSBURY ACADEMIC
Bloomsbury Publishing Plc
50 Bedford Square, London, WC1B 3DP, UK
1385 Broadway, New York, NY 10018, USA

BLOOMSBURY, BLOOMSBURY ACADEMIC and the Diana logo
are trademarks of Bloomsbury Publishing Plc

First published 2015 by I.B. Tauris & Co. Ltd.
Paperback edition first published by Bloomsbury Academic 2020

A catalogue record for this book is available from the British Library.

A catalog record for this book is available from the Library of Congress.

ISBN: HB: 978-1-7845-3087-7
PB: 978-1-3501-5469-8

Series: International Library of Colonial History, vol 19

Typeset by GS Typesetting Services

To find out more about our authors and books visit
www.bloomsbury.com and sign up for our newsletters.

In memory of my father (a judge during the British Raj) whose rare collection of 100-year-old picture postcards of Imperial India and London provided the main illustrations for this book

The people love show and want to be
impressed by their rulers and feel awe
for them. A great ruler must be like
the sun – too dazzling to look upon but
the source of all light and hope and
warmth without whom existence would
seem impossible.

> Akbar (1556–1605), cited in Alex
> Rutherford, *Empire of the Mughal:
> The Tainted Throne*, 2012

The glory of our blood and state
Are shadows not substantial things;
There is no armour against fate;
Death lay his icy hands on kings;
Sceptre and Crown must tumble down,
And in the dust be equal made
With the poor crooked scythe and spade.

> James Shirley, *Death the Leveller,
> in The Contention of Ajax and
> Ulysses*, 1659

My name is Ozymandias, king of kings:
Look on my works, ye Mighty and despair!
Nothing beside remains. Round the decay
Of that colossal wreck, boundless and bare
The lone and level sands stretch far away.

> Percy Bysshe Shelley, *Ozymandias*, 1817

Contents

Part IV Conclusion

List of Illustrations

Figures

ix

Colour Plate Section

Tables

Chart

Preface

India has been under foreign rule for centuries, starting from the twelfth century when Muslims established the Slave Dynasty there. The British East India Company which began as a commercial enterprise, soon developed political and military designs and ambitions. The British defeated the Mughals and started ruling India on behalf of the Imperial Crown in London. They also defeated the Sikhs in two wars which ended this brief period of domestic rule after the collapse of the Mughal Empire.

The book presents an illustrated account of India and its royal monuments under different rulers. The long span of foreign rule is divided into three parts: (1) The Hindu empires (Mauryan and Gupta), kingdoms (for example, Vijayanagar in the south and Ranjit Singh's Sikh kingdom in the north) and princely states such as Baroda, Patiala and Hyderabad; (2) The Mughal Empire, the pre-Mughal Delhi Sultanates and the Deccan Sultanates, and (3) the British Raj.

It contrasts the wealth and splendour of emperors and kings with the abject poverty of their subjects. It discusses royal vainglory, power and ostentation under different empires, and considers whether some rulers were less ostentatious and more benevolent than others, and if they responded to people's economic and social needs as well as religious sentiments.

Illustrations in the book come from several different sources. The first is a rare collection of 100-year-old picture postcards of pre-Mughal, Mughal and British India which I inherited from my late father. He made this collection through generous help from two friends, who spent several years in London before World War I. The collection of postcards was a popular hobby at the time as photography was not so common. The second source consists of photographs of John Burke and William Baker taken during the period 1860–1900 and obtained from different sources. The third source is the British Library and the Victoria and Albert Museum in London which kindly supplied several images. Finally, I have used my own photographs of ancient monuments (in Agra and Mandu, for example) taken during several trips to India from 2000 to 2006.

I owe a debt of gratitude to a number of friends and relatives: Parminder Bedi who contributed a note on Lawrence School, Sanawar (Himachal Pradesh, India), where he studied in the 'fifties; Harpreet Duggal, a former student of Mayo College, Ajmer (1983–5), who contributed a write-up on the College. As a former pupil of the College, he was instrumental in obtaining old College photographs; Vijay Bhalla who provided information on Doon School where he studied in the early fifties; Ravi Ahooja who obtained photographs of a number of the surviving monuments of the British Raj in Old Delhi; Rajagopalan Sampatkumar and Dilip and Shobhana Lahiri who engaged in stimulating discussions about Indian history; Ingvar Åhman who helped with the scanning and editing of many images. Others who helped in identifying Mughal and British monuments of the Raj in Mumbai (Bombay), Kolkata (Calcutta), New Delhi and Chennai (Madras) are Atul and Sandhya Sondhi, Santoshi Arora and Dr M.S. Swaminathan and his colleagues. My wife, Praveen Bhalla, skilfully edited the entire manuscript in record time despite other pressing commitments.

Syed Babar Ali, a student at Aitchison College, Lahore, Pakistan (1934–43), and a current Member of the Governing Body of the College, clarified many points about the history of the School. Naveed Riaz (Lahore) and Noorjehan Bilgrami (Karachi) helped dig up old material and images from the British Raj relating to Lahore, Karachi, Peshawar, Quetta, and Rawalpindi. Ardeshir Marker of Quetta, who lives in Karachi, was most helpful in identifying several images of Quetta buildings dating back to the 1880s, most of which were destroyed in the 1935 earthquake but were later rebuilt.

Professor James Mayall, Fellow of Sidney Sussex College, Cambridge (and former Director of the Centre for International Studies, Cambridge University) kindly read Parts III and IV of the book and gave valuable comments. Professor Lindsay Greer, Fellow of the same College and former Head, Department of Materials Science and Metallurgy, Cambridge University, provided useful material and references, and Nicholas Rogers, Archivist, Sidney Sussex College, Cambridge dug up useful historical information from old archives. Hemani Singh, an architect based in Gurgaon, India, reviewed Chapters 1 to 4 and 10 and suggested improvements. Khawaja Khalid (Murree, Pakistan) reviewed the draft on Murree in Chapter 7. Fariq Aijazuddin, Principal of Aitchison College, Lahore, provided valuable inputs to the discussion of this school in Chapter 8, and gifted his book: *Aitchison College Lahore 1886–1986:The First Hundred Years*. Lindsay Greer, James Mayall and Gordon Johnson (former Master of Wolfson College, Cambridge) were a constant source of encouragement throughout my research.

Finally, I would like to thank the staff of the following libraries in Switzerland and the United Kingdom respectively for their tireless efforts in tracing old and rare books required for my research: History and History of Art Sections of the Library of Geneva University; the Library of Art and Archaeology of the City of Geneva; the Library of the University of Lausanne at Dorigny; and Cambridge University Library.

A.S. Bhalla
Commugny, Switzerland

Glossary

Achkan	A knee-length coat buttoned in front worn in India
Aigrette	A headdress consisting of a white egret's feather or other decoration such as a spray of gems
Ashrafi	A gold coin also called Mohur
Atrium	Open central court
Bangala	Sloping roofs
Baradari	Pavilion
Begum	Indian princess
Belvedere	Summer house
Bibi	Indian mistress
Burj	Tower
Campanile	Bell tower
Cenotaph	Monument to someone buried elsewhere
Chhajjas	Overhanging eaves
Chhatris	Domed kiosks on pillars
Chimney pot	Pipe at the top of a chimney narrowing the aperture and increasing the updraught
Chummery	Bachelors' accommodation; boarding house
Chunam	White polished stucco made from burnt seashells which when polished resembles marble
Civil Lines	Area outside a native city inhabited by British civilians
Cloister	Covered walk
Crore	Ten million
Dharamsala	Rest-house for pilgrims
Diwan-i-Am	Hall of Public Audience

Diwan-i-Khas	Hall of Private Audience
Durbar	Public audience of king or viceroy; court
Eurasian	Person of mixed descent; an Anglo-Indian
Garb Griha	Sanctum sanctorum, the most sacred part of a Hindu temple
Gend Khana	Racquet Court
Ghi/Ghee	Clarified butter
Gora sahibs	White men
Guldasta	Slender ornamental minaret (pinnacle) on a dome
Gumbad	Pre-Mughal tomb; dome
Gurdwara	Sikh temple
Hammam	Bath
Harem	Separate part of a Muslim household reserved for wives, concubines and female servants
Hookah	Water pipe or hubble-bubble
Howdah	Seat for the back of an elephant
Jali	Latticed stone screen, usually with an ornamental pattern
Jatakas	Stories of Buddha's former lives
Jaziya	Tax on non-Muslims
Kalassa	Pinnacle on top of a *shikhara* of a Hindu temple
Kama Sutra	Ancient Sanskrit treatise on the art of love and sexual technique
Khana	House; dwelling
Khind	Pass
Kiosk	Open pavilion
Lakh	Hundred thousand
Lal Bazaar	Red-light (brothel) area for Indian army regiments during the Raj
Lat	Pillar
Lingam	The phallus; male genitalia; symbolic form in which Hindu god Shiva is worshipped
Madrasa	Theological college
Mahout	A person who rides and tends an elephant
Maidan	Large open space often used as a parade ground
Mandir	Hindu temple
Mansabdar	Mughal nobleman and office holder

Marhi	Place at high altitude
Masjid	Mosque
Memsahib	European (English) lady in India
Mihrab	The prayer-niche of a mosque which contains *qibla* indicating the direction of Mecca
Mofussil	Rural hinterland; countryside
Mohur	A gold coin used in pre-Mughal, Mughal and British India; also called 'Ashrafi'
Nabob	Person from Indian princely class; English corruption of the Hindustani *nawab*; in England used as a derogatory term for Englishmen returned from India
Nahar	Canal
Naib	A senior officer of the Delhi Sultan above the rank of Wazir
Naqqar Khana	Music Hall; place where drums are beaten
Nautch	Dance performance popular in the early nineteenth century
Nautch girl	Professional dancer and courtesan
Nawab	Viceroy or governor
Porte cochère	Porch for vehicles to pass through
Punkha	Fan
Qazi	A Muslim legal expert
Qibla (Kiblah)	The direction of the Kaaba (the sacred building of Mecca) to which Muslims turn at prayer
Raiyat	Peasantry; Landholder paying revenue to zamindars or to government
Residency	Official residence of the Resident
Resident	British Government agent, especially Governor-General's Representative at the court of an Indian (princely) state
Safaa	Turban
Sangha	Buddhist Order
Sanjeevni buti	Life-saving herb
Sati	Former Hindu practice of a widow immolating herself on her husband's funeral pyre
Sepoy	Indian soldier in the service of the British East India Company

Shamiana	Marquee
Shikhara	Temple spire
Sijda	Prostration before a Mughal emperor
Sola	An Indian swamp plant whose stems yield the pith used to make sola topis
Soneri	Golden
Stambha	Pillar
Syce	Groom
Takht	Throne
Tehkhana	Cool underground room
Tiffin	Luncheon
Topi	Hat, Helmet
Trabeated	Constructed with horizontal beams or lintels rather than arches
Venetian arch	Arch flanked by tall and narrow square openings
Veranda	Porch in front of a bungalow
Volute	The spiral scroll on an Ionic capital
Voussoir	Brick or wedge-shaped stone in an arch
Wazir	Prime minister
Yoni	Hindu vaginal symbol; usually represented cupping the Shiva lingam
Zamindar	Indian landowner
Zamindari	The system under which Indian zamindars held land
Zenana	Women's secluded quarters of a Muslim household; harem

Introduction

The head of a mighty Empire ought to conform himself to the prejudices of the country he rules over, and that the British in particular, ought to emulate the splendid works of the Princes of the House of Timur.

(Lord Valentia,[1] 1809)

Imperial India is not an abstract concept but a reality. Since time immemorial, India has been ruled by emperors, maharajas, sultans, British East India Company governors and, finally, the British Crown in London represented by Her Majesty's viceroys. The story of imperial India came to an end in August 1947 when the country became independent of foreign rule which had lasted 800 years, from the twelfth to twentieth century. During this period, India was ruled by Turks, Afghans, Mughals and the British.

Much has been written about these various empires and their grandiose monuments, and so does not warrant repetition. This book seeks to examine the vainglory and ostentation of different emperors and kings in the midst of the poverty and misery of ordinary citizens. However, well-documented information on the pomp and glory of the early empires and kingdoms is harder to find. The following are the main sources for piecing together that story: (i) literary sources, (ii) archaeological and architectural remains, (iii) accounts of foreign travellers, and (iv) inscriptions and numismatic sources. In varying degrees, this book relies on all these sources, but particularly on the first two listed here.

Empire and Imperialism

The creation of an empire generally involves the conquest and sub-jugation of one dominant state over a weaker state. This process of 'establishing and maintaining an empire' is called imperialism (Doyle, 1986:19).

The terms 'empire' and 'imperialism' conjure up both positive and negative emotions. On the positive side, empires have been defended for providing political and social stability, law and order, and scientific progress (Lal, 2002). On the negative side, they are associated with socioeconomic exploitation and oppression, racial hatred between the ruler and the ruled, concentration of wealth in the hands of a few, the subjugation of people through wars and brute force.

However, not all empires were created through military conquests alone. For example, the British Colonial Empire in India started in 1600 as a commercial venture of the British East India Company.

Different empires may be characterized by some or all of the following features:

(1) Territorial expansion through wars and alliances to demonstrate power and domination;
(2) centralization of political and military power;
(3) hierarchical power and authority;
(4) a political metropolitan centre and periphery as in the Roman, Ottoman and British empires; and
(5) concentration of wealth and ostentatious spending on monuments as symbols of imperial power and vainglory.

Empires may be global or national. Colas (2007:19) defines the former as having 'frontiers and boundaries, but no external borders', whereas national empires (for example, the Ashoka, Gupta or Mughal) were 'built on territorially exclusive borders'. They may rule both directly and indirectly. For example, the British ruled India directly from the metropolitan centre in Britain, but also indirectly through alliances with native Indian princes who were allowed autonomy as long as they remained loyal to the Crown.

Empires can be autocratic, totalitarian or benevolent. Were the three Indian empires – Hindu, Muslim and British despotic or benevolent?

Was their creation attributable to the victory of foreigners over the indigenous population? The Hindu empires of the Mauryas and Guptas did not involve foreign intervention. In this sense, they differed from the Muslim (especially the Mughal) and British empires whose creation involved military intervention and commercial interests respectively.

While the Hindu and Muslim empires in India were land- and revenue-based, the subsequent British Empire first began as a commercial operation of the East India Company (henceforth, the Company). Initially, it grabbed land through annexation, but later it became a revenue-extracting imperial power characterized by economic and trade relations between the metropolitan centre in Britain and the periphery in India. The earlier empires (Mughal, for example) were also engaged in long-distance trade with the West. Alam (1994) describes commercial and trade relations between the Mughals, Persians and Uzbeks, and Santen (1991) discusses a Mughal export promotion policy. But the Mughal Empire did not involve the kind of centre-periphery relationship associated with British colonialism. Colonialism was characterized by the export of raw materials from the periphery to the centre and the mobilization of Indian indentured labour across continents for the development of other colonies of the British Empire. This process reinforced Britain's imperial domination.

'Eurocentrics' view India under the Mughals as a case of 'oriental despotism' which is a rather exaggerated opinion. Hobson (2004:79–88) debunks the notion of 'oriental despotism' as a myth and presents eight anti-Eurocentric propositions in support of his argument.

Theme of the Book

The book highlights the vainglory and lavish spending on grandiose monuments as symbols of power which characterized all three major empires of India. In particular, it shows how the Hindu, Muslim and British rulers of India all indulged in grand displays of wealth in contrast to the poverty and misery of their subjects.

It attempts to compare and contrast the different styles of the rulers. For example, were ostentation and wasteful expenditure common to all empires or were some empires more benevolent than others? It seems that the Ashoka (Buddhist) and Gupta (Hindu) empires were less ostentatious, and more utilitarian and benevolent than the later empires. Ashoka built rock edicts and pillars throughout his kingdom to spread information about imperial tenets as an attempt at administrative expediency rather than vainglory. He and the subsequent Gupta emperors built temples (stupas) to promote religion and thus responded to people's spiritual needs and religious sentiments (Chapter 1). Thus not all the monuments they built were intended as symbols of their fame and glory.

However, some of the later Hindu rulers (for example, the Chandelas and the kings of Vijayanagar) built a large number of ornamental and elaborate temples in small and limited areas which may not have responded to the religious needs of their subjects. For example, the erotic temples of Khajuraho built by the Chandelas stand close to each other in one big garden. An extreme concentration of temples for a small population could hardly be considered a utilitarian project; it was more likely a display of extravagance and ostentation. Similarly, other chroniclers describe the splendour of the royal palace of Vijayanagar and the pomp and ceremony of its kings and queens.

The contribution of the Delhi sultans (Slaves, Tughluqs and Khaljis, for example) to architecture and infrastructure was significant, as exemplified by the Qutb Minar complex in Delhi, as well as the monuments of Daulatabad and Mandu in the Deccan (Chapter 2). The Deccan sultans (Bahmanis, Adil Shahis, Qutb Shahis and Asaf Jahis) also indulged in ostentatious building projects (Chapter 3).

The monuments built during the three empires are illustrated in the following matrix.

Some monuments (temples, churches and mosques, for example) may be considered utilitarian as they responded to popular needs. For example, the Mughals built sarais for pilgrims and other travellers (Chapter 4). The British built clubs and gymkhanas for social interaction (Chapter 5), as well as cantonments and garrison towns which were symbols of power but at the same time necessary for national security and for running the Empire (Chapter 7). Although expensive structures, they were not in the same class as palaces, government houses and such memorials as the Taj Mahal in Agra (Chapter 4) and the Victoria Memorial in Calcutta (Chapter 6).

Table 1.1. A Matrix of Monuments and Empires

Monuments\empires	Hindu		Muslim	
	Maurya (Ashoka)	Gupta	Mughal	British
Palaces	x	x	x	x
Palatial houses and lodges/sarais	x	x	x	x
Temples/mosques/churches	x	x	x	x
Forts and fortresses			x	x
Memorials			x	x
Tombs/cemeteries			x	x
Statues		x		x
Pillars/rock edicts	x	x		
Clubs, cantonments				x
Educational edifices		x	x	x

Thus, the royal monuments presented in the matrix can be grouped into the following three categories:

(1) *Ostentatious:* Royal palaces, forts and fortresses, government houses, memorials, tombs and cemeteries.
(2) *Utilitarian:* Pillars and rock edicts; temples, mosques and churches; sarais and water tanks.
(3) *Ostentatious-cum-utilitarian:* Educational institutions/edifices, such as Nalanda University, and palatial public schools (for example, Mayo College in Ajmer and Aitchison College in Lahore).

The Mughal and British empires are compared: both have left a rich legacy of art and architecture. Their extravaganza is presented in juxtaposition with the misery, poverty and squalor of the native subjects. During the Mughal period, ordinary subjects were poor and their living conditions largely squalid. Yet the Mughal Empire was 'almost certainly the richest empire in the world at the time' (Paxman, 2011:72). Bernier (1901:252) writes of 'wretched mud and thatch houses in Delhi'.[2] However, some observers believe that ordinary people during the Mughal period were better off than those during the later British period at least in terms of nutritional status (Chapter 10). During the British Raj also, similar opinions have been expressed about the poor socioeconomic condition of the subjects. For example, an observer (Ed Brown of the 2nd Battalion of the Royal Warwickshire Regiment) writes of 'squalor, hunger, filth, disease and beggary at the back of the jewel in the Crown of the Raj'. Indeed, health and sanitary conditions were far from adequate or satisfactory. In 1863, reviewing health conditions in the Indian Army, Florence Nightingale wrote:

> Bombay [. . .] has a better water supply; but it has no drainage. Calcutta is being drained but it has no water supply. Two of the seats of Government have thus each one half of a sanitary improvement, which halves ought never to be separated. Madras has neither [. . .]. At Agra it is proof of respectability to have cess-pools. The inhabitants (152,000) generally resort to fields. (cited in Judd, 1972:82)

Contrast these wretched conditions with the pomp and grandeur of the ruling classes during the Mughal and British empires. The British viceroys in India 'were supplied with the robes and carriages, decorations and retainers, to give them an appropriate viceregal appearance' (Paxman, 2011:193). Even junior colonial officers in India enjoyed the luxury of a large retinue of servants, cooks, maids and nannies.

Chapters 4 and 10 show that in these empires, the native Indians were oppressed and subject to high land and other taxes to build lavish monuments, finance wars or to fill the imperial coffers. For example, during the British Raj, the cost of the Empire was borne largely by the Indian taxpayer. The British monopoly of salt on which a high tax was imposed is a case in point. A great hedge extending over 2,000 miles was built as a Customs Line to prevent the smuggling of salt (Moxham, 2001).

During the Mughal period (*c.*1600) also land taxes (the main source of revenue) were quite high. Mughal noblemen and officers, Indian princes and landowners extracted large surpluses from the rural population. Watson (1979:118) notes that during the reign of Shah Jahan the rural Indian peasant in north India suffered from one of the worst famines (1630–2) when the Taj Mahal was nearing completion. The social and caste structures were such that the Indian economy suffered from stagnation and lack of productive investment.

Historical Context

The Mauryan Empire of the fourth century BC was perhaps the first Indian empire to cover a vast territory (see Chapter 1).[3] Chandragupta Maurya of the Moriya tribe ascended the throne in 321 BC at the age of 25. His Empire stretched across the Indus and Ganges plains and the far northwest, covering a very diverse group of inhabitants.

The Mauryan Empire lasted till 185 BC, when the Sungas took over the reins of power. They were succeeded by the Kushanas and Guptas. However, the early kingdoms succeeding the Mauryas and the Guptas did not have an easy ride. Different families, tribes and social groups started asserting their independence, thus weakening the political and social fabric of society, and leading eventually to the gradual disintegration of the Indian Empire.

Not much trace is left of the royal monuments of the early Hindu empires of the Mauryas and Guptas. For example, the only extant symbols of Ashoka's Empire are the pillars and edicts in Brahmi or Sanskrit written on rocks throughout his kingdom. The Guptas left behind a few temples, monasteries and statues of Buddha. Much more significant and well-documented are the monuments of the later Muslim and British empires.

The Muslim presence in India can be traced to the Arab conquest of Sind in 712. The Arab expansion towards India did not meet with much resistance, since the Sind region was largely a desert. Al Hajjaj, Governor of Basra, sent Muhammad bin Qassim to Sind who conquered the port of Debal. However, the Arabs did not bring with them any significant Muslim architecture. This appeared first with the arrival of the Mamluk slaves in the thirteenth century. Their royal monuments are illustrated in Part II of this book which deals with the pre-Mughal Muslim kingdoms. The term 'kingdoms' rather than 'empires' is preferable when referring to their reign, because their territories were rather small. For example, the Delhi Sultanate was confined mainly to the north, although it ruled parts of the Deccan for a while. Nor was the Delhi Sultanate a unified kingdom.[4]

Between the arrival of the Arabs in the eighth century and the Mamluks in the thirteenth, several small independent Rajput rulers and others in northern India campaigned against each other. This internal strife encouraged Muslim overlords to invade, including Mahmud of Ghazni (Afghanistan) in the early eleventh century and Muhammad Ghuri in the late twelfth century. While Mahmud was satisfied with looting the country's wealth and destroying temples, Muhammad was clearly more interested in territorial aggrandizement. These attacks marked the beginning of Turkish and Afghan rule in northern India until Babur, the first Mughal emperor, appeared on the scene in the sixteenth century.

Undoubtedly, the longest running empire was that of the Mughals starting with Babur and followed by Humayun, Akbar, Jahangir, Shah Jahan and Aurangzeb. Covering a vast territory, it contributed most significantly to the country's art and culture. It is also credited with bringing the Persian influence to bear on Indo-Islamic architecture. The Mughal Empire lasted for three centuries. In 1857, the British Empire took root with the dethronement and exile of the last Mughal emperor, Bahadur Shah II.[5]

It is surprising that a trading company with limited military, manpower and financial resources managed to take over a vast territory from the Mughal Empire.[6] Lloyd (1984:148) notes that 'the British found the process of conquest and expansion a bit surprising and for some years after the completion of Lord Hastings's wave of conquests they remained uncertain whether they could keep the political power they had gained . . .'.

The British East India Company (henceforth, the Company) practically ruled many parts of the country well before the British Crown replaced the Mughal Empire by the Government Act of 1858. Robert Clive's victories over Siraj-ud-Daula, the Mughal Nawab of Bengal, and over Joseph-Francois Dupleix, the French governor of Pondicherry, marked the beginning of the British supremacy in India. In 1756, a dispute broke out between the Nawab and the British, resulting in the withdrawal of concessions to the Company by the Mughals. The Nawab ransacked Bengal and captured Calcutta Fort. Lord Clive was sent from Madras to recapture Bengal, which he did after the Battle of Plassey in 1757, and the Nawab was overthrown and replaced by Mir Jafar, a general hostile to Siraj.

Lloyd (ibid.) maintains that the Indians accepted British rule because it was better than anything they had seen, and that the British alone could bring peace to the continent. This view seems exaggerated considering that the British (as their predecessors) did not do much for improving the lot of the ordinary people. The Indian subjects had no real choice, and, in any case, apart from a few educated elite, they would not have been very discerning about whether the British rule was more favourable to them than that of the Mughals. After all, the Mughals had fully integrated into the social fabric of India, which the British tried to destroy by importing British norms and rules. Furthermore, they may have alienated the Indian subjects by treating them as inferior and by maintaining a policy of apartheid. The clubs (Chapter 5) and the cantonments (Chapter 7), two exclusively British institutions in India, were clear manifestations of the separation of the rulers from their subjects: the natives had no access to either.

In 1803, the Mughal ruler became a nominal sovereign confined to the Red Fort when the British took over Delhi and Agra. His powers had long been curtailed by the British Resident (Agent to the Governor-General) at the Mughal Court. From this time till the 1857 uprising, the economic and social conditions of the Indian subjects were no better than they had been during the earlier Mughal period. Forbes (1813:61) wrote of Faiz Bazar in Chandni Chowk as a 'long street of very miserable appearance' and many houses looking 'low and mean'. The socioeconomic situation of the natives of Delhi became even worse in the post-uprising period.

The formal transfer from the Mughal to British rule was not bloodless. In May 1857, 300 sepoys from Meerut marched into Delhi in revolt. This uprising is often given a military interpretation, since the Hindu and Muslim sepoys in the British Bengal Army (based in Meerut, Lucknow, Calcutta and Cawnpore) formed the backbone of the revolt. The British had worsened caste consciousness in the army by establishing regiments along caste and religious lines. One cause of the uprising was the outrage felt by the sepoys who had to bite into cartridges for Enfield rifles that were greased with fat from beef and pork, abhorrent to Hindus and Muslims respectively. Both Hindu and Muslim regiments were up in arms before the mistake could be corrected. The sepoys massacred Christians in Delhi, Calcutta, Cawnpore and elsewhere before the British rulers were able to quell the uprising. The British were unprepared and their troops were outnumbered by the native troops.[7]

The damage done to British property during the 1857 uprising can be seen in the bullet-ridden image of the Residency in Lucknow, which was

Fig. 1.0. Residency, Lucknow (Author's Private Collection)

one of its epicentres (Fig. 1.0). The figure appears to be a photograph to which the Union Jack has been inserted (rather crudely) by hand. Residencies (the official homes of Residents[8]) were the third most important symbol of the expanding power of the British Raj after the Government and Council Houses.

In their revenge, the British were no less brutal and merciless. They massacred a large number of sepoys who saw themselves as freedom fighters. Most were hanged in public. Dalrymple (2009:402–3) gives gory details of the British revenge: 'fourteen rebels were strung up opposite the Kotwalee [. . .]'; 'there has been nothing but shooting these villains for the last three days, some 3 or 400 were shot yesterday'. Short ropes were used for hanging in order to prolong the death of rebels.

What was initially seen as a military revolt soon became a popular uprising against British rule which might have been prompted by the rapid westernization of social, political, cultural and economic life. For example, in 1829 the British rulers hastened to abolish the age-old practice of Sati (the burning of Hindu widows), which alarmed orthodox Hindus. At the same time, the religious Evangelical missionaries from Britain were busy converting Indian Hindus and Muslims to Christianity. Further-more, Indians had suffered several defeats during the British wars against the Afghans and the Sikhs. The British had annexed the Muslim state of Oudh (part of present-day U.P.) and several Maratha territories. To add insult to injury, 'the British were becoming increasingly hostile toward traditional survivals and contemptuous of anything Indian' (*The New Encyclopaedia Britannica*, 1981:407). British educational policy (Chapter 8) based on the western model, with English replacing the Persian language, offended the traditional custodians of Indian education. However, the modern Indian natives welcomed English education, which they saw as an opportunity not only to understand British actions and policies, but also to interact socially with the ruling elite and to obtain government employment. An unintended consequence of the English education of Indians in India and the UK was to encourage them to fight for autonomy, thus sowing the seeds of an independence movement.

Indian princes were disgruntled as the British annexed their kingdoms on the pretext of mismanagement under the 'Doctrine of Lapse'. This doctrine allowed the Company to expand its territory by annexing any princely state which was 'incompetently administered' or where the ruler did not leave behind any natural heir to succeed him.[9] The annexation of Oudh and many Maratha territories sent shivers through the spines of local rulers. Thus, the climate was ripe for a popular uprising.

The British Empire in India lasted nearly 100 years, from 1857 to 1947 when India became independent. But the Company had been virtually ruling the country for about a century prior to the Crown taking over in 1857. Although the Mughals ruled at the time, they did not wield much power. From 1757 to 1857, the Company exercised a strong influence on the Mughal court.

The Company, which owed allegiance to the Mughal Crown for 200 years, eventually rebelled against it. The British forces took control of the Red Fort, the seat of the Mughal Empire. The Hall of Public Audience (*Diwan-i-Am*) and the Hall of Private Audience (*Diwan-i-Khas*) became the British officers' mess and offices respectively. Thus ended the Mughal Empire, known for its outstanding contributions to Indian art and architecture, not to mention its Persian culture.

When the British Crown took over the administration of India from the Company, a permanent Indian Civil Service (ICS) and a unified

Indian army were established. These two institutions may have more or less maintained the day-to-day administration and security of British rule in India when the Viceroy and the Commander-in-Chief moved every year from Calcutta, the then seat of the government, to the hills of Simla for six months during the summer (Chapter 7). It is remarkable that this remote summer capital was established only a few years after the 1857 uprising. Were the British rulers fully confident that a similar uprising would not recur when they were up in the hills? Or did they have full faith in the ICS and the army to maintain law and order? Perhaps they wanted to establish their presence in the north close to the trouble spots.

In 1877, Queen Victoria was proclaimed Empress of India, and Disraeli, the Prime Minister, 'believed that if his government gave Queen Victoria the new title it would make the Indian princes (who ruled one-third of India) even more loyal in their support of the Raj' (Judd, 1972:77). Indeed, concrete efforts were made to ensure their continued loyalty and allegiance to the Crown. For example, princes were given new coats-of-arms which could be displayed on silk banners.

Structure of the Book

The book is divided into four parts. The first three parts deal with three major empires: the Hindu, Muslim and British. Besides the Maurya Empire, Part I covers the Gupta Empire and some of the lesser ones in the medieval period, such as the Kingdom of Vijayanagar in the south and the Sikh Kingdom of Maharaja Ranjit Singh in Lahore in the north.

Part II covers the Mughal Empire, the various pre-Mughal Kingdoms in the north and the Deccan kingdoms of Ahmadnagar, Bijapur, Golconda and Hyderabad (Chapters 2 to 4).

Part III discusses the British Raj and its legacy in India in the form of Presidency palaces and memorials, educational edifices, summer capitals and hill stations, as well as clubs and sports and garrison towns and cantonments (Chapters 5 to 8). Chapter 9 offers glimpses into the lifestyles of British public servants serving the British Raj in India, comparing them with those of London. Contrary to expectations, they enjoyed a better quality of life, living in spacious and luxurious houses and indulging in active social entertainment.

Part IV concludes with a comparison of the extravagance of the two major empires in India – the Mughal and British (Chapter 10). Whatever the differences between these two empires (and there were many as discussed in Chapter 4), they had one feature in common. They were both driven by a building spree to erect symbols of power, vainglory and imperial majesty. The extravaganza of both these empires embodied an ostentatious display of imperial power in sharp contrast to the misery and squalor of the natives, a paradox discussed and illustrated at length in this book.

Part I

The Hindu Empires and Kingdoms

1

Maurya and Gupta Empires and Later Kingdoms

Amidst the tens of thousands of names of monarchs that crowd the columns of history [. . .] the name of Ashoka shines, and shines almost alone, a star [. . .]. More living men cherish his memory today than have ever heard the names of Constantine and Charlemagne.

(H.G. Wells, 1920)

The Mauryan and Gupta empires were the only two empires of ancient India. Although based in the north, with Pataliputra (present-day Patna) as their capital, they extended beyond the Deccan in the south. Bussagli (1978:57) notes that the Mauryan Empire was 'the first national Indian empire on the models furnished by both the Persian empire of the Achaemenids [. . .] and of Alexander the Great . . .' The ruins of a Maurya palace in Pataliputra show that the Mauryans may have been inspired by Persian art and culture.

Did the Maurya and Gupta emperors and later kings of smaller kingdoms indulge in pomp, extravagance and ostentation at the expense of their subjects? Were the monuments of the period (temples, rock edicts and other structures) symbolic of their vainglory?

The Mauryan (Ashoka) Empire

The extant Mauryan structures consist mainly of Hindu and Buddhist temples (for example, the cave temple of Karna Kauphar and the Vishnu temple in the Barabar caves in Bihar) and pillars, which 'symbolically represented the world's axis, or better, indicated the magico-religious nature of the places where they were erected' (ibid.). The pillars and inscriptions are known to be the earliest surviving stone monuments since the collapse of the Indus civilization. During Ashoka's reign, many monuments were also built of wood, rather than stone, and have perished.

The Mauryan Empire is remembered mainly for the reign of Ashoka, also known sometimes by his other title, *Devanam-piya* (dear to the gods) *Piyadassi*, mentioned in old inscriptions. Not much was known about Ashoka's reign until 1837 when James Princep, a British officer at Calcutta mint, deciphered the earliest Indian script known as '*Brahmi*'.

Ashoka was known to be a great builder who may have even imported craftsmen from abroad to build royal monuments. Megasthenes, the Greek ambassador, mentioned a wooden Mauryan palace set in a big garden in Pataliputra, capital of the Mauryan Empire (Watson, 1979:47). Not much remains of this palace except a hall with many pillars, which was excavated in 1913 by David Spooner of the Archaeological Department of India who, in a report, noted that the pillared hall was 'in almost incredible state of preservation, the logs which formed it being as smooth and perfect as the day they were laid, more than two thousand years ago' (cited in Nehru, 1946:103). It is remarkable that the wooden logs survived for so long. Either it was a special kind of wood or the builders gave it a special treatment.

His two other contributions to architecture are the pillars (or *lats* and *stambhas*, as they were called) and the rock edicts, which were found scattered throughout his empire and even beyond, in Afghanistan, Ceylon and Nepal. These simple monuments have contributed significantly to the piecing together of Indian history of the time.

Two kinds of inscriptions on the Ashoka pillars and rock edicts are the main sources of information about his reign. One describes his declarations concerning the adoption of Buddhism and his relationship with the Buddhist Order.

When Ashoka inherited the throne from Chandragupta Maurya, he was not a Buddhist but a Hindu Brahmin. Apparently, the transfer of power from Chandragupta to Ashoka was not bloodless. In his early life, Ashoka was known to be cruel and vindictive in his ruthless pursuit of power. In order to accede to the throne, he must have eliminated his older brother, who was favoured by his father to be his successor, as well as his other brothers. Fratricide of this kind appears to have been quite common among the royal families at the time.

The Ashoka pillars and rock edicts were built only after he became a Buddhist following bloodshed at the battle of Kalinga. Ashoka ruled over a big empire extending from the north to the south of the country. The only hostile territory in the East was Kalinga (present-day Orissa). The Battle of Kalinga which he fought to gain supremacy of the trade routes involved the loss of thousands of innocent lives. This single event seems to have changed him from a ruthless and power-hungry emperor to a benevolent and humane ruler. He also changed his religious faith from Brahminism to Buddhism. His conversion to Buddhism may not have been a direct consequence of the war, but there is little doubt that the mass human suffering caused by it left an indelible mark on his conscience. That Ashoka became a strong believer in Buddhism which preached *ahimsa* (non-violence) is amply recorded in his edicts and rock inscriptions.[1]

Buddhism received royal patronage under Ashoka who went on his first royal pilgrimage to Bodhgaya where Buddha attained enlightenment, and later to Lumbini, Buddha's birthplace. However, at no stage during his reign did Ashoka declare Buddhism a state religion. He was not a religious fanatic, but a pragmatist who continued to tolerate other religions. He was careful to distinguish between his own personal religious beliefs and his duty as an emperor, according fair treatment to all religions (Thapar, 1990:73). His inscriptions did not mention any Buddhist religious discourses, but they did cite dharma as a simple and tolerant way of life based on ethical principles.

Ashoka's concept of dharma was different from that preached by Buddha.[2] He interpreted it not as a religious dogma but as 'an attitude of social responsibility' (ibid.:85–8). The three principal forms of his concept of dharma were:(1) humanitarian social spirit and sense of responsibility, (2) social welfare, and (3) non-violence. It is these principles, rather than Buddhism, which Ashoka propagated through inscriptions and edicts.

The second type of Ashoka pillars contain proclamations to the public in different local dialects, which were intended to propagate Buddhism. Perhaps their main purpose was more administrative than religious. Some observers have argued that Ashoka had a simplistic understanding of the Buddhist concept of dharma, which may explain the absence of religious sermonizing.

The pillars date back to the middle of the third century BC. Only about a dozen have been discovered so far, but many more may have been buried or destroyed. The most notable pillars were found in Lumbini in Nepal, and in Vaishali (Plate 1), Sarnath and Sanchi in India. Two Ashoka pillars were discovered in Delhi. Originally located in Meerut (Uttar Pradesh, U.P.) and Topra (Ambala) in Haryana, they were brought to Delhi in 1356 by Firoz Shah Tughluq.

They were made of sandstone and were polished, invariably crowned with bell-shaped capitals topped with figures of animals such as bulls (as the pillar in Rampurva) and lions as in Sarnath. Indeed, the latter was to become the official national emblem of India, showing four lions back to back. This devotion to animals may have derived from Hindu rituals and idol worship, not only of cows but also of other animals.

The style of all pillars is uniform, which suggests that craftsmen from the same region may have built them. Their shiny polish and the quality of stone bear testimony to the artistic sophistication, craftsmanship and technological genius of the architects of that time. The stones were quarried in Chunar, south of Varanasi, and were moved to different places, perhaps using the Egyptian techniques for carrying obelisks over long distances. Some (in Lumbini, for example) may have been built to commemorate events, for example, to mark the emperor's visit to Buddha's birth place. But most were designed to propagate his reforms as well as to commemorate Buddha's relics, as suggested by the inscriptions on them.

Like the pillars, the rock edicts were used to inscribe Ashoka's moral principles to create a just and humane society. They have been found in several countries, including Afghanistan, India, Nepal and Pakistan, and in different languages, the most common being the Brahmi script. Some edicts discovered in the eastern part of India use Magadhi, possibly the official language of Ashoka's court. Those discovered in the western part of India are inscribed in a language similar to Sanskrit. Remarkably, one discovered in Afghanistan is bilingual, written in both Aramaic and Greek.

Ashoka is known to have built many Buddhist stupas for holy relics, as many as 84,000 according to Pali sources. This number may be a gross exaggeration; a more realistic number seems to be a hundred or so. Hsuan Tsang, a Chinese traveller to India in the seventh century, mentions having seen more than 80 Ashoka stupas and monasteries. The most notable stupa was the Great Stupa in Sanchi (Madhya Pradesh), but nothing remains of the original version. The one standing today is believed to have been rebuilt by a Sunga king of the Andhra-Satavahanas dynasty. Some observers suggest that the Mahabodhi temple in Bodhgaya was also built by Ashoka. Cunningham (1892) saw the remains of an ancient shrine (which may have belonged to the original one built by Ashoka) while renovating the temple floor.

Art historians (such as Niharanjan Ray) believe that the Ashokan architecture and sculpture were not entirely indigenous. The Sarnath lion pillar and the Pataliputra palace, in particular, reflect Persian and Hellenistic influences. For example, the pillared hall of the palace resembles the Hall of a Hundred Columns in Persepolis. It is quite possible that Persian stone carvers were employed in building the palace and in making the stone pillars. This hypothesis is not so far-fetched considering that Persians migrated to India for work when the Achaemenid Empire collapsed (Eraly, 2005:344).

That the welfare of the people was Ashoka's main goal is suggested by his inscriptions and edicts. His policy of dharma is interpreted as including social welfare of the citizens. Some pillars spell out welfare measures adopted by the emperor for the benefit of the people. Pillar edict VII (translated by Thapar as Ashoka and the Decline of the Mauryas) mentions the following welfare measures (1) Planting of banyan trees for providing shade to the citizens as well as animals; (2) planting mango groves; (3) building rest houses; (4) digging wells and other sources of water supply; and (5) provision of medical facilities for human beings and animals.

This humane orientation of his reign and policies was a significant departure from the earlier precepts which dealt mainly with ruthless administrative efficiency. It may in part (along with a long period of peace) explain the happiness and prosperity of the emperor's subjects.

The standard of living is known to have been high during the Mauryan Empire. Consumption of meat and domestic and imported wines mentioned in the contemporary literature further suggest people's prosperity. This is not surprising considering that the Mauryans (at least Ashoka) did not build any ostentatious and costly monuments. Therefore, there must have been enough resources at the disposal of the royal court to look after the economic and social interests of the subjects.

Many inscriptions on Buddhist monuments such as the Sanchi stupa indicate the names of wealthy merchants in the Mauryan period who sponsored such monuments as well as their maintenance and repair (Bhalla, 2014). The Buddhist and Jain chronicles also mention their immense wealth, which may be attributed to a long period of peace as well as to the growth of domestic and maritime trade. Industry was organized into different craft guilds which also wielded significant economic and political power (Panikkar,1947:35–6).

During Ashoka's reign, the economy was largely agrarian, with most people living in villages and cultivating the land. Small-scale ownership of land existed even though, in principle, all land belonged to the king (Thapar, 1990:77). Irrigation for agriculture was provided in the form of canals, dams and water tanks. Prices were controlled in order not to cause any economic hardship to ordinary people. It may, therefore, be concluded that there was no rural poverty. Thapar (ibid.:83) notes that 'the higher officials were extremely well-paid' which would suggest that there was no urban poverty either. India was known to be prosperous at the time.

Did Ashoka seek fame and glory like most kings? He probably did, but sought it as a means to an end, the latter being the dharma he propagated. In one of his inscriptions, Ashoka notes: 'His Sacred Majesty does not regard that fame and glory bring much profit, unless my people obediently hearken to dharma and conform to its precept now and in the future' (cited in Eraly, 2005:328). It is claimed that Ashoka 'was the first monarch to make an attempt to educate his people into a common view of the ends and way of life' (Wells, 1920:401–2).

After Ashoka's death, the Mauryan Empire did not last very long. It may have collapsed and disintegrated under its own weight, as it covered a vast area. Other reasons given for its collapse include poor transportation and communication, breakdown of law and order, financial stress and a revolt by powerful Brahmins who resented the royal patronage of Buddhism. Some observers blame Ashoka's pacifist policy (guided by the adoption of Buddhism) for having emboldened his enemies, since the long years of peace may have caused Ashoka's army to lose its martial spirit and fighting skills.

The Sungas took over from the last Mauryas when the dynasty's founder, Pushyamitra, assassinated the Mauryan king and usurped the throne. Another powerful empire in India did not emerge until the fourth century with the Guptas.

The Gupta Empire

The Gupta Empire lasted from the fourth to sixth century. Founded by King Chandragupta I, it matched the Mauryan Empire in terms of its size, importance and contributions to art and culture. It was the only great Hindu Empire in India's history. Pataliputra, the capital of the Mauryas, remained the capital of the Gupta Empire, which extended to the south and east of India, and eventually also to western India.

Although the Guptas continued to build monuments in the Mauryan style, their main contribution lay in the stone sculptures of Buddha images of the Sarnath and Mathura Schools. Their sculpture is known for its grace and skilful representation of the human form. Noteworthy are the two standing Buddhas with halos at the Mathura Museum and the National Museum, New Delhi. A third example is the standing Buddha turning the Wheel of Law, which is displayed in the Sarnath Museum. A large number of Buddha statues excavated in Sarnath belong to the Mathura School.

The iron pillar in the courtyard of the Quwwat-i-Islam mosque in the Qutb Minar complex in Delhi may have been one of those at the Hindu and Jain temples in Udayagiri in the vicinity of Vidisha in Madhya Pradesh. It is believed that the pillar was brought to Delhi by a Rajput ruler of the Tomara dynasty (Sharp, 1921:43). Judging by the Sanskrit inscriptions on the pillar dating to the fourth century, it may have been built in memory of the Gupta King Chandragupta II or in honour of Lord Vishnu. The capital of the iron pillar is bell-shaped, as are most pillars of the Maurya dynasty. Metallurgists remain puzzled about the nature of the iron and alloys used in the manufacture of the pillar. Why has the iron not rusted for nearly 2000 years?

The Gupta emperors are known to have built wooden temples, but none has survived. However, some Gupta sandstone temples are

still standing. For example, temple no.17 in Sanchi, though unpretentious and small, is characterized by well-balanced proportions and harmony, which were the hallmark of Gupta art and architecture. Marshall
(1928:105) notes that this balance, as well as external ornamentation,
are similar to those of the Athenian Acropolis, for example. This simple
temple, described by Thapar (1990) as one of the most 'unimpressive
shrines', can hardly be considered an ostentatious monument. Neither
this temple nor the Sanchi stupa attributed to Ashoka can be classi-
fied as symbols of pomp and power. They are more like symbols of
religious zeal and sentiment. In grandeur, the temples of this period
do not match the mosques and churches built during the Mughal and
British empires.

Although no trace remains of ancient palaces, there is evidence to
suggest that ancient Hindu rulers did indeed build them, albeit modest
ones compared to those built during later dynasties. In *Mayamatam*,
a treatise on housing and architecture, a chapter is devoted to four
types of palaces: (i) small palace, (ii) palace of narendra or padmaka,
(iii) sambala palace, and (iv) Adhiraja palace (Dagens, 1994, Chapter 29).

Scholars have described the Gupta Empire as the Golden or Classical
Age of ancient India. However, this was true mainly of north India; a
high-level civilization in the south began only in the post-Gupta period.
Furthermore, although the period was marked by rich cultural achieve-
ments, the role of the Gupta emperors is not clear (Eraly, 2011:47). In
fact, very little is known about the origin of the Gupta dynasty. Many historians believe that the Gupta family did not enjoy any royal antecedents.

An inscription of the Gupta period found in Junagarh (part of present-
day Gujarat) claims that 'no man among his (Skanda Gupta's) subjects
[. . .] is distressed, in poverty, in misery' (cited in ibid.:192). This claim
is supported by the discovery of large hoards of gold coins of the Gupta
period. Similarly, Fa-Hsien, a Chinese traveller who visited India at that
time, found Indian people to be very well-off.

Contemporary literature suggests that 'the standard of living was high'
during the Gupta Empire. Thapar (1990:151) notes that 'prosperous urban dwellers lived in comfort and ease with a variety of luxuries in the
way of jewels and clothes'. Did the high standard of living also prevail
in rural areas? Living standards may have been lower there as might be

expected, but historical accounts suggest that there was less disparity. Foreign travellers noted that the villages 'were reasonably prosperous'. Eraly (2011:392) observes that in India the 'first half of the first millennium AD was a period of vigorous economic growth and rapid urbanization, and was characterized by vibrant city life, with the urban upper classes enjoying especially high living standards'.

At the time India enjoyed economic prosperity thanks to commercial trade with Europe. During the Maurya and Gupta empires, agricultural expansion improved the lot of the ordinary people and generated demand for domestic and imported manufactured goods. Infrastructure and irrigation facilities were built for the promotion of farming and the village economy in general. Small-scale irrigation and water tanks in villages were also built by local people. The state offered incentives to farmers to bring new land under cultivation. It also offered land grants to religious institutions and to royal courtiers/officers to help propagate new agricultural techniques.

The Roman Empire in Europe was a major market for such Indian exports as textiles and luxury goods. Gradually, trade with Europe declined following the collapse of the Roman Empire. Later, the Middle East became a major source of demand for these goods. In the post-Gupta period, the economic well-being of the common people deteriorated despite India's rich natural resources and wealth.

Before the glorious Mauryan and Gupta empires, India consisted mainly of tribal republics which are unlikely to have indulged in vainglory or pompousness. The concept of kingship during the early Aryan polity defined a king as first among equals, more like a chieftain. The powers of the emperors in the pre-Mauryan period were restricted by the myriad rules and regulations of guilds and local communities as well as by the customs of the caste system. However, Eraly (ibid.:103) notes that even the small kingdoms which were limited in power 'flaunted grandiose titles like *Maharajadhiraja* (Great King of Kings), *Parama-bhattaraka* (Supreme Lord), *Samasara-bhuvnasvaya* (Refuge of the Whole World) and so on . . . ' Contrast these with the modest title of 'Raja' for Ashoka.

The pomp and vainglory of kings may have increased over time, especially when the relationship between them and the people changed. As Eraly (ibid.) states, this relationship was reversed so that the king no longer belonged to the people. He now 'ruled the people instead of ruling for the people'.

The royal lifestyle in those days included a daily durbar where formal business was conducted. According to historical accounts (such as those by Bana, a celebrated writer at King Harsha's court), the audience hall of the emperor was sprinkled with sandalwood water and carpeted with flowers (ibid.:119–20).

However, royal customs and extravagance differed from king to king, and from one place to another. In general, kings in north India demonstrated their pomp and glory a lot more than those in the south. In the north they sat on high and bejewelled thrones, whereas in the south they sat on carpets on the floor.

Like the later Muslim sultans of the north and the Deccan, the earlier Hindu or Buddhist kings marched in lavish and colourful processions with large retinues and such lavish objects as golden drums, expensive cooking utensils and pottery from which they ate, as well as dancing girls. This is described by such historical chroniclers of India as the Chinese Hsuan Tsang. Eraly (ibid.:123) observes: 'The royal camp was always elaborately laid out, so that the king and the courtiers and their favourite ladies [. . .] would not miss any of the luxuries they normally enjoyed in the state capital.'

Many kings lived in palaces that have not survived but they are mentioned in the literature. Some examples are listed below:

(1) The kings were expected to live in large and magnificent palaces regardless of the size of their kingdoms. *Manasollasa*, a twelfth-century document, specifies that the king should have different palaces for different seasons, and that these palaces should be from one to nine storeys high with golden pillars and mirror walls.

(2) *Silappadikaram*, a Tamil literary work of the time, notes that the royal Chola palace in Pihar, the capital, was so grand that it was believed to be the creation of the divine architect, Maya (ibid.:123).

(3) *Jataka* stories note that the king's palaces were furnished with all sorts of luxuries such as perfumed floors, gold-studded starry ceilings and garlanded walls.

Sumptuous feasts of food of many delicate flavours and imported wines are mentioned in historical chronicles. Royal recreation included polo playing, hunting, hawking and animal fights, as well as harems of many wives and concubines who were more for 'pomp and ceremony' than for sexual pleasures. Vatsayana, a Hindu Vedic philosopher, describes how the upper class enjoyed the pleasures of life including music, festivals (flower festivals and Diwali, for example) as well as gambling.

Regional Hindu Kingdoms

There were no *national* Hindu empires following the end of the Gupta Empire. Between the fall of the Gupta Empire and the rise of the Delhi Sultanate, north India went through a period of political instability and turmoil. Several small kingdoms emerged, namely, the Guptas of Magdha (a minor dynasty bearing the same name as the earlier empire), the Maukharis, the Maitrakas, and the Pushyabhutis. Harsha of the Pushyabhuti dynasty in Thanesar (north of Delhi) ruled for four decades. There were also smaller principalities constantly fighting each other.[3]

Many Rajput kings (for example, the Pratiharas, Chauhans and Paramars or Pawars) ruled in Rajasthan in the ninth and tenth centuries. The Pratiharas kingdom extended to the Ganga – Yamuna Doab and southern Rajasthan. The Chauhans ruled in eastern Rajasthan. Internal conflicts between different Rajput clans for supremacy and territorial expansion must have drained the resources of each kingdom. Little remains of any major monuments of that period. Lack of resources may have been the main reason for an absence of royal pomp at the time. The Rajput palaces of Ajmer, Amber, Jaipur and Udaipur were built much later in the seventeenth and eighteenth centuries.

The Chandelas who ruled central India from Khajuraho are known for the famous erotic temples there. Controversy surrounds the erotic postures of the sculptures that adorn these temples. One theory is that these *kama sutra* positions were designed to educate newly married couples in the art of love-making; others argue that they sought to depict the real, everyday life of the times.

The temples of these medieval Hindu kingdoms are far more ornamental and symbolic of power than those built during the Ashoka and Gupta empires. Therefore, it is doubtful whether their construction was inspired mainly by the religious needs of ordinary people.

The Pala kings, who ruled Bihar and Bengal, were keen on art and learning. Nalanda University belongs to this period, as do several bronze statues of such Hindu gods as Vishnu. The art of painting also flourished during the Pala period (Sivaramamurti, 1978).

Yazdani (1960:134) notes that 'some of the Satavahana Kings (of the Deccan) [...] displayed keen interest in promoting the welfare of the people'. They gave large sums of cash as well as goods in kind to Brahmins and Buddhist monks. They also organized rest houses and places for drinking water for their subjects.

The Southern Kingdom of Vijayanagar

The kingdom was founded by two local princes, Harihara and Bukka. In 1336, Harihara became the king of Hasinavati (Hampi today) and made the city of Vjayanagar his capital. In 1346, the Hoysala king was defeated, thus enabling the kingdom to reinforce its hold on the south. The Madura sultans were also defeated, allowing its extension to the whole of south.

Foreign visitors to the kingdom describe the lavishness of the royal court, and of the pomp and extravagance of the religious festivals. They saw numerous palaces, fortresses and temples in the city of Vijayanagar. Abd-ur-Razzaq[4], an emissary of the King of Persia to the Vijayanagar court, has written a detailed account of the palaces, forts and temples that he visited. He was received by the Vijayanagar king seated on a huge throne made of gold and embellished with expensive precious stones. He remarked that the city of Vijayanagar was 'unparalleled in the world' and noted that the seventh fortress in the city was ten times the size of the main market of Herat in Afghanistan (cited in Ghoshal,1960b:657). Domingo Paes, a Portuguese chronicler,[5] described Vijayanagar to be as large as Rome, and very beautiful, because of its groves of trees and its gardens with water-conduits and lakes. He noted that within the inner city, all streets were bordered by very beautiful rows of well-decorated houses (cited in ibid.).

From the fourteenth to sixteenth century, Vijayanagar was the most powerful Hindu capital in the Deccan, built as an entirely new city 'with lavish temples, but what remains, shows that it was characterized by sumptuous and rich ornamentation' (Thapar, 1990:333).

Paes writes about the costly establishments of the Vijayanagar queens, their rich jewellery and lavish clothes as well as the large number of their female attendants (Sastri and Aiyar, 1966:315). The king also enjoyed a lavish lifestyle. Sastri and Aiyar (ibid.:314) remark that 'the King and his court led an extravagant and luxurious life in striking contrast to the modest living standard of the rest of the population'. Abd-ur-Razzaq and Duarte Barbosa[6] (who lived in Vijayanagar) mention that the high and low people wore jewels and ornaments and costly cotton and silk clothes.

There does not appear to be any information on the living conditions of ordinary people, on their wages and incomes, for example. However, there is some indication that agricultural and other taxes were low, suggesting that people's real incomes were higher than they would have been under a higher tax regime. Hsuan Tsang notes that 'the taxes on the people are light, and the personal service required of them moderate' (Eraly, 2011:141).

Fernão Nuniz, a Portuguese horse trader who lived in Vijayanagar for several years during the sixteenth century, states that nobles there 'were like renters who hold all the land from the King [. . .] the common people suffer much hardship, those who hold the lands being so tyrannical' (Eraly, 2007:279).

Barbosa mentions the king and nobles living in palaces and the common people in thatched but well-built houses. He also notes that a large number of the city's inhabitants were very wealthy. In general, 'the life for the upper class was comfortable if not luxurious' (Thapar, 1990:334).

Ranjit Singh's Sikh Kingdom

A number of monuments are attributed to Maharaja Ranjit Singh, notably the marble pavilion in Lahore, and Govind Garh (the fort) and Ram Bagh in Amritsar. It is alleged that the marble used in the pavilion in the Royal Gardens (Huzuri Bagh) was taken from the fort or possibly from Jahangir's tomb, though there is no conclusive evidence of this latter possibility. Moorcroft (1841) believed that the marble from Jahangir's tomb was removed by Aurangzeb instead. The pavilion in Lahore, where Ranjit Singh used to hold court, does not show any trappings worthy of a king. It was a two-storey building whose upper storey collapsed in 1932 when lightning struck it.

Ranjit Singh, also known as the Lion of Punjab, ruled Punjab and the North-West Frontier Province (NWFP) from 1799 to June 1839 when he died at the age of 57. In 1792, at the age of 12, he succeeded to a local chiefship. He first acquired Lahore from Shah Zaman of Afghanistan who had invaded north India and captured Lahore. When Zaman returned to Kabul, he agreed to grant Lahore to Ranjit Singh for services rendered in recovering 8 out of 12 of Shah's guns that had been lost in the River Jhelum (Latif, 1892:80). Gradually, the Maharaja went on to capture several northern cities, namely Amritsar, Kasur, Ludhiana, and Multan in the Punjab, Kashmir further up north, and Attock and Peshawar in the NWFP.

He recovered the famous Koh-i-Noor diamond from Shah Shuja, the ex-king of Kabul. In 1809, he entered into a treaty with the British Government (the Treaty of Amritsar) under which his territorial boundary in the Punjab was confined to the north and west of the River Sutlej. Ranjit Singh created a formidable and disciplined Sikh army with 40,000 infantry, 12,000 cavalry and a powerful artillery. It was considered highly efficient and motivated, and compared favourably with the forces of the Company (*The New Encyclopaedia Britannica*, 1981:404).

He employed members of the Hindu and Muslim communities in the army and civil administration. Most of the state revenues were devoted to the creation and strengthening of the army, which may have meant that few resources were left for development.

The simple living of Maharaja Ranjit Singh was proverbial and marked a sharp contrast to the lavishness discussed above. During his nearly 40-year rule, he did not attach his name to any monument or coins; nor did he assume any royal titles, which is a remarkable example of modesty. He was known to be inquisitive and 'remarkably humane'. William Osborne, who visited the maharaja, noted that 'his reign will be found freer from any striking acts of cruelty and oppression than those of many more civilized monarchies' (cited in Thompson, 1943:157–8). Grewal (1990:113) states that 'he revived prosperity and minimized oppression. He created opportunities for members of several sections of the society to improve their social position.'

Indian Princely Kingdoms

Nearly half the territory of the Indian sub-continent during the Mughal and British empires was governed by Hindu (Rajput and Maratha) and Sikh rajas and maharajas. There were more than 560 autonomous princely kingdoms scattered throughout India.

The Rajputs built many fortresses and palaces in Rajasthan. The Sikh princes built fortresses and palaces in the north of the country, and the Marathas in the west.

There were two phases of palace building by the maharajas: (1) from the sixteenth to early eighteenth century during the Mughal rule, and (2) from the nineteenth to early twentieth century during the British rule. The Hindu palaces during the Mughal period were almost all built by the Rajputs who had accumulated considerable wealth through Mughal patronage. Many Rajput rajas forged alliances with the Mughal emperors (particularly Akbar) who used their help to conquer the south. During the British rule, the Sikh maharajas built palaces in the Punjab, in Faridkot, Kapurthala (in a Louis XIV style inspired by Versailles) and Patiala.

The Maratha palaces in central India included those in Gwalior and Indore. The Jai Vilas Palace of Gwalior built in the 1870s has a facade comprising a mix of Doric, Tuscan and Corinthian styles, while its interior is in Italianate style. The enormous Durbar Hall has two big chandeliers with 248 candles each. The main gate of the Lalbagh Palace in Indore, built in English style, resembles that of Buckingham Palace in London.

Many palaces of the Indian maharajas are still standing as living memory to their pomp and grandeur, wealth and power, pretentions and self-indulgence. The Maharaja of Baroda (1980:15) notes:

> There were some palaces where the demands of sumptuous grandiosity and its dictates of conspicuous display overtook any notions of stylistic accuracy, integrity or restraint [. . .]. They were deliberately out of place in the Indian landscape.

A sample of palaces in the north, central and western parts of India are described below to illustrate the pomp and glory of the Indian maharajas.

The Udaipur city palace was built in the seventeenth century on Lake Pichola. It contains an endless number of rooms 'built for no purpose other than royal pleasure' (ibid.:16). Its marble walls are painted with friezes, dancing girls and hunting scenes. The stylistic features of the decorations are a blend of Rajput and Mughal architecture.

Jul Mandir or Water Palace, Oodeypore.

Fig. 1.1. Water Palace, Udaipur (Author's Private Collection)

In the middle of Lake Pichola was the summer palace of the royal family (water palace) built of white marble (Fig. 1.1).

The Jaipur City Palace of the Amber Rajput family of the Kachwaha clan (the first of the Rajputs to give a daughter in marriage to Akbar) surpasses the Udaipur palace in its imitations of Mughal decorations. Jaisingh II (who also built the pink city of Jaipur) built the palace in the early eighteenth century, since the palace in Amber was considered too small. While the walls of the palace painted in pink are Rajput in style, the layout of the buildings surrounded by gardens, is typically Mughal. As in the Mughal palaces, the Jaipur palace contains Halls of Public and Special Audience.

Old Motibagh Palace (Patiala), considered one of the largest residences in Asia, belonged to Bhupinder Singh, the Sikh maharaja of Patiala, whose excesses are proverbial. The palace grounds extend over 11 acres of gardens. Maud Diver (a popular author) described the palace as an 'immensity of rose pink sandstone that would make Versailles look like a cottage' (ibid.:189).

Jagjit Palace (Kapurthala), inspired by Versailles palace, was built between 1900 and 1908 by Maharaja Jagjit Singh who ascended the throne in 1890. Educated by English and French tutors, he toured

Fig. 1.2. Laxmi Vilas Palace, Baroda (Author's Private Collection)

Europe where he fell in love with France, French food and its architecture. Built by a French architect, the palace was called the Elysée as a testimony to France and as homage to the Louis XIV style. A European visitor to the palace remarked: 'one mass of gold with nymphs disporting themselves on vaulted ceilings and innumerable Sèvres ornaments and vases and objets d'art about'. Artists from abroad painted the ceilings, lapis lazuli columns were transported from Italy and Aubusson carpets were specially woven to fit the rooms (ibid.:195).

Laxmi Vilas Palace (Baroda) belonged to the Maratha military clan (Fig. 1.2). Maharaja Sayajirao built a new Laxmi Vilas palace as the old Nazar Bagh palace was not considered suitable. It attempted to combine native Rajput detail with Mughal domes and a touch of European modernity. Workmen from London created the stained glass windows and gilding on the walls and ceilings.

The rulers of the independent princely states are known for grandiose palaces described above. But these palaces were only one among many symbols of wealth and extravagance. Other symbols included jewels, diamonds, pearls and gold. Among the possessions of the Maharaja of Baroda. was the Star of the South, the seventh biggest diamond in the world. Various symbols of the lavish style of the Maharaja of

Patiala included a private cricket club and orchestra, a fleet of 72 cars, including three dozen Rolls Royces, and jewels and diamonds. In 1924, at a Viceregal Ball in Delhi, he arrived 'in a brocaded coat entirely concealed by diamonds [. . .] he made sure that he became the owner of a necklace that had once belonged to the Empress Eugenie of France' (ibid.:188).

The Indian princely kingdoms survived during the Mughal and British empires through collaboration and treaties. Many Rajput princes gave their daughters to Akbar in marriage, and a few even worked for the Mughal emperor. Later, the British rulers wooed the native princes, extending control over them by giving them an English education and by advising them (through Residents and Agents) and by awarding them honorific titles.

The British used the princely states to achieve political stability and avoid a repeat of the 1857 uprising. Before the uprising, Lord Dalhousie's policy was aimed at political unification by annexing princely states on the pretext of their poor governance (so-called 'Doctrine of Lapse'). After the uprising, this policy was abandoned in favour of continued autonomy of the princes who were free to appoint any heirs as long as they swore allegiance to the British Crown. This new policy was motivated by a desire to avoid another uprising, and to use the support of princes in meeting any such threat.

The princes retained autonomy in exchange for their recognition of the Paramountcy of the King Emperor of Britain represented by the Viceroy in India. But they ceded control of defence and foreign affairs to the Viceroy. Two princes, of Hyderabad and Kashmir, were entitled to a 21-gun salute, whereas others (of Baroda, Gwalior and Mysore, for example) were awarded fewer gun salutes, thus grading their status by their importance to the King Emperor.

The Indian princes did not survive independent India for very long. In 1947, the departing British rulers urged them to merge with either India or the newly-created Pakistan. In 1948, the Indian Government persuaded the princes to give up their territories, but it allowed them to keep their palaces. In 1971, the princes lost their incomes and privileges through an act of Parliament. Thus, nearly 600 Indian princes disappeared into the archives of history.

Part II

The Muslim Kingdoms and Empire

2

The Pre-Mughal Muslim Kingdoms

The tradition of constructing palaces in the history of Islam goes back to
the Omayyads[1] who built them to overawe the public mind by their glory
and grandeur. The sultans of Delhi were zealous builders of palaces [...].
The first concern of every new ruler was to construct a magnificent new
palace for himself.

(Nizami, 1997)

The early Islamic monuments in India consisted of palaces, victory towers, mosques and mausoleums. In principle, Islam forbade the glorifi-
cation of death through the construction of mausoleums. The orthodox
Islamic law (Shariat) prohibits even masonry graves. Therefore, it is paradoxical that many countries, Islamic as well as non-Islamic, are replete
with tombs and royal mausoleums.

The Muslim sultans and emperors may have ignored religious injunctions since they enjoyed absolute religious and political power. They
may have regarded themselves as descendants of the Prophet through
his son-in-law, Ali. As the rulers were considered divine by their subjects,
they felt free to leave a legacy in the form of mausoleums in the tradition
of the earlier Greeks and Romans, such as Halicarnassus and Augus-
tus. However, no equivalent memorials to such emperors as Ashoka and
Gupta were ever built, although a modest mausoleum (*samadhi*) was
built in more recent times in honour of Maharaja Ranjit Singh. Non-
royal Muslim tombs also grew with religious believers' desire to honour their saints and Sufis: the general population was quite religious at
that time.

The long history of tomb construction originated with the first Islamic mausoleum of Qubbat-i-Sulabiya (863) in Samarra (Iraq) which was built for three caliphs. It marked the beginnings of Islamic mausoleums in Egypt, Persia, southern Central Asia and India. The tomb of the Samanids in Bokhara was built soon after (905) and many others followed, the Gur-i-Amir in Samarkand (1404), for example.

In India, both the pre-Mughal sultans and the Mughal emperors built mausoleums as symbols of vainglory and power. That of Iltutmish, built in 1235 by Iltutmish himself, was the first Muslim mausoleum apart from Sultan Ghari, the tomb of his eldest son, Prince Nasir-ud-din Mahmud.

Other structures built by the Delhi sultans included mosques (Sikandar mosque in the Lodi Gardens and Begumpura mosque in Jahan Panah), and religious schools (madrasas). Mosques were not just prayer halls; they also served as community centres and meeting places.

Each sultan tried to demonstrate his power and glory by building victory towers (Qutb Minar and Chand Minar), palaces (Hazar Sutun in Jahan Panah and Hanging Palace in Mandu) and fortresses (Tughluqabad and Daulatabad). Sometimes even entirely new cities (Tughluqabad and Jahan Panah) were built to satisfy the sultans' whims, ego and vanity.

In the Delhi sultanate, successive sultans belonged to different dynasties whose interests in architecture and building activity also varied (Table 2.1).

The pre-Mughal Turko-Afghan sultans were attracted to India by its immense wealth. Unlike Mahmud who died in 1030, Ghuri came to India to stay and establish a kingdom. He defeated the then Rajput ruler of Delhi, Prithviraj III, who was killed in battle.[2] He conquered Sind, Lahore, Delhi and Ajmer in quick succession and created a foothold in the north of India. He was assassinated in 1206, but his Turkish-Afghan interests in India survived, thanks to his General, Qutb-ud-din Aibak, who managed his Indian acquisitions and established what is called the Slave (or Mamluk) dynasty.

In the twelfth century, the Muslim conquerors of north India built victory monuments such as those in the Qutb Minar complex. These are the oldest architectural specimens of Muslim India. They lie on the foundations of the old city of Lal Kot built by the Tomara and Chauhan Rajputs. No doubt, there were earlier Muslim invasions into India by Mahmud of Ghazni (Afghanistan), but these raids were largely for the

Table 2.1. The Sultanate Rulers and their Architecture

Date	Dynasty and Rulers	Architecture and Related Features
1206–90	*Mamluk or Slave dynasty*: Qutb-ud-din Aibak (1206–10); Shams-ul-din Iltutmish (1211–36); Nasir-ud-din Mahmud (1246–66); Balban (1266–87).	Utilization of existing temples as mosques; tentative attempts at creating such Islamic forms as arches and domes (Qutb Minar; Iltutmish's tomb); decline in building activity after the fall of Iltutmish.
1290–1320	*Khalji dynasty*: Turko-Afghan kings from the village of Khalji near Gazhni; Firuz Shah (1290–6); Ala-ud-din Khalji (1296–1316); Mubarak Shah (1316–20).	Development of Islamic architecture in Delhi and Malwa (Mandu); introduction of ornamental decoration.
1320–1413	*Tughluq dynasty*: Ghiyas-ud-din Tughluq (1320–5); Mohammad bin Tughluq (1325–51); Firoz Shah (1351–88); Muhammad Shah (1389–94); Muhammad Shah II (1401–12).	Greater building activity (restoration of the two top storeys of the QutbMinar which had collapsed); building of hospitals, mosques and schools under Firoz Shah.
1399	Timurid invasions and capture of Delhi.	Cessation of migration of craftsmen to India; migration of Indian skilled craftsmen to Samarkand.
1414–1451	*Sayyid dynasty*: Khidr Khan (1414–21); Mubarak Shah (1421–34); Muhammad Shah (1434–43); Alam Shah (1443–51).	Restricted building activity; Muhammad Shah's tomb in Lodi Gardens.
1451–1526	*Lodi dynasty*: Bahlol Lodi (1451–89); Sikandar Lodi (1489–1517); Ibrahim Lodi (1517–26).	Revival of construction of tombs (*gumbads*), especially under Sikandar Lodi.

purpose of looting wealth rather than for any territorial gains or long-term stay in the country.

Slaves and the Qutb Minar Complex

Although many buildings were completely destroyed, in the Qutb complex in Delhi four still survive and are in excellent condition, namely the Qutb Minar (Victory Tower) (Plate 2), the Quwwat-i-Islam mosque, the Alai Darwaza and Iltutmish tomb. Qutb-ud-din Aibak built the Qutb Minar to commemorate Muhammad Ghuri's victory over the Rajput Chauhans.

Iltutmish of the Slave dynasty (1206–46) was one of its greatest master builders. He built his mausoleum in red and grey stone, which has a square plan with three doors, while the fourth wall has a *mihrab* instead of a door. It has several Hindu features, including a simple exterior but a lavishly decorated interior, similar to many Hindu temples. However, the motifs are largely Islamic with a few Hindu symbols such as the lotus. The interior is characterized by profuse and intricate carvings in red sandstone with inscriptions from the holy Qur'an representing such themes as the oneness of Allah. The tomb may have provided inspiration for subsequent Muslim buildings in India.

It is believed that the tomb was once covered by a dome which later collapsed, most likely due to structural flaws, as the Hindu craftsmen who built the tomb were unfamiliar with the construction of domes and Islamic building techniques. Hindu influence on Islamic architecture is largely attributed to these local Hindu craftsmen, because, initially, the Delhi sultans relied almost entirely on them.

Ala-ud-din Khalji left a legacy behind in the form of Alai Darwaza (Gateway) located near the Qutb Minar. The gateway represents an important building in several respects. It influenced later structures, such as the tomb of Ghiyas-ud-din Tughluq. Its pointed 'horseshoe' arches are its unique feature not repeated in any other subsequent buildings (Bhalla, 2009). The architectural style, the conception of the dome and the shape of its arches suggest an external influence, possibly of the Seljuk Turkish dynasty of Asia Minor. The Mongol invasions may have led to the break-up of the Seljuk Empire, forcing its architects and craftsmen to move to Delhi to work for the Khalji sultans.

Alai Darwaza looks more like a mausoleum. It has latticed red sandstone screens embellished with marble. Its purpose and origin are unclear. Was it the main entrance to a mosque, or did Ala-ud-din build it
as a memorial to celebrate his success in chasing the Mongols out of
India? There are no clear-cut answers to these questions.

Close to the Alai Darwaza and Iltutmish's tomb is a mosque, Quwwat-
i-Islam, the first mosque to be built in India. Aibak built it by using the
pillars and columns of several Hindu and Jain temples. The Hindu motifs (bells and chains) on the pillars in the mosque interior and the
indigenous, corbelled arches, bear testimony to local Hindu craftsmanship.[3] Since Islamic law forbids idol worship (allowed under Hinduism),
all the figures carved into the Hindu columns were removed. Qur'anic
calligraphy adorns the facade of the mosque along with Hindu decorations, such as bells chains and lotus flowers.

Khaljis, Daulatabad and Mandu

Khalji sultans indulged in building lavish monuments. Several noteworthy royal monuments of Daulatabad associated with the Khaljis, namely
the fort, the Jami Masjid and Chand Minar, are still standing. Striking
features of the fort include: (i) a sequence of traps for intruders and
armies of enemies, (ii) a moat infested with man-eating crocodiles, (iii)
three cannons – two Persian and one Dutch – which lie in the fort's
courtyard, (iv) Chini Mahal, (v) Jami Masjid, and (vi) Baradari on the
hilltop which was used by the Mughal emperor, Shah Jahan, during
his visits to Daulatabad. It is believed that a Yadavi queen originally
lived there.

In 1296, the Delhi Sultan, Ala-ud-din Khalji, invaded Deogiri (hill of
the gods) and captured the fort. However, he allowed the Yadava raja
to continue to rule as a vassal.[4] Deogiri was founded in AD 1187 by the
Yadavas who initially ruled over modern Dhulia and Nasik districts under
the Chalukyas of Kalyani. Deogiri's prosperity drew the attention of the
Delhi sultans who saw it as a perfect base from where to launch their
campaigns to conquer the Deccan further south of the country.

Later, Qutb-ud-din Mubarak Shah Khalji annexed Deogiri. The im-
pregnable nature of the fort may have encouraged him to move there.
But it was not a move of good fortune; in less than 17 years, the Sultan

was forced to return to the north, following draught, famine and threats of Mughal invasion.

Other Khalji monuments (palaces, madrasas and a mosque) were built in Mandu. However, a white-marble mausoleum there is associated with the Ghuri sultan Hoshang Shah. It was completed by his successor, a Khalji ruler, several years after his death. It is of special significance as a rare example of an Indian tomb built entirely of white marble which caught the attention of Shah Jahan (ibid.). One of the door jambs carries an inscription recording his visit along with four architects who came here to study the building before starting work on the Taj Mahal. It is believed that the marble dome of the tomb provided inspiration for the architects of the Taj. Hoshang's tomb also served as a prototype for many other tombs in Malwa.

It forms part of a building complex with the Jami Masjid on one side and Ashrafi Mahal on the other. The Ashrafi Mahal was not a residential palace but a theological college (madrasa) which Sultan Muhammad Shah later converted into a tomb. The building complex around the Mahal once included a seven-storey victory tower whose base has survived. On the left of the Mahal is the Jami mosque.

Mandu became a walled city of 12 gates which were built to protect it from the invading armies of the enemies. The Delhi Gate provided the main fortified entrance to the walled city, which still looks grand even today, with its palaces, pavilions, mosques, tombs and gates. It is similar to the magnificent dead city of Fatehpur Sikri in the north.

At the end of the fourteenth century, Mandu became part of the Delhi Sultanate. When the Mughals captured Delhi in 1401, Dilawar Khan Ghuri, the governor of Malwa who was working for the Delhi sultans, took advantage of the situation and declared independence. He became the Sultan of Malwa with Mandu as his capital. Dilawar's reign lasted only four years. He was succeeded by his son, Hoshang Shah, who ruled Mandu for three decades. This was Mandu's golden period during which many palaces, mosques and step wells were built.

With Hoshang Shah's death in 1435, Ghuri rule in Mandu ended and Mohammad Khalji went on to rule for over three decades. In 1469, his son, Ghiyas-ud-din, a debauch and womanizer, succeeded his father. He maintained a large harem in the Jahaz Mahal which accommodated thousands of women. Jahaz Mahal, derives its name from its unusual

Fig. 2.1. Jahaz Mahal and the Lake, Mandu (Author's Private Collection)

shape of a long ship (Fig. 2.1). It is built on a narrow strip of land between two lakes. Originally, it accommodated the Sultan's harem protected by women soldiers and doorkeepers. The palace has a large roof terrace surrounded by four domed pavilions, and offers a beautiful view of the bathing pools, the lakes and the countryside.

Another palace with sloping walls is called Hindola Mahal or the Swinging Palace. It may have been designed as an audience hall during the reign of Ghiyath Shah, a hedonistic sultan of the Khalji dynasty. Built on a T-shaped ground plan, it has delicate stone windows with ornamental work.

The palace of Baz Bahadur, the Sultan of Mandu from 1551 to 1561, is situated on a hill above the sacred water tank, Rewa Kund. It combines Islamic and Rajput styles of architecture and opens out onto a large courtyard with halls on all four sides. Its northern side has an octagonal porch with arches and its southern side has two pavilions (*baradaris*) overlooking a garden. Baz Bahadur built a pavilion on a steep hill for Rupmati, his beloved mistress, a Hindu singer of Rajput origin. The Sultan was interested more in love and romance than in affairs of the state.

Lavishness characterized the Khalji reign. The building of palaces and other royal monuments is only one example. Ala-ud-din Khalji's accession to the throne was marked by lavishness and extravagance. When he ascended the throne, 'gold and silver were showered for crowds from catapults; gifts of gold were given to nobles by weight and one gift did not debar the recipient from receiving another' (Ashraf, 2000:161). When the Khaljis invaded south India in the fourteenth century, their soldiers looted such large amounts of gems that they hardly bothered to pick up the silver objects that were not considered worth much! (Eraly, 2007:178).

However, little is known about the social and economic conditions at that time. According to Barani, during Ala-ud-din Khalji's reign, three kinds of taxes were imposed on the peasantry on cultivation, milch cattle and houses. Tax imposition and collection were vigorous, and payment was to be made in cash, which meant that quite often peasants were forced to sell their produce immediately. As the tax was heavy and regressive, a new system had to be introduced to lighten the burden on poor peasants.

Sometimes the rural producers suffered because of controlled low prices for their crops. For example, Ala-ud-din Khalji controlled prices and supplies of essential commodities for the benefit of his army officers who did not receive very high salaries. The sultan found it difficult to maintain a large standing army with the resources available. As taxes were already high, additional revenue could not be generated through new taxation. Chitnis (2009:246) observes that 'the interests of the peasants and the merchants were sacrificed mercilessly on the altar of the soldiery'. Neither the peasants nor the merchants had any incentive to produce or trade because they earned a bare minimum. Writing about the Khaljis, Lal (1967:219) notes that 'the spirit of the Turkish government in general and of Ala-ud-din's in particular' was to 'rule by force' and their rule 'was not based on the will or well-being of the people'.

Ordinary people may not have benefited much from controlled prices, since, as Barani notes, their wages were extremely low. He cites what at the time was a popular saying: 'A camel sells for a *dang* (copper coin); but who has got a *dang*?' (cited in Habib, 1982b:87).

Goldsmiths, jewellers, blacksmiths, tailors and shoemakers who supplied luxury goods for the sultans and the royal family and other nobility, may have enjoyed a higher standard of living than that of the peasants. Many artisans were employed in the royal workshops and thus contributed to the maintenance of royal splendour and extravagance. Writing about the Muslim wage-earners (artisans such as weavers and carpenters), Mirza (1960:614) notes that 'they were fairly well off and could earn enough to keep themselves and their families in tolerable comfort [. . .] because the essential commodities were cheap and plentiful . . .'

Foreign travellers' accounts about different parts of the country in the fifteenth and sixteenth centuries suggest that economic prosperity was quite widespread. The general population is known to have lived a life of ease and comfort. Eraly (2014:130) observes that 'people on the whole led a better life under Ala-ud-din than under any other king of the Delhi Sultanate.'

Tughluqs, Tughluqabad and Jahan Panah

The Tughluq sultans were fond of architecture. For example, Firoz Shah built palaces, mosques, religious schools and roads and bridges. He made a significant contribution to architecture, as did Shah Jahan during the Mughal period. But his buildings were of a simpler design than any built by his predecessors, especially the Khaljis. Financial considerations may have necessitated the use of simple designs and cheap materials.

Within a year of his reign, Ghiyas-ud-din decided to build a new fortified capital, Tughulqabad, where he moved from Delhi three years later. After his death, his son and successor, Mohammad Tughluq, moved back to Delhi leaving the new fortified city to crumble.

Tughluqabad is located at a distance of about 8 kilometres east of the Qutb Minar complex and 13 kilometres from the old city of Siri. The city was divided into several parts, the most important being the citadel with its high walls. It had 13 gates and several halls and towers to protect the city. Not much remains of the city except a few ruined walls of the fortress and palace.

The Tughluq palaces were made of bricks. According to Ibn Batuta,[5] an Arab traveller who lived in India from 1333 to 1341, the bricks in Ghiyas Tughluq's palace were gold-plated and 'at sunshine they shone with such brightness and lustre that one could not gaze at it' (cited in Nizami, 1997:42). The palace consisted of a tank filled with molten gold. He also describes the palace of Mohammad Tughluq as having many gates.

While the palaces, fortresses and victory towers were the symbols of power and glory of kings during their life time, mausoleums immortalized them after their death. The tomb of Ghiyas is the only royal monument of the Tughluq period to have survived without any damage. Unlike that of Iltutmish earlier, this monument is rather heavy and without ornamentation. It looks more like a fortress with thick walls surrounding it.[6]

Mohammad Tughluq, who had moved his capital to Daulatabad (see below), returned to Delhi in 1327, perhaps because he realized that he could not govern his kingdom from the Deccan. Instead of moving back to Tughluqabad, he moved to a new capital city, Jahan Panah (Refuge of the World), which he had commissioned. It lies between Lal Kot (built by the Tomar ruler, Anangpal I, in around AD 731) and Siri (built by Ala-ud-din Khalji in 1311). Historical evidence is not conclusive concerning the date of its construction or its purpose, especially as it was built close to the old city of Tughluqabad. It may have served as recompense by the Sultan for his mistake to move to Daulatabad, which had caused a lot of suffering.

Jahan Panah is now in ruins. The only surviving monument is a large mosque and ruins of a palace, observation tower and a dome. Bijay Mandal is a terraced, tower-like structure which may have formed part of Sultan Firoz Shah's palace, Hazar Sutun, (with 1,000 pillars) right next to it. On top of Bijay Mandal, there seems to be an observation post, presumably for the Sultan to watch military exercises and monitor troop activities. Near the Bijay Mandal is a tomb-like structure whose purpose and origin remain a mystery. It is rather puzzling to find an unnamed mausoleum close to a palace. Could this structure have served some purpose other than that of a tomb?

The palace horseshoe arches, believed to be copies of the Khalji prototypes, are still visible although no pillars are intact (Marshall, 1928:587). The palace has intersecting vaults which became an important feature of Tughluq architecture. In the early twentieth century, excavations at the site found precious objects, including old coins, gold and rubies, which would suggest that a palace did indeed exist. Tadjell (1990:162) attributes the palace to Mohammad Tughluq, and believes that the Sultan built it 'to outdo Ala-ud-din'.

Royal Extravagance

Besides building towns and palaces, the Tughluq sultans spent large sums of money on elaborately decorated robes of honour with costly brocades and velvet, which were presented to their nobles. One account estimates that 200,000 robes were distributed by Mohammad Tughluq who was particularly known for offering lavish gifts. The Sultan's own requirements for goods also cost an exorbitant amount of state funds (Ashraf, 2000:159). He and his successor, Firoz Tughluq, spent large sums of money on their ceremonies of accession. Later, this extravagance was emulated by the Mughal emperors.

Ibn Batuta describes the extraordinary pomp of Mohammad Tughluq and the splendour and extravagance of his capital, Tughluqabad. At that time, Delhi was the largest of all the Islamic cities in the East. The sultan's wealth may have been accumulated through campaigns against the independent Hindu kingdoms in the south. His opulence may be illustrated by the following examples:

(1) the Sultan's public audiences included a lavish display of horses and elephants decorated with silk and gold-covered seats;
(2) the Sultan's high throne of pure gold was studded with precious jewels;
(3) the Council Hall had artificial trees of silk and gold chairs; and
(4) there were sumptuous processions of decorated and bejewelled elephants during the Sultan's Id durbars and accession to the throne (Ghoshal, 1960a:655).

The royal expenditures included maintenance of the royal court, wardrobe, standards and ensigns, furniture, carpeting and furnishings of the palace, the harem, the bodyguards and domestic servants, not counting the cost of building various palaces and forts. Estimated costs of a few items are presented below by way of illustration (Ashraf, 2000:159):

— Royal wardrobe: annual expenditure of 600,000 *tankas* for cold weather alone.
— Royal shoes: 70,000 *tankas* for a single pair.
— Furnishings and carpeting: 200,000 *tankas* per year.
— Royal stable: 60,000–100,000 *tankas*.
— Standards and ensigns: 80,000 *tankas* per year.

Firoz Tughluq built Firoz Shah Kotla, a new palace and a pleasure pavilion when four already existed: at Siri, Jahan Panah, the Qutb and Kilokheri near what is Maharani Bagh today. The palace consisted of halls for special and public audience, a step-well for the king to keep cool in summer besides a large number of rooms. In addition, he is known to have built 200 towns, 40 mosques, 30 colleges, 30 reservoirs, 50 dams, 100 hospitals, 100 public baths and 150 bridges (Watson, 1979:98).

It is not clear why Firoz Shah would decorate his palace with a Buddhist pillar brought from outside Delhi. Did he aim to show that he ruled over both Hindus and Buddhists? Or was the pillar symbolic of his respect for and recognition of an ancient ruler? Historical records do not provide any clues.

The royal palaces were the centre of pomp and splendour during the Muslim rule in India (Nizami, 1997). They have not survived but their ruins are a reminder of the extravagant lifestyles of the sultans whose ambitions, whims and fancy were almost insatiable. Superfluity was the hallmark of an extravagant civilization.

Apart from the sultans, the aristocracy also indulged in pomp and extravagance, thanks to their large landholdings and fiefs, besides their high salaries. During the reign of Mohammad Tughluq, his Naib (deputy) 'enjoyed the income of a province as large as Iraq; the wazir (Prime minister) was paid a similar amount; the four ministers received from 20,000 to 40,000 tankas each, every year' (ibid.:163). During Firoz Tughluq's reign, the salaries were much higher: his wazir received a million and a half tankas and other personal allowances. This allowed the nobles to pursue a life of luxury, as reflected in the rich garments, jewellery, perfumery and artistic articles produced for them. Their houses and courts imitated those of the sultan. Indeed, the wealth and splendour of the nobles 'occasionally excited the jealousy of the kings themselves' (Mirza, 1960:613–4).

However, not much is known about the economic plight of ordinary people during the Tughluq rule. Lavish expenditures on royal monuments as well as on ceremonies may have left little for the improvement of the standard of living of the subjects.

In general, the economic history of northern India during the period of the Delhi Sultanate is extremely patchy. Information sources are scarce. Economic historians have to rely on travellers' accounts as well as on archaeological ruins, inscriptions and coins of the period. For the medieval period relating to the Muslim rule, archaeological excavations have not thrown as much light as they have of the much earlier periods (Digby, 1982:45). Therefore, it is difficult to assess whether the royal extravagance occurred at the expense of ordinary subjects in the sultanate.

Literary sources and travellers' accounts give some indication of the wealth and splendour of the upper classes and the misery and poverty of the common people. There did not seem to be any prosperous middle class so that 'the wealth and splendour of the upper strata of society formed a strange contrast with the poverty and squalor of the masses both Muslim and Hindu' (Mirza, 1960:608).

Peasants did not enjoy private ownership of land, a fact noted in a document pertaining to the reign of Firoz Shah Tughluq. Habib (1982a:54) states that they were 'no better than semi-serfs'. Their plight 'often became miserable owing to oppression and heavy taxes' (Chitnis, 2009:43). However, during the Sultan's reign, most commodities such as wheat and barley as well as silk were known to be very cheap (Ghoshal, 1960a:655).

Some inferences about the economic situation of the general population can be drawn by examining the state of the agrarian economy. At that time, most Indians lived in villages, and agricultural production was the mainstay of the Delhi Sultanate along with some handicraft industry. The majority of the population must have been engaged in subsistence farming. Barani notes that canal irrigation was provided during the reign of Ghiyas-ud-din Tughluq. And, according to Ibn Batuta, Mohammad Tughluq dug wells for artificial irrigation and provided loans to peasants for cultivation. Firoz Shah Tughluq extended the canal irrigation network further. In fact, Habib (1982a:49) found that 'Hisar was so well-irrigated by new canals that while previously only the rain-watered autumn crops (kharif) were grown here, now the spring (rabi) crops, especially wheat, could also be raised.' Artificial irrigation and knowledge and use of the Persian wheel allowed double irrigation, which may suggest that rural people probably had enough food to eat.

A contemporary observer (ibid.:55) suggests that 'peasants were generally 'affluent' and prosperous. He writes:

In the houses of the raiyat (peasantry), so much grain, wealth, horses, and goods accumulated that one cannot speak of them. Everyone had large amounts of gold and silver and countless goods. None of the women folk of the peasantry remained without ornaments. In every peasant's house, there were clean bed-sheets, excellent bed-cots, many articles and much wealth.

Firoz was a benevolent sultan who cared for the poor, even setting up a free hospital for them. His sultanate 'was the closest that any government in medieval India came to being a welfare state' (Eraly, 2014:173).

Sayyid and Lodi Tombs in New Delhi

All that is left of the legacy of the Sayyid and Lodi sultans from Afghanistan are their modest tombs in Lodi Gardens. Sayyids did not leave behind many architectural monuments with the exception of a few square and octagonal tombs which are scattered all over Delhi. The two known ones are those of sultans Mubarak Shah (in Kotla Mubarakpur) and Muhammad Shah (in Lodi Gardens). Unlike several other tombs in India (mostly Lodi), the tomb of Muhammad Shah is octagonal in shape, with numerous Hindu-style *chhatris* around the central dome, several arches, verandas and sloping buttresses. Other examples of Hindu elements include ornamental pinnacles (*guldastas*) and *chhajjas*. The octagonal tomb is a good example of a blend of Hindu and Islamic styles of architecture in India. Many believe that the royal tombs of sultans were generally octagonal whereas those of nobles and princes were square.

Several years later, Sikandar Lodi's tomb was built also in the Lodi Gardens on the model of the above Sayyid tomb. However, unlike the Sayyid tomb, it has no *chhatris* which appear in the outer precincts. Other Lodi tombs include the Shish Gumbad (glazed dome) and the Bara Gumbad (big tomb). The former has two storeys of blind arcades with central frieze of square panels, which show remnants of the original glazed tiles of turquoise blue colour. Some observers believe that it is Bahlol Lodi's tomb. Bara Gumbad with an adjoining mosque is located quite close to the Shish Gumbad. These structures lead one writer to observe that 'this complex of buildings is on a scale befitting a royal personage' (Digby, 1975:553).

The interior of Bara Gumbad with its Tughluq-style minarets consists of painted tiles and Qur'anic inscriptions. A mosque, known as Jami Masjid built by Sikandar Lodi, is attached to the tomb. Why was it attached to Bara Gumbad and not to Sikandar Lodi's tomb? What purpose did Bara Gumbad serve? Historical records do not throw much light on these questions. While it may have been a tomb, some scholars and historians believe that the high-domed edifice may have been taken over by Sikandar Lodi and converted into a gateway to the mosque (Alfieri, 2000:55).

Lodis built many more royal as well as non-royal tombs than those built in Firoz Shah Tughluq's reign, for example. The Lodi nobles and chiefs were quite powerful and were allowed to build their own tombs along with those of the sultans. The Lodi sultans considered themselves as first among equals. In fact, the Lodi ruling tribe was only one among many other powerful tribes whose loyalty was needed to govern effectively. According to one scholar, Bahlol Lodi, the first Lodi sultan, was 'at best the chief leader of the Afghan tribes and not a king of all the peoples of his kingdom' (Tripathi, 1936:84).

However, under the Tughluq reign the nobles did not have an independent authority, as the sultan wielded absolute and autocratic power. This situation is attributed by one observer to 'the power relationship among the Afghan class which was diversely different from the power structure of the Turks (Tughluqs), and particularly to the attitude of the Turkish nobles who regarded the sultan as absolute' (Ara, 1982:78).

There is no trace of any Sayyid and Lodi palaces or fortresses like those in Tughluqabad, Mandu and Daulatabad discussed above. The Lodis may not have built any, which may have something to do with their particular concept of kingship and its interpretation. Also the treasury of the Sayyids and Lodis was empty, which might also explain why no new forts and palaces were built during their reign. One author observes that 'the Sultans of the first half of the fifteenth century (Sayyids) were comparatively poor both financially and in personal attainments [. . .]. By the latter half of the fifteenth century much of the glory and prosperity seems to have returned as is clear from the description of the coronation Darbars of Sikandar Lodi and Ibrahim Lodi' (Lal, 1963:262).

However, as the Lodi sultans were more egalitarian than their predecessors, they looked after the socioeconomic interests of the common people in the sultanate. Sikandar Lodi abolished the corn duties and made sure that the prices of basic commodities were kept under control. Abdulla notes that during the reign of Ibrahim Lodi, 'Corn, cloth and other things were cheaper than they had been in any other reign, excepting the closing years of Alauddin's reign' (ibid.:258).

Conclusion

The royal monuments described above illustrate the pomp and conspic-uous consumption of the Delhi Sultanate. While there are traces of Tughluq and Khalji palaces, forts, towers and tombs, Lodis built only modest gumbads and mosques, and no palaces. This suggests that the earlier sultans were more pompous and conscious of their legacy and royal status than their successors.

The Delhi Sultanate included the early Turkish sultans (Slaves, Khaljis and Tughluqs) and the later Lodi Afghans. The Turks and Afghans adopted different concepts of kingship and the royal court. Therefore, the style and degree of pomp, luxury and lavishness is likely to have differed during the earlier and later periods.

The Turkish rulers were known to be absolute monarchs who kept a distance from their subjects. They felt racially superior to the local people of Indian origin. Non-Turks were given low positions in their courts (Chitnis, 2009). On the other hand, Afghan society was divided into a large number of important and independent tribes who considered their ruler as only first among equals. There is evidence to suggest that the Lodi sultans did not behave like absolute monarchs, their power being restricted by the influential tribes and clans.

The Tughluqs built a whole new city of Tughluqabad which contained palaces, forts, mausoleums, lakes and water tanks, but they built very few royal tombs for themselves and their immediate families. They did not allow any tombs of nobility to compete with their own glory and power. In contrast, the Lodis, the last of the Delhi sultans, built no such lavish structures. Instead, they built a large number of simple tombs, including those of sultans as well as of amirs, princes and senior officers who did not have any royal blood. This may suggest their egalitarian attitude and simple life style.

The building of simple mausoleums by the Lodi sultans is unlikely to have been associated with a desire to show power. Lodi sultans were not known to be ostentatious. At social gatherings, Bahlol Lodi did not sit on a throne, but on a carpet, and did not allow his nobles to stand. This was in contrast to Sher Shah Suri, a low-ranking Afghan sultan who wanted to raise his and his family's social and political status by building impressive mausoleums.

Some scholars (for example, Rahim, 1961) suggest that Bahlol Lodi had to win the support of his strong tribal chiefs by lavishing upon them large *jagir* (land). Tripathi (1936:84) goes further in commenting that he 'lowered the dignity of the sultan and reduced kingship to a sort of exalted peerage'.

The accounts of Badaoni,[7] Barani and Ibn Batuta suggest that most of the Delhi sultans indulged in pomp and ostentation. Chitnis (2009:41) notes that 'they indulged in unnecessary pomp, wasteful luxury and vanity'. The display of banners, beating of drums and blowing of trumpets were important symbols pomp and vainglory during their campaigns.

The extravagant lifestyle of the rich contrasted with the poor living conditions of ordinary Indians. Ercly (2014:358) believes that the common people in medieval India lived at a bare subsistence level even though India was rich in natural resources, including fertile lands.

3

The Deccan Muslim Kingdoms

Palaces, arches, tombs, cisterns, gateways, minarets, [...] (of Bijapur) all carved from the rich basalt rock of the locality garlanded by creepers, broken and disjointed by peepul trees, each in its turn is a gem of art and the whole a treasury.

(Philip Meadows Taylor,[1] 1866)

Like the Delhi sultans, the Deccan sultans also left behind their legacy in the form of palaces (Farah Bagh), forts and fortresses (Golconda fort) and royal tombs (Qutb Shahi tombs and Gol Gumbad). The building of palaces and to a lesser extent, mausoleums (especially by the Qutb Shahis) was their main preoccupation.

Bijapur, Gulbarga and Bidar were the three most important cities which depicted the Deccan style of architecture. Two outstanding examples of this style are Gol Gumbad in Bijapur and Char Minar in Hyderabad. Initially, during the fourteenth and fifteenth centuries, plaster was used for decorations on Bahmani monuments, but it was replaced by stone in the sixteenth and seventeenth centuries (Michell and Zebrowski, 1999). However, the Qutb Shahi sultans retained plasterwork for decorative purposes.

The Bijapur Sultanate founded by the Adil Shahis grew out of the Bahmani kingdom.[2] It surpassed all the others in the Deccan in terms of its contribution to art and architecture. As eulogized by the poet, Iqbal Asif, 'There are many good cities in the world, but you cannot find in any other the domes of Bijapur, talking to the sky' (cited in Werner and Wells, 2013).

During their long rule, the Bijapur sultans built several fortresses, palaces (Gagan Mahal and Asar Mahal) and mausoleums. Two of the finest examples of mausoleums in Bijapur are those of Muhammad Adil Shah (Gol Gumbad) and Ibrahim Adil Shah II (Ibrahim Rauza). An unfinished mosque, Jami Masjid, is one of the oldest monuments of the Adil Shahis. Each sultan tried to outdo his predecessor in architecture, so much so that Bijapur is sometimes called Agra of the Deccan, and Ibrahim Rauza its Taj.

Tajuddin Firoz (1397–1422), one of the most powerful Bahmani sultans, contributed significantly to art and culture. He invited to his court several Persian, Arab and Turkish artists and scholars, as well as architects and craftsmen. They worked with local architects and craftsmen, leading to the creation of a distinct Deccan style, which blended local styles with those of Persia, Turkey and Arabia. He also built a new city, Firuzabad (known as the palace city), and several royal monuments.

Early Bahmani monuments used the Persian-style geometric and floral motifs found in Daulatabad and Firuzabad palaces. It is also likely that the crown and wing motifs in the arches were inspired by the earlier Hindu monuments in the Deccan.

From the fourteenth to sixteenth century, the history of the Deccan, like that of the Delhi Sultanate, was ridden with conflicts, which might in part have arisen from the political instability and uncertainty caused by the frequent campaigns of the Delhi Sultanate to conquer and annex the Deccan, all of which ended in failure.

Ala-ud-din Hasan, who was an able military commander of the Deccan Sultanate of Mohammad Tughluq, the Delhi sultan, revolted against his master and established an independent Muslim Bahmani kingdom. It was the first such kingdom in southern India, with its capital first at Gulbarga (1347 to 1425) and then at Bidar (1425 to 1527). By1526, it had broken up into five independent kingdoms of Ahmadnagar, Berar, Bidar, Bijapur and Golconda, known as the Deccan Sultanates.[3]

Nizam Shahis of Ahmadnagar[4]

The Nizam Shahi rulers built many palaces, forts and mosques. They are also known for miniature paintings, which are scattered around the world, with some fine examples on display at the San Diego Museum in California and the Bibliothèque Nationale in Paris.

The large number of palaces discussed below suggests that each Nizam felt compelled to build his own, presumably to out-do his predecessors. It would seem that extravagance and vainglory were the underlying motives for building so many palaces so close to each other. Even the nobles built palaces in attempts to emulate their masters.

The Farah Bagh palace complex on the outskirts of Ahmadnagar stands out as the most impressive of the palaces. Built in the typical Persian style of architecture, it is more grandiose than similar palaces built in Persia at that time (Michell and Zebrowski, 1999:11). Its construction was begun by Burhan Nizam Shah I (1508–53) and completed in 1583 after his death. It was a favourite residence of Murtaza Nizam Shah. Chand Bibi[5] also stayed in the palace from time to time.

The octagonal palace, originally built in the middle of a lake, has a flat-roofed upper storey, which offers a view of the entire central hall. Its facades on four sides have double-height arched portals flanked by smaller arched recesses. It is built of rough stone and lime masonry and is plastered with stucco both inside and outside.

Other palaces in Ahmadnagar are:

(1) Kasim Khan's palace, built at the beginning of the sixteenth century during the reign of the first sultan, Ahmad Nizam Shah (1490–1508). A long flight of steps leads to its central hall, which is adorned with black-stone pillars, a dome and a carved ceiling.

(2) Khan Zaman's palace and mosque, located quite close to Kasim Khan's palace, built in 1559 during the reign of the third sultan Husain (1553–65).

(3) Nyamat Khan's palace and mosque completed in 1579 during the reign of the fourth sultan Murtaza I (1565–88). It is almost completely in ruins; only its foundations have been traced (*Ahmadnagar District Gazetteer*, 1884). However, the mosque remains intact.

(4) Sarje Khan's palace and mosque built in 1561, presumably by a local nobleman whose tomb is also situated nearby.

(5) Kavi Jang's palace built in 1750 by the Nizam's commandant.

Invariably, palaces contained mosques some of which have survived. Other mosques outside the palaces were also built, such as the *Soneri* (golden) mosque built by Nizam-ul-Mulk (1720–48). Many nobles also built mosques.

Nizam Husain Shah is said to have built a strong fort which was successfully defended by Chand Bibi in November 1595 against the invading Mughal army. In 1600, the fort was again besieged by the Mughal forces. This time the Mughals succeeded in occupying it and in murdering her when many fort defenders mutinied.[6] Apart from the strong fortifications, barracks and garrisons, the fort included the Nizam's palace similar to those of the Delhi sultans of the north. The palace was quite grand with a large public room and a roof of multiple domes, a badminton court, stables and a state prison. However, the British destroyed many palace buildings when they took possession of the fort.

Bagh Rauza (garden of the shrine), in which the first Nizam Ahmad is buried, is considered to be one of the finest buildings of Ahmadnagar. It is made of black stone with a dome on top. Inside the tomb building the text from the Qur'an is inscribed in gold letters. Other mausoleums in the complex include those of Shah Tahir, a minister of Husain Nizam Shah, an elephant (named Gulam Ali, which captured Ramraja of Vijayanagar in the Battle of Talikot, 1565) and its mahout.

The Nizam Shahis built pleasure gardens and resorts like those of the Mughals. One example of such a resort is the Hayat Behisht Garden in the north of Ahmadnagar, which contains a two-storey pavilion in the middle of a pond. The central chamber of the pavilion is surrounded by an arcade. They also designed extensive water systems in the Iranian tradition, drawing water from dams and springs in the hills to keep palaces and pavilions cool.

The above lavishness appears in sharp contrast to the poverty of ordinary citizens. One scholar notes that 'the ordinary rural folk used to live in mud huts thatched with straw' (Fukuzawa, 1982b:471). Anecdotal evidence indicates that most common people were barefooted and scantily dressed, more out of poverty than for climatic reasons.

Frequent famines in the Deccan (1630–1, 1655, 1682 and 1684) due to scant rainfall must have further pauperized the rural poor. In the famine of 1630–1, a million people are known to have died in Ahmadnagar district alone. The famine was so acute that state revenue of the Mughal Deccan provinces was too inadequate to meet their administrative expenses not to speak of providing for serious remedial measures.

It is hard to find any robust information on the wages of rural artisans and labourers. Fukuzawa (ibid.:471–2) presents some crude data on cash payments to artisans on the basis of which he concludes that they were 'remarkably small in amount as compared with urban wages'. Many weavers were often poor and had to depend on advance payments from their buyers. This situation suggests a high degree of rural-urban income inequality in the medieval Deccan.

As expected, urban living conditions were much better than the rural. Fukuzawa (ibid.:474) notes that 'the urban poor were not always paupers in normal times. Rather, some of them seem to have been fairly well-to-do.' In the seventeenth century, the urban population consisted of many rich merchants, bankers and jewellers especially in the larger cities.

Other well-off classes included the military and civil functionaries who received revenue from villages and sub-districts, besides their regular salaries and some land. Senior officials, who maintained a retinue of soldiers and servants, were ranked according to the number of soldiers they were entitled to maintain. The larger the number of soldiers, the higher the rank of the officer (Fukuzawa, 1963).

Adil Shahis of Bijapur

The Adil Shahi sultans excelled in building palaces and mausoleums. *Gagan Mahal* (Heavenly Palace) is part of a building complex within a walled fortress consisting of other structures such as the Sat Mahal (Seven-Storey Palace). It was built in 1560 by Sultan Ali Adil Shah (1557–80) as a palace and as a hall of public audience. The palace included the royal residence and a *zenana* (harem) with latticed windows. It's important features include a grand arch and a gateway.

In his novel, *A Noble Queen*, Philip Meadows Taylor describes a royal audience at the Gagan Mahal thus:

> It was a sight at once gorgeous and impressive in itself; the costumes and banners of the ranks of infantry interspersed with cavalry Deccanis, Arabs, Persians, Oozebeks, Circassions, Tatars of many tribes and Georgians, Turks, and many other foreigners . . . (cited in Werner and Wells, 2013:9)

Anand Mahal (Joy Palace) was also built by Sultan Adil Shah, in 1589, 29 years after the Gagan Mahal. Apparently, it was built especially for his queens, its main features including splendid archways in the foreground, fountains and gardens, ornamental walls and lofty roofs.

Asar Mahal (or Athar or Dad Mahal) was built in 1646 by Sultan Muhammad Shah. Originally, it was built as a palace or hall of justice. It is the best preserved of all the Adil Shahi palaces in Bijapur. In 1646, it was converted into a sacred place to keep two hairs of the Prophet Mohammad.

Chini Mahal within the fort complex is decorated with locally-available glazed tiles, which explains its name. The palace consists of a 40-metre long hall followed by suites of rooms.

Sat Manzil (Seven-Storey Building) is also located inside the fortress. Only four of its original seven storeys are still standing. Water basins and murals suggest that it was a pleasure pavilion.

Kummatgi, a pleasure resort 16 kilometres from Bijapur, consists of pavilions, tanks and cisterns overlooking a big lake. A double-storey tower is one of the most important buildings of the royal complex.

Gol Gumbad is a round mausoleum of Muhammad Adil Shah. According to an inscription on it, Muhammad died in 1656, when the construction may have stopped, which is suggested by the fact that the attached mosque has no parapet. It is simple in design and has a massive hemispherical dome above a square chamber unsupported by any pillars. It is one of the largest dome structures in the world, comparable to that of St Peter's Basilica in Rome. The dome has several arches. Each corner of the square structure has seven-storey towers. Its short octagonal minarets are similar to those decorating the Qutb Shahi tombs. They stand in sharp contrast to the tall and tapering Mughal minarets of Humayun's tomb, Jahangir's tomb and the Taj Mahal. Jehan Begum, Sultan Muhammad's queen, is buried at nearby Ainapur in a mausoleum similar to Gol Gumbad but half its size.

Ibrahim Rauza, the mausoleum of Ibrahim Adil Shah II (Fig. 3.1), consists of a chamber 'roofed by a horizontal vault divided into nine squares with curved sides'. The outer walls of the mausoleum 'are covered with panels of geometric and calligraphic designs' (Michell and Zebrowski, 1999:90–1). Henry Cousens, an expert architect, called this tomb the Taj Mahal of the south. Although it was built before the Taj, such a comparison is suggested probably because the tomb was originally intended for the Sultan's wife, Taj Sultana. Others noted that it was one of the finest buildings 'which rivals those of the Mughals' (Haig and Burn, 1937:573).

Fig. 3.1. Ibrahim Rauza, Bijapur (Author's Private Collection)

Most of the Bijapur Sultanate buildings are simple unadorned structures. For example, neither Gagan Mahal nor Gol Gumbad has any ornamentation. According to one scholar, 'the dark brown local trap used in Bijapur lacked sophistication in tone and texture, and the builders themselves lacked sophistication, paid little attention to aesthetics' (Eraly, 2007:378). In general, the sultans tended 'to substitute size for elegance'.

However, the Ibrahim Rauza is an exception; it is well ornamented and full of bulbous finials, intricate roof brackets and minarets, and calligraphic decorations of Qur'anic verses as well as Persian poetry.

Adil Shahis lived long and were related to such Mughal emperors as Akbar and Aurangzeb, which may explain why Bijapur had so many royal palaces and mausoleums as symbols of glory and power. As the Sultanate was situated between the Mughal Empire in the north and the Hindu kingdom of Vijayanagar in the south, Hindu and Muslim (Ottoman) cultural and architectural influences are understandable. Examples of such influences include stone-carved chain links hanging from vestibule ceilings invoking pulls of temple bells. The Ottoman influence is visible in such elements as crescent finials on the tombs of the Adil Shahi sultans.

Asaf Beg, Akbar's courtier, has given a detailed and vivid account of Bijapur as one of the most prosperous cities of India in early Mughal times. However, it lost its prosperity following the wars imposed by the Mughals. The rule of the Bijapur Sultans came to an end when Aurangzeb, the Mughal Emperor, conquered Bijapur after a siege that lasted more than a year.

Qutb Shahis of Golconda[7]

Qutb Shahi architecture (and that of the Bahmanis and Adil Shahis) broke with the northern tradition of Afghan and Tughluq architecture introduced by the Khaljis and Tughluqs in the Deccan. It is rather surprising that, despite their presence in the Deccan, their northern style did not have much influence on the Deccan style, possibly because the Deccan plateau separates the two regions. It may also have been due to the fact that, although Mohammad Tughluq shifted his capital to Daulatabad, he did not stay there long enough to have had much influence on its architecture. Such Muslim cities as Golconda, Bidar and Bijapur were not built near any sites of thriving Hindu culture, presumably for historical and political reasons. Therefore, building materials from the Hindu temples were not as readily available to the Deccan sultans as they were to their counterparts in the north.

Deccan architecture was influenced more by Persian and Turkish styles than by Indian Hindu or Muslim. This influence may be explained by a thriving trade route between the Deccan and the Arabian Sea during the fourteenth and fifteenth centuries, which must have brought skilled craftsmen and artisans to the western Indian ports. The Persian influence is seen in the stone calligraphic panels. Stone and plaster inscriptions on the Qutb Shahi tombs are described by Michell and Zebrowski (1999:123) as 'some of the finest stone epigraphy from the sixteenth and seventeenth centuries in India'. Stone work is also done on the polygonal platforms inside the royal baths (*hammams*). It is generally believed that these platforms were intended for mortuary baths. However, Michell and Zebrowski argue that they were used by visiting courtiers and nobles for bathing.

The Qutb Shahis built several palaces, forts, mausoleums and mosques. The Golconda Fort, expanded by the successive Qutb Shahi sultans, was their seat of government for several years before they moved their capital to Hyderabad. It contained palaces for the kings and queens, Shahi Mahal and Rani Mahal, respectively, as well as audience halls, commercial streets, ceremonial portals, mosques, gardens and defensive gates (such as the Fateh Gate and the Bala Hisar Gate).

Qutb Shahi monuments used plaster for decoration, for example, on the Bala Hisar Gate, which is the main entrance to the Golconda fort, and on the Qutb Shahi tombs and mosques. Arabesque medallions, peacocks with long feathers and lions with curly tails on Bala Hisar are Hindu symbols. It is paradoxical that Islam forbade the use of such symbols in Muslim tombs of holy places, but the Muslim sultans nevertheless used them, flouting religious injunctions.

Golconda is known for its unique necropolis in Ibrahim Bagh (Garden) located about two kilometres from the fort. It represents the highest concentration of royal mausoleums anywhere. All the Qutb Shahi sultans, except the last, are buried there. The Garden also contains tombs of relatives, commanders and singers, which are almost identical in plan, each with a square base supporting a Persian-style dome built in white stone. With a few exceptions, the original blue and green colours, which adorned the tombs, have now faded.

The Sultans' mausoleums were fitted with golden spires to distinguish them from those of other members of the royal family. Originally, the tombs were furnished with carpets, chandeliers and canopies supported by silver poles. All these furnishings have now disappeared. It is believed that the royal mausoleums were originally covered with mosaics and blue tiles, some of which have survived till today in Ibrahim Qutb Shah's tomb, for example. Unlike the earlier tombs of the Slaves, Tughluqs and Lodis in the north, the exterior of the Qutb Shahi tombs is finished with moulded plaster, not carved stone. The end of the Qutb Shahi reign led to a total neglect of the Golconda necropolis. It was not until the nineteenth century that the tombs were restored, with a garden laid and a wall built around them.

Qutb Shahi architecture differs from the Bahmani in several respects. It has different kinds of arches, ornamental finials and corner minarets adorned with balconies. Bulbous domes and turnip-shaped orbs of small finials rising from double rows of petals are its other special features (Bawa, 2002:330). In Golconda, the long reign of Ibrahim Shah, who ruled for more than 30 years, must have provided the political stability necessary for architecture to flourish. Bawa attributes the continuity, autonomy and identity of Qutb Shahi architecture to the ruling family and the Sufi saints who were linked to it.

Mosques are found adjacent to some tombs, such as the one next to Jamshid Qutb Shah's tomb. Originally, each tomb was accompanied by a mosque next to it, but some may have been destroyed, though it is uncertain when and by whom.

Mosques of Hyderabad (the second capital of the Qutb Shahi dynasty after Golconda) include Mecca Masjid built over 400 years ago by Muhammad Qutb Shah, the sixth sultan of Hyderabad. It has three arched facades built from a single granite stone. The elegant *Toli Mosque*, built in 1671, has a prayer chamber with five arches on the facade and attractive calligraphic medallions.

The Char Minar (Four Towers) in Hyderabad, built by Muhammad Qutb Shah and his successor, is one of the most well-known Deccan monuments. It had a mosque and a madrasa at the upper levels.

Golconda was known for its elephants and diamonds. In the sixteenth and seventeenth centuries, some of the most valuable diamonds, such as the Regent, the Koh-i-Noor and the Orloff, were found there. Tavernier, who visited Golconda fort in 1645, described it as a rich store of precious diamonds.

The Golconda sultans gave gifts of elephants and diamonds to Mughal emperors such as Shah Jahan (Bijapur submitted to Shah Jahan in 1636). Akbar sent Asaf Beg to collect elephants and rare jewels from the Deccan Sultanates (Eraly, 1997:530). When Golconda Fort fell to Aurangzeb's army, a large number of jewels, inlaid articles and gold and silver vessels were seized as well as property worth Rs 68 million (ibid.:495).

Asaf Jahis of Hyderabad

The last Asaf Jahi Nizam of Hyderabad was considered to be one of the richest men in the world. He and his family used their wealth to build dozens of palaces in Hyderabad, a city which perhaps has more palaces per capita of population than any other city in India. The building of such a large number of palaces shows the Nizams' penchant for an

Fig. 3.2. Chowmahalla Palace, Hyderabad (Author's Private Collection)

ostentatious display of wealth, vanity and vainglory besides an exalted status. A few palaces are briefly described below.

Chowmahalla Palace (Fig. 3.2) was the seat of the Asaf Jahi dynasty. Modelled on the palace of the Shah of Iran in Isfahan, it was the official residence of the Nizam where he held ceremonial functions such as his accession and receptions in honour of the British Governors-General and Viceroys.

Chowmahalla literally means four palaces: Aftab Mahal, Afzal Mahal, Mahtab Mahal and Tehniyat Mahal, in the southern courtyard. A clock tower adorned the main entrance gate to the palace which has disappeared.

The Maharaja of Baroda (1980:134–5) notes that the sprawl of out-buildings of the palace 'housed almost ten thousand persons [. . .]. There were relatives, wives, concubines and their offspring, courtiers, func-tionaries, some two thousand servants, and a platoon of Amazons dressed in brown uniforms of French design standing guard over the zenana.'

King Kothi Palace was the residence of the seventh Nizam, Osman Ali Khan, who moved there as a young boy of 13 years of age. In 1911, after his accession to the throne, he preferred to stay in the palace rather than move to the Chowmahalla palace where his father had lived.

Fig. 3.3. Falaknuma Palace, Hyderabad (© Centre for South Asian Studies, Cambridge University)

It consists of three main buildings: the eastern half, the western half and a royal library used by the last Nizam. The eastern half was used for official functions, whereas the western half consisted of such residential buildings as Nazri Bagh and Mubarak Mansion. The palace treasures, which included diamonds, rubies, sapphires and precious stones, were stored in steel trunks fastened with English padlocks.

Falaknuma Palace (Mirror of the Sky) located on a hill five kilometres from the city centre is one of the most lavish palaces of Hyderabad. It has now become a Heritage Hotel of the Taj Group (Fig. 3.3). It was built by Vikarul Umra, the Prime Minister of Hyderabad (1894 to 1901). In 1897, the sixth Nizam (Mahbub Ali Khan) bought it for his favourite queen and added several new structures such as the Coronation building where he died in 1911. Later a new wing was added when it was converted into a royal residence.

The palace became the royal guest house when the queen became tired of it and moved out. British royalty and various viceroys often stayed there as royal guests. They included the future King George V and Queen Mary, the Prince of Wales and Lord Wavell. In 1906, Queen

Mary's bathroom was fitted with a perfume spray. In 1912, electric lights were fitted for the future Duke of Windsor who also stayed there.

Murray's guide notes that the palace is 'considered the finest in India'. It has a Grecian facade with a cornice resting on a double row of Corinthian columns. In its interior, white marble was used copiously to combat extremely hot temperatures. The marble staircase has beautifully carved balustrades adorned with figures of muses from Greek mythology made of Italian Carara marble.[8] The staircase was lined with the portraits of governors-general and viceroys. A ceremonial gateway to the palace was topped by the Nizam's crown, and music was played in a chamber above the gateway.

Bashirbagh Palace was built by Sir Asman Jah, the Prime Minister of Hyderabad (1887–94). It was destroyed after India's independence. However, the area is still known as Bashirbagh.

Chiran Fort Club in the centre of Hyderabad is part of a former palace of the Nizams built in the 1890s. The portion in which the Club is located is part of the Seven Palace Begumpet complex.

Asmangarh Palace, now St Joseph's Public School, was built in 1885 by the Prime Minister Asman Jah of Hyderabad. It is designed as a Gothic European castle.

Saroornagar Palace, now the Victoria Memorial School, was originally built as a palace.

The Asaf Jahis (Nizams) preserved the earlier Persian influence in architecture in Golconda and Hyderabad. They outlasted the British Empire and remained independent until India's independence in 1947. But the tenth Nizam (Mir Usman Ali), who ruled from 1911 to 1949, was not interested in joining either India or Pakistan as was proposed by the departing British rulers. He wished to remain an independent ruler despite pressure from the Indian leaders to join India. In 1950, the Indian Government annexed the princely state of Hyderabad through a quick and easy military intervention.

Some scholars (such as Michell and Zebrowski, 1999) have compared Hyderabad to the Persian Safavid capital of Isfahan, as many royal buildings in the city are designed in the Persian style of architecture.

The princely state of Hyderabad was in constant turmoil on account of conflicts over royal succession. In the eighteenth century, it lost territory to the French, the British and the Marathas. In 1779, it entered into a peace treaty with the Company. The Nizam was a faithful ally of the British who remained loyal during the 1857 uprising despite being a Muslim. In recognition, the British called his kingdom of Hyderabad, 'the premier native state' and referred to the Nizam as 'His Exalted Highness'.

Muhammad Shah (1719–48), the Mughal Emperor, appointed Nizam-ul Mulk as his Prime Minister, conferring on him the title of Asaf Jah after his victory over rebelling Mughal nobles. Appointed governor of the Deccan, he was left 'to rule virtually free of any interference from Delhi' (ibid.:19). He also became rich and powerful thanks to a large income from the six Deccani provinces over which he ruled. However, he avoided conferring upon himself any royal title despite his wealth and opulence. He preferred to call himself Nizam, a practice followed by his successors until the tenth and last Nizam of Hyderabad.

The last Nizam is rumoured to have owned 'stacks of gold bricks, chests of diamonds and pearls and three hundred expensive cars presented to him by his admirers' (Maharaja of Baroda, 1980:135–6). As the last standard-bearer of the Muslim power in India, he received all types of gifts and offerings from rich Muslims in India and abroad. The expensive cars received as a gift are believed to have rusted in the stables of King Kothi and the Nizam continued to ride in an old Buick. Despite being very wealthy, he was known to be parsimonious.[9]

It is believed that the Nizam used a diamond called 'Jacob' as a paperweight. His collection of jewels and pearls was so enormous that 'the pearls alone would cover all the pavements of Piccadilly Circus' (Collins and Lapierre, 1976:144). Besides, he had 'over two million pounds in cash – sterling and rupees – wrapped in old newspapers' (ibid.:145).

His Falaknuma palace was built with imported Carara marble from Italy when cheaper Makrana marble (used in the Taj and Victoria Memorial) could have been used, which testifies to his lavishness and extravagance. Its ballroom contains a manually-operated organ (weighing two tons), which is considered to be the only one of its kind in the world. The palace has over 200 richly decorated rooms and 22 large halls. The dining hall can seat 100 guests at a single table and the tableware was made of gold and crystal. It boasts a unique collection of jade along with other treasures (paintings, statues, furniture, and books and manuscripts) collected by the Nizam. The inlaid ceiling and walnut panelling was inspired by those in Windsor Castle.

Conclusion

It is clear from these descriptions of the various monuments, that the Deccan sultans, be they Nizam Shahis, Adil Shahis, Qutb Shahis or Asaf Jahis, all had their fair share of grand palaces and mausoleums to match those of the sultans in the north. Although their architecture did not match that of the Slave and Tughluq dynasties in terms of ornamentation, the Bijapur monuments such as Ibrahim Rauza were quite well decorated.

However, it is difficult to make such a comparison partly because the royal monuments of the Deccan are still standing and are much better preserved than those of the sultans of the north. Not many royal monuments of the Slave, Tughluq and Lodi sultans have survived the ravages of time.

Bijapur, Golconda and Hyderabad were well-known and prosperous cities. Hyderabad had the reputation of being a hedonistic city despite its Muslim origin. Plenty of drinking bars were found alongside brothels. Tavernier[10] notes that several thousand horses carried jars of toddy to Hyderabad every day. Toddy was freely available despite the Islamic prescription against drinking (Eraly, 2007:102).

Muslim civilization in the north and south of India developed independently and differently. In the north, Turks and Afghans were the Muslim sultans, whereas in the south, the dominant Muslim ethnic groups were Persian and Abyssinian, with a different language and religion. While Persian was the official language in the north, Urdu flourished in the Deccan, and while the Sunni faith was popular in the north, Shias occupied pride of place in the Deccan.

These differences may have influenced the attitudes, ostentation and cultural attachments of the Deccan sultans, and differentiated them from those in the north. The monuments discussed in this chapter certainly depict a stronger Persian influence in their architecture than what is found in the north. However, the legacy of the Deccan sultans is surpassed by the Mughals who excelled in the building of lavish monuments of all kinds, from fortresses, palaces, mosques mausoleums and madrasas, to entire new cities.

Was the above pomp and extravagance of the Deccan sultans accompanied by prosperity among ordinary people in the Sultanates? This is not clear, owing to the lack of adequate and reliable information. In principle, in the absence of any systematic economic data, it is possible to form some impression of the prevailing living conditions on the basis of the following sources: (1) European travellers' accounts, (2) the agrarian and revenue systems, (3) prices and availability of foodstuffs, (4) wage payments in cash and kind to artisans and other workers, and (5) quality of housing. On all these counts, living conditions in the Deccan, in both rural and urban areas, were quite poor, with few exceptions.

Available evidence points to tyrannical and exploitative behaviour of the Deccan sultans and nobles towards peasants. For example, Eraly (ibid.:279) mentions such exploitation in the Bahmani kingdom. But some Deccan sultans (Ibrahim Qutb Shah, for example) were benevolent towards their subjects. They built irrigation facilities (dams, canals and water tanks) for agricultural development and shared the increased income from irrigated lands with peasants and religious bodies. In case of crop failures due to famines or wars, they exempted the peasants from the payment of land tax (Fukuzawa, 1982a:200–1).

The majority of peasants had only ten or fewer acres of land, and may thus be defined as rural poor; others had as many as 30 acres. As land was the main economic asset, the latter were generally considered affluent and might have represented a class of hereditary landlords who were also entitled to a certain share of the revenue from the villages. The unequal distribution of land within villages accounted for vast inequalities in rural income (Fukuzawa, 1982b).

4

The Mughal Empire and Beyond

During Akbar's reign, Mughal architecture achieved its distinct character and the intense architectural activity surpassed even the building frenzy of Tughluqs two centuries earlier.

(Blair and Bloom, 1994)

The Taj deserved to be numbered among the wonders of the world much more than pyramids of Egypt which were 'unshapen masses' and 'heaps of large stones'.

(Bernier, 1901)

The Hindu empires of Mauryas and Guptas and the Muslim Sultanates did not match the pomp and splendour of the Mughal Empire. In opulence, splendour and wealth, it was unmatched especially during the reign of Akbar and Shah Jahan. In his Memoirs, Ralph Fitch, one of the first English merchants to visit Hindustan (as India was then called), describes the beauty and splendour of Mughal buildings in Agra and Fatehpur Sikri, the two Mughal capitals. He observes that 'either of them was much greater than London' and both were very populated (cited in Smith, 1892:395).

These thriving Mughal cities as well as Delhi (Shahjahanabad) and Lahore were the living symbols of Mughal art, architecture and culture. Of course, Agra was already the capital of the Lodis which Babur adopted as the Mughal capital. Akbar demolished the Lodi fort in Agra and built a new one on the same site, thus stamping his own imprint on the city. He lived in the new capital, Fatehpur Sikri, for 14 years before moving to Lahore for another 14 years. Delhi became the capital of Shah Jahan and later, of Aurangzeb and his successors.

Babur and Humayun, the first two Mughal emperors, did not contribute much to Mughal art and architecture. Only a few traces of royal monuments built by them remain: they were preoccupied with consolidating the empire. Moreover, they were not as rich as their successors.

Akbar, who succeeded Humayun, was the first Mughal emperor to undertake large-scale building projects throughout India. Important monuments associated with his reign include: Humayun's tomb in Delhi, Agra Fort (Akbari Mahal and Jahangiri Mahal despite its name) and Fatehpur Sikri (or Fathabad, the City of Victory). However, Shah Jahan not Akbar, was the most reputed among all the Mughal emperors for ambitious building sprees. Jahangir did not show much interest in architecture.

Jahangir was not a master builder in the class of Akbar or Shah Jahan. He did not build a new royal city perhaps because of ill-health as one scholar has suggested (Prasad, 1922:322). The only imperial monument to his credit is Akbar's tomb in Sikardra near Agra.

Building activity revived again when Shah Jahan became Mughal emperor in 1627 after Jahangir's death. He is known as one of the greatest Mughal master builders whose appetite for grand monuments was almost insatiable (Plate 3, a water-colour miniature painting dating to c.1800).

Aurangzeb's reign following Shah Jahan's, is known more for the destruction of buildings (especially Hindu temples) than their construction. For example, he destroyed the Kesev Rai temple in Mathura which had been built at a very high cost (Richards, 1993:175). His Deccan wars to annex the sultanates of Bijapur and Golconda were very costly, and may have drained his resources so much that very little building activity was reported towards the end of his reign. The only significant royal building of Aurangzeb's reign is *Bibi ka Maqbara*, a mausoleum for his wife, which he reluctantly built under pressure from his son. As a poor imitation of the Taj, it cost only Rs. 0.65 million. Mughal architecture lost its erstwhile grandeur and glory, perhaps due partly to his narrow outlook and philistinism (Haig and Burn, 1937:566).

After Aurangzeb's death, the Mughal Empire started to decline for lack of financial resources and strong rulers. So did the building of lavish monuments.

Below are presented first of all, the glimpses of Delhi, since it was also the capital of the Delhi Sultanate as well as that of the earlier Rajput kingdoms. This is followed by descriptions of monuments in the other major cities noted above.

Delhi (Shahjahanabad)

The seven cities of Delhi were built during different periods of its imperial history: only Din Panah (World Refuge) and Shahjahanabad (Shahajahan's City) belong to the Mughal period. Humayun built Din Panah in 1533, three years after he ascended the throne. The sixth city of Delhi, it consisted mainly of Purana Qila (Old Fort).[1] Shah Jahan built Shahjahanabad as the new capital of the Mughal Empire where he moved from Agra in 1638. It was built as a walled city with 14 gates: many have since disappeared. Its main historic monuments are the Red Fort, the palace inside the fort and Jami Masjid (for more details, see Blake, 1991; Singh, 2010).[2]

The Mughal forts and to a lesser extent, the mosques in different capitals were similar in design, content and architecture. For example, each of the three Mughal forts in Delhi, Agra and Lahore had halls of private and public audience, *Naqqar Khana* (where the imperial band played), baths (*hammam*), royal residences and a mosque. This may be explained by the need to economize but it is also possible that different monuments were built by the same architects.[3]

The forts were not merely defensive fortifications for protection against the enemy. As they included royal palaces, they represented important symbols of power and grandeur as well. The Red Fort in Delhi (Fig. 4.1) is one such palace fort, a walled township containing palaces, private residences for princes, Pearl mosque (Moti Masjid) for the emperor to pray, reception halls such as the Diwan-i-Am, a rectangular hall with nine arches for public audiences and Diwan-i-Khas for private audiences with visiting dignitaries.

Diwan-i-Khas is highly decorated and has ornamental pillars with floral pietra dura panels (Plate 4). It contains a marble dais which is said to have supported the Peacock Throne[4] (Plate 5 shows a watercolour painting of it on ivory by an unknown artist which dates to *c.*1850). Tavernier (1889, vol. I:381–4) describes it in great detail, noting that canopy of the throne had the famous: 'Peacock with elevated tail made of blue sapphires and

Fig. 4.1. Red Fort, Delhi (Author's Private Collection)

other coloured stones, the body being gold inlaid with precious stones, having a large ruby front of the breast, from whence hangs a pear-shaped pearl of 50 carats . . . ' Behind it was a smaller throne in the form of an oval bathing tub.

After he moved to the Red Fort in Delhi, Shah Jahan would be seated on the Peacock Throne in the Diwan-i-Khas (Spear, 1994:3). Originally, he used to sit on it in the Diwan-i-Am dais in the Agra Fort.

The fort palace contained the Khas Mahal, the emperor's private chambers and a covered market for the inhabitants of the fort. Although similar to the Agra and Lahore forts, it is different in one respect. Here, unlike in the other forts, the emperor's apartments contain several inscriptions in Persian that compare the palace to paradise, eulogizes the emperor and cites the date of commencement of the fort's construction (Asher, 1992:198–9). Built of red sandstone on the outside, copious use is made of white marble inside the royal palaces and the Diwan-i-Khas. The fort is octagonal in shape with two longer sides on the east and west. It had several gates, for example, Delhi Gate (formerly called the Akbarabad gate), Kashmiri Gate, Ajmeri Gate and Lahore Gate. The Delhi Gate led to the Jami mosque.[5] The inscription on the Lahore Gate, which is the main entrance to the Red Fort, may be translated from Persian as: 'Entrance to the Palace at Delhi'.

Shah Jahan's successors made some extensions to the Red Fort. For example, Aurangzeb added the Pearl Mosque (Moti Masjid) to the west of the baths and a great wall in front of the Lahore Gate. A small balcony of the Mussaman Burj was added by Akbar Shah II in 1808, and Zafar Mahal in the Bagh was added by Bahadur Shah II in around 1842.

Red Fort was considered a 'wonder' of the times (Blake, 1991:44). Amir Khusrau, the poet laureate, eulogized it as 'a paradise on the face of the earth'. The marble palace inside the Red Fort, especially the Rang Mahal (Palace of Colours) is resplendent with its pietra dura inlays of diamonds, gold ceilings and white-marble water fountains.

Most other Mughal monuments in Delhi are mausoleums intended to mark the emperors' legacies. Notable among these is *Humayun's tomb* (Plate 6) built by Akbar, Humayun's son. A well-deserved UNESCO World Heritage site, it pioneered the Safavid Timurid style of architecture in India. The Persian influence is not surprising considering that the tomb's architect, Mirza Ghiyas, was Persian (although originally from Herat in Afghanistan) as was Haji Begum, Humayun's senior queen.[6]

Humayun's tomb is the first Mughal tomb to be built in Delhi with a double dome, its unique feature. It is rather unusual in that it does not have any interior decorations or Qur'anic verses typical of most other Mughal mausoleums. While Humayun introduced the Safavid style of architecture in India, Akbar blended it with indigenous Hindu elements to create an Indo-Mughal style reflected in his tomb in Sikandra (Fig. 4.4). Unlike Babur and Humayun, Akbar had the time and resources as well as the inclination to promote art and architecture during his long reign.

Agra

Most Mughal emperors (with the exception of Aurangzeb) lived in Agra at one time or another. Their royal residences were inside the Agra Fort. Akbar built an entire new city, Fatehpuri Sikri, as his new capital about 30 kilometres from Agra. But he was forced to return to Agra on account of a serious shortage of water there and possibly for other reasons. Agra remained the capital of the Mughal Empire for over a century.

The Agra Fort was the seat of the government and residence of the emperors. Akbar and Jahangir ruled from here; so did Shah Jahan before he built Shahjahanabad. No wonder then that many Mughal monuments

INTERIOR SAMAN BURJ IN FORT AGRA.

Fig. 4.2. Summan Burj Interior Decorations, Agra Fort (Author's Private Collection)

are found in Agra, notably, palaces in the Agra Fort, Fatehpur Sikri, Akbar's tomb in Sikandra (outside Agra) and the Taj Mahal.

Akbar built several fort palaces the first of which was in Agra: Jahangiri Mahal. It is the only building of Akbar's time that has survived. Its exterior resembles other monuments built by him, notably, Jodh Bai's palace in Fatehpur Sikri. Its entrance opens to a large courtyard flanked by pillared halls.

The Agra Fort was extensively renovated and extended with three new courts: halls of public and private audience, a house for treasures (Machhi Bhawan) and a residential court known as Anguri Bagh (Garden of Grapes).

Apparently, Shah Jahan destroyed many fort buildings built earlier by a Akbar and built several new ones with marble, notably, the public and private audience halls; his own living quarters near the Summan Burj (Fig. 4.2) and the Pearl Mosque (Fig. 4.3). Did he not like his grandfather's architectural taste? It was his prerogative to build a palace for himself, especially since it is considered inauspicious to take over a

Fig. 4.3. Pearl Mosque (Author's Private Collection)

predecessor's. He may have also preferred the cool and glistening marble to the sandstone used in Akbar's monuments.

Akbar's mausoleum is located in Sikandra a few kilometres from Agra (Fig. 4.4). Akbar himself started its construction in 1600; after his death,

Fig. 4.4. Akbar's Mausoleum, Sikandra (Author's Private Collection)

its construction was completed by his son, Jahangir. Apparently, Jahangir added four tall marble minars to the entrance gate (separate from the main mausoleum) built on the model of the victory gate in Fatehpur Sikri. He wanted to see 'an edifice which travellers would pronounce to be unrivalled in the world'. It is suggested that on special occasions the famous Koh-i-Noor diamond was displayed on top of the tall pillar on the north side of the emperor's cenotaph.

The location of Akbar's mausoleum in Agra is not surprising as it was the capital for most of his reign. Perhaps he had unhappy memories of his father's (Humayun's) defeat and subsequent death in Delhi. It is similar to that of Humayun in the sense that it is also built on a raised platform in the midst of a charbagh-style garden. But its architectural style is very different. It is a pyramidal structure of five storeys, each successively smaller than the one below. Four flights of steps lead up to the tomb in the centre of a terrace with black and white marble.

Shah Jahan's major imperial building, the Taj Mahal, is a mausoleum built in honour of his queen, Mumtaz Mahal (Fig. 4.5). Its stunning beauty, symmetrical proportions and the setting, surpass all the royal monuments built including those of the British Raj.

Any discussion of the Taj Mahal needs to cover at least three S's: Symmetry, Setting and Story of love and romance. The beauty of the Taj is enhanced by the remarkable symmetry of the various buildings around it, the four minars as well as its gardens in front. The mausoleum is located in a charbagh-style garden along the Yamuna River. Each of the four quarters of the garden is sub-divided into 16 flowerbeds by stone-paved pathways. There is a high degree of perfection in its proportions.

The beautiful setting of the Taj, its location by the bank of river Yamuna, the charming gardens, and the light of the setting sun, magnify its charm. Even Aldous Huxley, its greatest critic, admits that 'nature did its best for the Taj' (Baker and Sexton, 2000:440).

Thirdly, the story of the Taj is a living symbol of love and romance of an emperor for his beloved queen. Few Mughal buildings evoke as much passion and interest as the Taj. Mumtaz died while giving birth to her eighth son. The devastated emperor (who is buried next to his Begum) decided to immortalize her by creating an unsurpassed mausoleum.[7] Indeed, love and passion, religion and political power, symbolize Islamic architecture in India.

Fig. 4.5. Taj Mahal, Agra (Author's Private Collection)

For the construction of the Taj, masons and goldsmiths were invited from several countries. The white marble used in the mausoleum was brought from Makrana near Jodhpur in Rajasthan, and precious stones and gold were imported from various countries, including Afghanistan,

Fig. 4.6. Fatehpur Sikri with Panch Mahal (Author's Private Collection)

China, Persia, Russia and Tibet. Its bulbous dome (somewhat similar to that of Humayun's tomb) is said to be modelled on the domes of Bokhara from where Shah Jahan's ancestors came. Apparently, the cenotaph was originally surrounded by a balustrade of gold studded with precious stones, which Aurangzeb might have removed to finance his battles with the Jats, Rajputs and Marathas. The balustrade was later replaced by marble screens.

Fatehpur Sikri

In 1574, Akbar built his new capital, Fatehpur Sikri, near Agra (Fig. 4.6). It was a city created from scratch to celebrate his victories in Bengal and Gujarat. But why did he need to build an entirely new capital? Did he feel claustrophobic in the congested Agra Fort? Or was he keen to celebrate his conquests? Historical accounts do not present any conclusive answers to these questions. However, there is no doubt that Akbar left behind a dead city of red sandstone of immense charm and beauty. The carvings on red sandstone palaces and houses (Birbal's and Sultana's) are rich and of high quality. Indeed, Ferguson (1910:579)

Fatehpur Sikri   Dewan Khas piller, Agra

Fig. 4.7. Diwan-i-Khas Interior (Author's Private Collection)

regards these two houses as 'the richest, most beautiful as well as the most characteristic of all Akbar's buildings'.

Fatehpur Sikri combines the artistic traditions of both Hindu and Islamic architecture and cultures. Akbar's Hindu chief architect, Tuhin Das, was responsible for the planning and design of the various buildings. As in Agra Fort, this other walled city also contains palaces, private and public audience halls, high gates (such as Buland Darwaza) and mosques (Jami Masjid and Salim Chishti mosque).

The Diwan-i-Khas in Fatehpur Sikri (Fig. 4.7) is different in concept as well as design from others in the Red Fort and Agra Fort, for example. From the outside, it looks like a two-storey building but in fact it has only a single chamber inside. Secondly, a circular platform with balustrades in the centre of the chamber, supported by a richly carved column, was built for the emperor's throne. The platform is connected by diagonal bridges to the four corners of the chamber signifying the four corners of the globe which the emperor commanded. Any dignitaries invited by him for a private audience would walk on one of the bridges and the courtiers would watch and listen from down below in the chamber.

A less important Mughal capital but still quite magnificent was Lahore in the Punjab, discussed below.

Lahore

The Mughal period in Lahore started with the conquest of Babur in AD 1530. Akbar made Lahore his capital in 1584. Although the lack of water in Fatehpur Sikri is often given as a reason for his departure, it is equally likely that he moved to Lahore 'to deal with the military and political upheaval' in the north following the death of his half brother, Mirza Hakim Muhammad, who was Governor of Kabul (Blair and Bloom, 1994:272). Akbar conducted several military campaigns from Lahore, against Kashmir, for example.

Many Mughal monuments in Lahore were destroyed and today bear the marks of their destruction. A few landmarks, which are still standing include the Fort, Jahangir's tomb, Nur Jahan's tomb, Badshahi Mosque and Shalimar Gardens. The Fort and its palaces and Jahangir's mausoleum were considered the jewels of the Mughal Empire.

Akbar built the Lahore Fort on the site of an old citadel where he also built a palace as his residence. Later his successors, Jahangir, Shah Jahan and Aurangzeb, extended it by adding more palaces and other buildings. For example, Shah Jahan built the Shah Burj (the Tower), and Aurangzeb erected the Alamgiri entrance gate flanked by semi-circular towers with domed pavilions.

The Shish Mahal (Palace of Mirrors) inside the Fort (Plate 7) is so-called because of its decorations of glass mosaics and small multi-coloured convex mirrors. In 1631–2, Shah Jahan built it as his private quarters. With its cusped marble arches and pillars inlaid with precious stones, it is one of the finest pavilions of the fort.

The Marble Pavilion is also called *Naulakha* meaning Rs 9 lakhs (or Rs 900,000), which is what it cost to build. It looks similar to the pavilion in the Agra Fort. Originally, it had sloping bangala roofs. The pavilion is associated with Shah Jahan who may have lived here as a prince. However, neither he nor his father, Jahangir used the fort as their long-term residence.

Enamelled pottery work decorated the facade of the fort. Like the Delhi and Agra forts, the Lahore Fort had both a Diwan-i-Am and a Diwan-i-Khas. The emperors held their council meetings and durbars in the fort there.

Shah Jahan built Jahangir's tomb on the site of Bagh-i-Dilkusha (Dilkusha Gardens), which were laid out by Jahangir's wife,

Nur Jahan. The entrance to it is through two gateways of stone and masonry opposite each other to the north and south.

Nur Jahan's and Jahangir's tombs are fine examples of Indian architecture inspired by the Safavid Persian style. Nur Jahan (née Nur Mahall), a Persian poetess, may have introduced the Safavid style to the Mughal Court, but rather than adopting it in its entirety, the Mughals made adaptations to it. For example, in Persia, external glazed-tile decoration covered the whole surface of a building, whereas in Mughal architecture it consisted of panels framed by thin ledges of unglazed bricks. The Persian and Mughal styles began to diverge even further when the Mughals started combining red sandstone and marble in the same buildings.

The Mughals (starting with Babur) were fond of Persian-style gardens such as the Shalimar Gardens. In 1634, Shah Jahan laid their foundations (ibid.:142). They are modelled on the Kashmir Royal Gardens, which were also established by the same emperor. They are laid out in a typical charbagh-style, with four-fold square gardens divided symmetrically into quarters, and containing features such as descending terraces, pavilions and water channels. It is thanks to the Shalimar Gardens and other Mughal gardens such as Dilkusha that Lahore came to be known as the city of gardens.[8]

The reception halls and marble pavilions in the Shalimar Gardens were Shah Jahan's private residential quarters and those of his daughter, Jahanara. The pavilions have two storeys. In the upper storey are the Royal (Turkish) bathrooms presumably for the emperor, his immediate family and the harem. These bath rooms were heated by firewood of which a substantial quantity was required.

Imperial Wealth and Power

The above royal monuments are living symbols of unmatched Mughal wealth and power, which was further reinforced by immense hoarded treasures. Akbar left behind a vast amount of wealth in the Agra treasury, in the form of imperial jewels and precious stones. Eraly (2007:166) notes that 'the revenue of the king of England at the close of the seventeenth century was only about one-seventeenth of Akbar's revenue of the same period'. At the time of his death, the royal Treasury was estimated to have Rs 7 crores (Rs 70 million) not counting gold.[9] The

list of jewels prepared by the Royal Treasurer for Jahangir 'amounted
to nearly three hundred and fifty pounds in weight of diamonds, pearls,
rubies and emeralds alone; over six hundred and twenty thousand carats
of the most precious gems [. . .] and semi-precious gems too numerous
to count, never mind all the gold and silver coin' (Rutherford, 2011:389).
Jahangir also amassed a large amount of treasure, with chests full of all
sorts of diamonds.

Shah Jahan was the richest of all the Mughal emperors and perhaps
the wealthiest man in the world at that time. He loved luxury as much
as his father, Jahangir. In 1628, at his coronation, he presented to his
wife, Arjumand (Mumtaz Mahal), 200,000 gold coins (*Ashrafis*) and
60,000 rupees. He fixed Rs 1 million as an annual allowance for her
(Eraly, 1997:301). Bernier reports that he built two deep caves under his
Red Fort palace, one to store piles of gold, and the other to keep silver.
His wealth included:

— Rs 50 million worth of jewellery.
— Rs 1.24 million worth of aigrettes (spray of gems) on the turban he
  wore on the anniversary of coronation.
— A rosary containing five rubies and 30 pearls worth Rs 80,000.
— The Peacock Throne worth Rs 30–40 million, decorated with a
  large number of gems including rubies, diamonds and pearls as well
  as gold.

The Mughal wealth and splendour was on display at the time of royal ac-
cessions to the throne. Aurangzeb's coronation ceremony was the grandest and most ostentatious of all. He sat on the Peacock Throne dressed
in gold and diamond-studded robes, the nobles and amirs sat under a
large tent in the courtyard of the durbar hall, and incense burned in
gold and silver burners. The royal festivities lasted for several months
(ibid.:375–6).

The rich and bejewelled dresses and robes of the Mughal emperors
were another clear symbol of their wealth and ostentation. Sir Thomas
Roe, the British ambassador at the royal court, notes that Jahangir used
to be 'clothed, or rather laden with Diamonds, Rubies, Pearles and other
precious vanities, so great, so glorious' (ibid.:245).[10] European visitors
to India such as Manucci,[11] a Venetian who also worked at the Mughal

court, believed that Mughal pomp and grandeur had surpassed that of any European court.

Opulence and wealth also extended to the nobles and senior officers who received high salaries and other benefits. Their conspicuous consumption almost matched that of the emperor. The palaces of Asif Khan, Nur Jahan's brother and Shah Jahan's wife's father, are estimated to have cost Rs 20 lakhs (or Rs 2 million). As Shah Jahan's Commander-in-Chief, Asif Khan commanded 9,000 personnel and an equal number of horses. He earned an annual salary of over Rs 4 million. His property in Lahore at the time of his death in 1641 was valued at Rs 25 million (Latif, 1892:109), despite being only a noble of the Mughal emperor. These figures give some rough idea of the opulence of not only the emperors but also of their nobles.

There were several motivations for ceremony, pomp and vainglory. First, the rich and ostentatious life style of the emperor set him apart from his subjects. Second, it created a mystique around him which was awe-inspiring for the subjects who could not but admire him for this display. Third, the pomp of the royal court was a symbol of state power and the absolute authority of the emperor who alone could decide whether his nobles and courtiers could participate in royal ceremonies. It was up to him to bestow on the nobles any privileges he might deem appropriate. The royal courtiers offered expensive gifts to the emperor as was customary at that time. Other customs suggesting subjugation of the subjects included prostration before the emperor (*sijda*).

How did the Mughals accumulate such vast amounts of wealth? Apart from trade expansion and industrial growth, much of this wealth may have been obtained by squeezing the peasantry, which was impoverished as a result of widespread corruption and extortion by Mughal officers (Victoria and Albert Museum, 1982:15). The police and judicial officers took bribes for providing any services.

All that wealth was not shared with the common people who were very poor, ill-clad and without decent shelter. Their scanty dress was due to poverty and the social environment rather than to climatic considerations (Eraly, 2007:114). Eraly (p. 112) states that the 'average Indian in Mughal times had advanced little from the conditions of life of his ancestors of a thousand or more years before his time' (for more details, see Chapter 10).

From the Mughal to the British Empire

In the eighteenth century, the above royal splendour and extravagance of the Mughals began to fade with the weakening of the Mughal Empire and the rise of the British Empire in India. Its decline resulted from several factors: depletion of the royal treasury, frequent and costly wars for territorial aggrandizement, and conflicts, intrigues and bloodshed caused by rival aspirants to the throne, as well as the rise of the Marathas, Rajputs and Sikhs.

The British power in India was well entrenched even before the fall of the last Mughal emperor, Bahadur Shah II. The British had been in control of Delhi since 1803 when they took it over from the Marathas. Although they 'had succeeded in making the emperor (Bahadur Shah) politically functionless [. . .] the mystique of the court kept Delhi essentially a Mughal town' (Gupta, 1981:3, 13). The British had a Resident, a representative of the Governor-General, at the Mughal Court.[12] When the Residency in Delhi was abolished in 1831, territory controlled by the British was administered by a Commissioner supported by a Board of Revenue and the Agra High Court

The power and authority of the British was so strong that the British Government at one time thought of removing the Mughal emperor from his palace at the Red Fort.[13] Plan failed to materialize when the 1857 uprising erupted. However, the British Army did move into the Red Fort after the emperor was deposed and captured.

There are several differences between the Mughal rule and the British Raj. First, the Mughal emperors built buildings for the benefit of their subjects, such as mosques, step wells, sarais and gardens. The British rulers were different from the Mughals in that they made no attempt to build places of worship or other kinds of buildings for the welfare of their subjects. Instead, they built churches only for themselves or others of similar Christian faith. True, they built schools and universities, but these were intended for the elite princely class and not for the common man (Chapter 8). Indeed, a total neglect of basic and primary education may, inter alia, partly explain abject poverty among the Indians at the time.

Secondly, the Mughal rulers came to India to stay and became integrated into Indian society. For example, Akbar treated local Hindus or Muslims on par with the powerful Central Asian and Persian nobles. He married Hindu Rajput princesses (Jodh Bai from Amber, for example) in order to ensure peace and stability. Political alliances with the Hindu ruling families enabled Akbar to bring about stability. Two Mughal emperors, Jahangir and Shah Jahan, had Rajput Hindu mothers and were thus half Indian.

Shah Jahan opened the Red Fort (which included his palace) to the ordinary people of Shahjahanabad in order to establish contact with his subjects. Furthermore, the royal family regularly visited the bazaars and mosques and intermingled with the subjects (Singh, 2010). In contrast, the British remained aloof and created a world of their own distant from that of their subjects.

Thirdly, the British brought the justice system, courts and the rule of law to India which had not existed before. But the Mughals brought a revenue and administrative system and bureaucracy from which the British rulers benefited (at least initially), as they did from various Mughal concessions. They inherited a Mughal tax system under which most of the income of the Mughal elite was derived from land. The elite kept a portion of the income for themselves and paid the rest to the central treasury in the form of cash or support to the Mughal troops. There were no hereditary landlords, only jagirdars who were granted jagirs (tax revenue from a collection of villages) by the emperor which could be forfeited on death (Maddison, 2007:122–3). The British eliminated this Mughal 'warlord aristocracy' and replaced it by a hereditary zamindari system.

Fourthly, the Muslim rulers (especially Aurangzeb) tried to transform India into a Muslim society whereas the British allowed Indians to pursue their traditional cultures and enjoy religious freedom despite conversion efforts by Evangelical missionaries.

Fifthly, unlike the Mughal rulers who came to India as invaders and conquerors, it was primarily commercial interests that drove the British to India before political interests took over.

Finally, the two empires differed in their scope and geographical spread. While the Mughal Empire was *national* in character, extending throughout India, the British Empire was *global* extending beyond India's national boundaries. This fact had important economic implications. The relationship between the British rulers and their Indian colony was characterized as a 'centre' and 'periphery'. As discussed in Chapter 10, resources from the periphery were drained out of the

country to the centre. Although the Mughal Empire was also exploitative, the nature of its exploitation and the draining of productive resources
were internal, not external. Potential productive resources which could
have been used for economic development were diverted for conspicuous
and ostentatious consumption.

There were also several similarities between the Mughals and the
British. Both were involved in battles and political intrigues to defeat the
enemy and to gain control of the territory. Both represented a minority
class from abroad ruling over a large majority of Hindu and Muslim natives. A small minority of Mughals managed to conquer vast territories
and people in the same way as a small number of British Company servants did later. According to Tavernier, 'a multitude of men [. . .] cowed
by a handful, and bowed so easily under the yoke of the Mohametan
princes' (cited in Eraly, 2007:25).

The subjects, mainly Hindus, were discriminated against by both the
Mughal and the British rulers. During the Mughal Empire, Hindus suffered humiliation and many restrictions in their every-day lives. With the
exception of Akbar, most Mughal emperors were devout Muslims who
maltreated their Hindu subjects through the imposition, for example, of
jaziya (a tax on non-Muslims) and many other restrictions. Hindus were
not allowed to marry Muslim women or to keep a Muslim concubine.
Those breaking the rules were severely punished.[14] The attitudes of the
British rulers towards their subjects were similar. As discussed in Chapter 7, Indian natives were denied access to the exclusive British clubs
and to private homes although there were some exceptions. Equally,
liaisons between Indian natives and English memsahibs were rare if not
non-existent (Chapter 5).

During the Mughal period, in general the Muslims lived in urban areas
as they were invariably employed in government services. On the other
hand, Hindus were mainly farmers and landowners who lived in rural
areas. The two groups rarely intermingled: every-day contact between
them was minimal.

The Mughals actively promoted Persian culture, which they considered superior to all local cultures and customs. They disdained local
people in the same way as the British rulers who riled against Anglicized
Indians. Although the Mughals hired Indian Rajputs in the army, most
of the senior positions in the royal court and civil administration went

to Persians who considered Indians as 'slaves' or 'blacks', according to Manucci.

The Mughal and British rulers enjoyed similar sports and leisure activities. The natives were debarred from them. Chapter 7 describes the exclusive sports clubs and the gymkhanas where the British indulged in various leisure activities. The Mughal emperors also considered these sports as their exclusive preserve. Abul Fazl, Akbar's biographer, notes that several hunting grounds and animals were reserved exclusively for the emperor. Even princes were not allowed to organize such sports as elephant fights without special permission. Polo playing was a popular sport among both the Mughal emperors and the British rulers.

Other sports involving horses, such as horse racing and polo were popular during the Mughal and pre-Mughal periods. For example, Aibak, the first Delhi sultan who built Qutb Minar (Chapter 2), died while playing polo. Fazl's *Ain-i-Akbari* (1894, vol. 1:298) notes that Akbar used to play polo and also encouraged his courtiers to play. He invented a luminous ball so that he could play even in the dark. Apart from being a keen polo player, Akbar enjoyed hunting and horse racing, as did Jahangir (*Tuzuk-i-Jahangir*, 1909:110) who wrote:

> I ordered them (his courtiers) to bring my race horses (*aspan-i-dawanda*) to the Khiyaban (avenue). The princes and the amirs raced them. A bay Arab horse ran better than all the other horses.

Polo playing, horse racing and riding were also common in many other countries because horse was an important animal in warfare. It is for this reason that betting on horses is the only type of gambling that is allowed in Islam.[15]

Both the Mughals and the British left behind grandiose and extravagant royal monuments. It is striking that both concentrated on religious buildings (mosques in the former case and churches in the latter) besides palaces and memorials. Both empires lasted for sufficiently long periods to leave behind a rich legacy in bricks and stones as well as in education, culture and customs.

The monuments of the two empires were similar in their objectives and intent. They were designed as symbols of power, authority and imperial presence. Therefore, lavish amounts were spent on them at the expense of their subjects (see Chapter 10).

Conclusion

That Mughal emperors, particularly, Akbar and Shah Jahan, were great monument builders in India has never been in doubt. Do these monuments (such as Humayun's tomb in Delhi, the Taj Mahal in Agra, for example) represent symbols of power, extravagance, superfluity and superiority of the rich rulers over their poor subjects?

Each Mughal emperor tried to surpass his predecessors in building royal monuments as symbols of his power and authority. Many Mughal emperors had implemented major building programmes. Indeed, a lavish such programme during Shah Jahan's reign may have contributed to the near bankruptcy of the empire. It is no wonder, then, that building activity dried up during the reigns of Aurangzeb and subsequent Mughal rulers.

Mughal architecture in India can be divided into two evolutionary phases. The first phase (from 1556 to 1628) relates to the reign of Akbar and Jahangir when mainly red sandstone was used in construction. White marble came in vogue much later. The monuments of this period (such as Humayun's tomb in New Delhi and Nur Jahan's in Lahore) were devoid of too many intricate decorations. The second phase (1628 to 1707) associated with Shah Jahan and Aurangzeb witnessed remarkable examples of marble buildings (the Taj Mahal, for example), that were known for their refined architecture, rich decoration and inlay work.

Questions have been raised (by Begley, 1979, for example) about the widely-held belief that the Taj was an expression of Shah Jahan's love for his beloved queen, Mumtaz Mahal. Begley argues that so grand a structure could not be 'purely and simply' a tomb. Is the mausoleum not too grand and imposing an edifice to commemorate a single woman? Indeed, Bernier (1901) and other European travellers have even suggested that Shah Jahan had an incestuous relationship with Jahanara, his eldest daughter. Could it be that the Taj was more a symbol of Shah Jahan's love for glory, political power and self-glorification?

Both the Mughals and the British rulers built lavish monuments to leave behind a legacy. Victoria Memorial in Calcutta is considered an 'enduring testimony to the Imperial connection [. . .] and it lay at the very heart of Britain's claim to be a world power' (Davies, 1985:210). The British builders in India were more inclined to copy British architecture than to adapt it to the local requirements and the environment. On the other hand, the Mughal builders developed an Indo-Islamic architecture

The following five chapters deal with the British Empire and its contributions before a comparison is made between the extravaganza and poverty in the Mughal and British empires in the final chapter.

Part III

The British Raj

5

Social Glimpses of the Raj

India becomes for the first time a political and economic appendage of another country. The establishment of British rule in India was entirely novel phenomenon for her, not comparable with any other invasion or political or economic change. India had been conquered before but by invaders who settled within her frontiers and made themselves part of her life.

(Nehru, 1946)

The British continued to build lavish structures of monumental proportions (fortresses, palaces, clubs and so on) in the tradition of the Mughals and Indian princes. They symbolized the power and glory of British imperialism: the Company Raj and the Crown Raj which ended in 1947 with India's independence.[1]

The genesis of British rule in India can be traced back to the establishment of the Company as a commercial enterprise, which obtained concessions from Jahangir, the Mughal emperor. What was Jahangir's motivation to grant land to the Company to build a factory in Surat and to allow it to maintain a small army? These are intriguing questions.

The Company was in competition with the Portuguese, the Dutch and the French who were all operating in India and the East Indies to procure spices, silk, textiles and diamonds. The Company defeated the Portuguese who were a menace for the Mughal emperor because they controlled the pilgrims' sea route to Mecca. Jahangir may have rewarded the British for defeating the Portuguese.

It kept an army in each of the three Presidencies (Madras, Calcutta and Bombay) to defend its territory against the enemies. An army was needed not only to ward off the Dutch, the French and the Portuguese but also to negotiate with local maharajas from strength. This may also explain why the Company built fortresses in the Presidencies with residential blocks inside.

The Two Cultures

The earlier Muslim rulers, who came from abroad, became part of Indian life. They were Indianized, but not the British rulers. A vast gulf existed between an average Indian and his British masters: differences in outlook, tradition, ways of living and culture. The gaps were unbridgeable.

Early Englishmen and Scotsmen on the payroll of the Company in India lived in squalor, heat, dust and disease. The hot climate in the plains combined with dust took its toll on the health of company men, army officers and other staff. Frequent deaths caused by malaria, cholera and other tropical diseases led to a search for hill stations (Chapter 7).

The young and single Company men were without wives or white female companions, which led to loneliness and boredom. Return to England frequently was impossible due to the limited and slow transportation facilities. So they were tempted to look for local women as mistresses or 'bibis'. (The situation of boredom and loneliness may have also led to the emergence of social clubs discussed below.) By the eighteenth century, the practice of English company officers keeping a native 'bibi' had been well-established (Wild, 1999:105). *Bibi khanas* (houses for bibis) at the back of bungalows for the Company officers were a living testimony to the practice.

It was not uncommon to find English officers having several Indian concubines and/or wives. In 1858, the future Sir Garnet Wolseley confessed 'that he managed to console himself with an attractive "Eastern princess" who answered all the purposes of a wife without any of the bother . . .' (cited in Lehmann, 1964:60). The practice of keeping a mistress was also common in the eighteenth-century Britain (Hyam, 1990:115).

The widespread practice of interracial liaisons worried the Company management in London. So in the 1670s the Company decided to send a boatload of English women to Madras to respond to the needs of the Company's officers. The boat carried a colourful name of the 'Fishing Fleet' since these women were in search of male partners or husbands in India (de Courcy, 2012). The scheme failed to achieve the desired result since many women were rather ordinary, unattractive and perhaps from common families. Few found husbands or partners. Many ended up in brothels and others decided to return to England in disgust and disappointment.

Another reason for the failure of the above scheme may have been the win-win situation of the white man (*gora sahib*) and the bibi. The former had no commitment to the bibi especially if he was not married to her. The latter, especially those from humbler backgrounds, found it quite comfortable being a mistress of a well-paid white ruler.

During the Company Raj, many Englishmen adopted the Mughal customs and attire. They were the so-called 'white Mughals', notable among them being Sir David Ochterlony who enjoyed the Mughal title of Nasir-ud-Daula (Defender of the State). His 13 consorts followed him around Delhi, each on the back of an elephant. He enjoyed wearing Indian dress and smoking hookah as a true 'White Mughal', a far cry from the stodgy stiff-lipped Englishman. He was known for his fondness for dancing (*nautch*) girls and social entertainment. A water-colour painting of Sir David by an unknown artist in c.1820 shows him at the Residency (he was a Resident twice)[2] in Old Delhi smoking a hookah and enjoying an Indian dance performance (Plate 8). This image sums up the free social interaction that existed between the British and the Indians in the early nineteenth century.

A Cambridge don argues that '. . . the easy range of sexual opportunities [. . .] provided the long-term administration and exploitation of tropical territories . . .' (Hyam, 1990:1). He adds: 'the expansion of Europe was not only a matter of Christianity and commerce, it was also a matter of copulation and concubinage' (p. 2) Writing about Calcutta women, Radclyffe Sidbottom of the Bengal Pilot Service notes: 'the Eurasians and the "poor whites" who were absolutely riddled with sex and very beautiful, were comparatively fair game. You hadn't got to marry them and they courted you' (cited in Allen, 1975:124). It is arguable whether sexual energy played an important role in the expansion of the British Empire. After all, many empire builders were quite repressed and pre-ferred matrimony to sexual adventures (Ballhatchet, 1980:1).

Easy social interactions discussed above did not last long. The social gulf between the English and the native Indians widened with the arrival of Lord Wellesley as the new Governor-General. He openly discouraged

Fig. 5.1. First Car in Madras, 1901 (Courtesy of M. Anbazhagan)

interracial mixing at social parties, not to speak of intermarriages, in the interest of maintaining high moral standards in the Presidencies. Wellesley and his men felt superior to the natives. Holding of responsible positions and exercising authority at an early age may have reinforced this sense of superiority and paternalism.

The separation of whites from the natives meant a growing isolation of the rulers. The only natives with whom the white men came into contact were servants, cooks, 'orderlies', and nannies. In the nineteenth century, especially after the 1857 uprising, social contacts between the ruler and the ruled became even less common. This gulf may have widened further with the arrival of the memsahibs and the motor car (an object of curiosity for the simple natives) in India. The car enabled the whites to live further away from the Indians (Fig. 5.1, the figures in the car are those of the owner and his wife).[3]

Before long, the senior management of the Company in London recognized that problems could arise from mixed marriages or cohabitation. With few exceptions, the Anglo-Indian community that grew out of such cohabitation was despised by the British as well as the Indians.

In the nineteenth and twentieth centuries, the memsahibs who replaced the bibis, were partly responsible for creating a social distance
between the British rulers and Indian subjects (Hyam, 1990:119). The
bibis had provided the rulers some social contact with those they ruled.
On the other hand, the memsahibs made sure that the British stayed
aloof and behaved like rulers by showing imperial etiquette and 'decent'
behaviour before the natives (Paxman, 2011:139).

The boredom of sahibs was overcome in various ways: gambling, hunting, drinking and womanizing, and receiving pedicure from Indian servants (Fig. 5.2). For example, at Fort St George in Madras drinking
and gambling were rampant among both men and women. In 1721,
the Company directors expressed their anxiety about these vices in the
following words:

> It is with great concern we hear the itch of gaming hath spread itself over
> Madras, that even the gentle-women play for great sums, and that Capt
> Seaton makes a trade of it to the stripping several of the young men there.
> We earnestly recommend to you (the President of the Council) to check
> as far as you can that mischievous evil. (*India Office Records*, Letter Book
> No.17, cited in Judd, 1964:39–40)

Although contacts with the Indians were frequent at the beginning (seventeenth and eighteenth centuries), subsequently they were discouraged. However, the British introduced double standards even in social
contacts. While the Indians in general were kept at a distance, the rulers
hobnobbed with Indian princes who were independent, had their own
armies and were very wealthy.[4] The princes were seen as a potential
threat which could be held at bay by bringing them into the fold through
the granting of Privy Purses,[5] social invitations and an English education
(Chapter 8).

The Indian aristocracy was often represented at the British parties
and other social events. The Mughal Court was also patronized. Judd
(ibid.:42) notes that the 'Indian aristocrats were quite acceptable to the
British both as hosts and guests. Early in the nineteenth century, the
Mughal courtiers and the leading lights of British society in old Delhi
mixed at official afternoon receptions. Indian princes and princesses
competed with the British rulers at their favourite games of hunting
and polo.[6] A painting shows the Governor-General of Fort William

Fig. 5.2. A Member of the British Ruling Class Receiving a Pedicure (Courtesy of Godoirum-Bassanensis)

(1813–23) visiting Ghazi-al-din Haidar, the King of Oudh (part of present-day U.P.) (1814–27).[7]

However, in general, the British rulers in India considered Indian princes and the Mughals as inferior natives. The Anglo-Indians of mixed blood, one of the legacies of the British Raj, were also despised. They formed a distinct hybrid community, which looked down upon Indians as inferior but which in turn was despised by the British. The Anglo-Indians were rarely allowed to mix with the British as equals even though they behaved as British adopting the same customs, dress, habits and language. But as with the Indian princes, exceptions were made for the Anglo-Indians.[8] For example, Col. James Skinner (1778–1841), an Anglo-Indian, was accepted since he provided support to the British Indian Army by establishing 'Skinner's Horse', an irregular regiment of cavalry troops which remained in existence even after his death in 1841. Skinner introduced a Mughal-style durbar where any of his soldiers could raise problems and air grievances in the presence of their immediate superiors and other senior officers.[9]

The Indians mistrusted the Anglo-Indians who felt allegiance to Britain rather than to India. Their life styles were also more British than Indian. Their size and importance in India diminished by the late nineteenth century when an increasing number of British women were sent to India to marry white men there.

Relations with Indian women were accepted in military circles. Special provision for the British soldiers, who generally came from the lower classes, may have been accepted as a means of building army morale and keeping the soldiers fit and motivated. The British Indian Army promoted regulated brothels of Indian prostitutes in most army cantonments. However, such relations were discouraged among civilians, which showed a contradictory attitude of the British towards their subjects. Some observers have argued that such a contradictory posture was accepted as a price for preserving 'the structure of power' (Ballhatchet, 1980:9).

Clubs

A large number of social and sporting clubs were established throughout India to reduce the boredom and loneliness discussed above. Between 1776 and 1865, more than a dozen clubs and societies were established in Bombay and Poona alone (Table 5.1).

The British concept of clubs is described colourfully as 'islands of Britishness in the great Indian sea, to which the imperialists might withdraw whenever they felt personal, social or ritual need . . . ' (Morris and Winchester, 1983:57). However, the gymkhana (discussed below), often attributed to the British Raj, may have actually preceded it.

The justification for the establishment of the clubs is aptly described in the following words in the *Bengal Club: 1827–1970*:

> In the tropical possessions of the British Crown the idea of the club makes a special appeal to the large number of men, who are compelled by circumstances to be separated from their wives and families for longer or shorter periods. These clubs afford some consolation for the pains of exile and loneliness, while at the same time, they offer a welcome solution of a difficult problem, to the many bachelors with distaste for housekeeping.

The exclusive social institutions included sporting clubs (the Golf Club in Delhi and Calcutta) the gymkhana clubs and others established by the Army in cantonments and garrison towns for its own officers

Table 5.1. Names of Clubs and Societies in
Bombay and Poona (1776–1865)

Name of Club/Society	Date Founded
Bombay Theatre	1776
Sans Souci Club	1785
Bombay Turf Club	1800
Bapre Hunt	1800
Highland Society	1821
Mason Lodge	1825
Byculla Club	1833
Bombay Yacht Club	1849
India Naval Club	1850
Poona Gymkhana	1853
Bombay Golf Club	1856
Bombay Gymkhana	1860
Poona Club of Western India	1865

Source: Douglas (1900).

(Chapter 7). These institutions represented the ruler's mentality and policy of apartheid and preserved a colonial atmosphere with liveried bearers and bars, snooker rooms and golf.

George Orwell noted the exclusiveness of the clubs thus: 'In any town in India, the European club is the spiritual citadel, the real seat of British power, the Nirvana for which native officials and millionaires pine in vain' (cited in Edwardes, 1988:225). Since these clubs were located in cantonments or English quarters away from the cities, this further isolated the British from their subjects.[10] The Indian natives were barred from access to the clubs on grounds of race. Most members agreed that it was undesirable to admit Indians because they were inferior, would not bring their wives with them and would ogle at English women.

Divisions existed between commercial clubs, united services clubs and those of army officers. Those eligible for the elitist Bengal Club would not be accepted by a united services club, for example. Occupation was one criterion for membership which fully preserved the British class structure.

The clubs offered their members all kinds of recreational facilities: bridge and billiards rooms, bars (some for men only), dance halls, dining rooms and restaurants, tennis courts and golf courses as well as libraries and reading rooms. Some clubs even provided temporary accommodation to its members.

Before the clubs came into existence in the nineteenth century, coffee houses and bars were the main meeting places which remain popular until today in continental Europe and the United Kingdom. While the exclusiveness of these clubs has diminished in post-British India, their membership has remained rather selective. High membership fees ensure that a person with modest means does not have access.

They are an important legacy of the Raj. Many clubs have not only survived but are actually thriving thanks to the highly-Anglicized Indian middle class. One only has to visit the Gymkhana Club in New Delhi or the Bengal Club in Calcutta to see how packed they are especially for lunches and dinners and bridge parties.[11]

The Madras Club, known as the Ace of Clubs (formerly known as Adyar) is one of the oldest and finest in India. The original building on the banks of the river Adyar was owned by George Moubray, an English merchant, and was popularly known as Moubray's Cupola. Founded in 1831, the Club was established for informal social activities of the British in Madras. It had residential quarters which hosted the Prince of Wales in 1875.[12] The Club provided 'tennis courts, swimming baths and hot and cold steam baths [...] conferring a reputation for luxury and relaxation which was unrivalled throughout India' (Davies, 1985).

Lack of ice was a major inconvenience for the Club. So in 1840 the Club took shares of the new Tudor Ice Co. In 1842, a special circular building had to be built to store ice imported from America (ibid.:38).

The Bengal Club in Calcutta was the second elitist institution of the British Raj (Fig. 5.3).[13] Unlike the United Services Club, it was a snobbish place built mainly for the upper echelons of the Company. Initially it did not accept army and naval officers as its members. That may have generated a demand for the army to create its own clubs. While the British merchant class and Company officers frequented the elitist clubs, senior Indian Civil Service (ICS) and army officers had to be content with the united Services Clubs.

Fig. 5.3. Bengal Club, Calcutta in 1870 (©Victoria and Albert Museum, London)

The idea of the Bengal Club was born in the Town Hall of Calcutta in 1826 when Lt Col. J. Finch called a meeting to discuss the creation of a meeting place for like-minded Englishmen. Finch regretted that 'nothing akin to a respectable hotel or a coffee house existed' in Calcutta. Founded in 1827, the Bengal Club was the first to be established in India. Until 1959, it was not open to Indian nationals. Similar Clubs in London were opened at around the same period as the Bengal Club: the Athenaeum (1824), the Oxford and Cambridge Club (1830) and the Carlton (1832).[14]

Other Calcutta clubs included the Tollygunge, with hundreds of acres of parkland. It was founded in 1895 by William Dixon Cruickshank, a Scottish banker, to offer facilities for games and sports on the outskirts of the city. The Club building originally belonged to Richard Johnson, an officer of the Company. Later it was owned by Ghulam Muhammad Shah, one of the sons of Tipu Sultan, the ruler of Mysore.

The Byculla Club, the first formal club to be founded in Bombay in 1833, was located in the isolated rural area of Byculla west of Mazagaon. In the evenings, wild animals would stray into the club compound. Earlier attempts to set up clubs in Bombay were not successful: the Sans Souci

Club founded in 1785 was intended mainly for dining, but apparently, did not last very long; the Highland Society established in 1821 did not survive either (Shepperd, 1916).

During the nineteenth century. Byculla was a fashionable district of Bombay inhabited mainly by the British and Parsis. Sir David Sassoon, the Iraqi Jew and a philanthropist, built a grand house in which the club was located. The opening of the Byculla Club in 1833 coincided with the building of a church and soon after a railway station was built. With better communications, mills and factories also began to grow. Today Byculla is a dilapidated lower-middle class district with a large Muslim population. Sandhya Sondhi, a Bombay resident since childhood, recalls passing through Byculla as a little girl.[15] She notes that 'the buildings out there were old and dilapidated, but it had lovely churches'.

Shepperd (ibid.:24) cites an article from the *Bombay Gazette* describing physical and moral benefits of the Byculla Club in a rather amusing manner. The article notes that 'the gentlemen arriving from the *mofussil* (countryside) either for health pleasure or business, will no longer be obliged to roam about like the babes in the wood in quest of a spot of rest . . .' The moral influence of the Club is described in the following words:

> They (people) will begin to think more justly of themselves when contrasted with others. Self and egotism will be battered down [. . .] the Esprit de Corps will itself be softened and merged in a far better Esprit de Société . . .

The Byculla maintained one of the oldest English traditions, which was to entertain dignitaries at a Club. Members of the Royal family were invited to dinners. So were the incoming and outgoing viceroys. Lord Curzon was invited to dine at the Club three times, the last occasion being two days before his final departure from India.

Although Delhi was not a Presidency (it was Residency at the Mughal Court), the British needed a place for social entertainment there as in Calcutta, Madras and Bombay. A club (known as the Delhi Club) existed in Old Delhi where the cantonment and Residency headquarters were located.[16] This club may well have been the precursor of the Delhi Gymkhana Club which moved to its present premises in New Delhi in 1913.

Gymkhanas

Gymkhana clubs dating back to the nineteenth century can be found throughout India. The concept of the gymkhana is believed to be British in origin, but in fact, the term originated in India. It is an adaptation of the Hindustani word 'gend-khana' literally meaning ball-house or racquet court. The British substituted 'gymnastics' for 'gend' and converted gend-khana to gymkhana.[17]

Before the Raj, the gymkhana was designed as a gymnasium, a place or a house (khana) where equestrian sports were held: barrel racing, pole bending and any other games played on a horseback. The New Oxford Dictionary of English defines Indian gymkhana as 'a public place with facilities for athletics'. A more general definition is given as 'an equestrian day event comprising races and other competitions on horseback, typically for children'.

Polo playing and horse racing were common sports played at the gymkhana clubs in India. Polo, which dates back over two thousand years, used to be played in the Persian royal court from where it may have gone to India and China. Like the Persians, the British encouraged polo playing to train cavalry for warfare. The gymkhana clubs were less formal than the more exclusive clubs discussed above. Here women and children and families were welcomed. Perhaps they had fewer stag parties and bar brawls![18]

In 1875, the Bombay Gymkhana Club was formed following an earlier decision to merge all sports facilities (such as hockey, football, golf, cricket and boating) into one club. The authorities granted permission for the construction of a pavilion on the Parade Ground for this purpose. Later, a Swiss chalet-style club house and pavilion were built. It is ironical that a Parsi philanthropist, Sir Cowasji Jehangir, who contributed to the construction of the Gymkhana buildings, was not allowed to become a member. Membership, which was restricted to white Europeans, depended on social status and interest in sports. Indians were not considered to be of a high enough social status to become members. During the Raj, money did not necessarily buy social status, but the colour of one's skin did.

The gymkhanas (like the Bombay Gymkhana) were built in a rural mock Tudor style with more verandas than usual since they hosted mainly outdoor sporting events. The verandas offered shade in the very hot and humid climates of Bombay, Calcutta and Madras. In Bombay, the barring of Indians from membership drove different Indian communities (Muslims, Hindus and Parsis) to establish their own gymkhana clubs.

In 1884, the Madras Gymkhana Club was opened, offering horsemanship and physical fitness, pig sticking (wild boar hunts), golf, tennis, rugby and football as its main sports. Its early members included British army officers and company executives. Royal patronage helped the club expand its buildings and facilities.

The Karachi Gymkhana was created two years later, followed by the Delhi Gymkhana (originally called the 'Imperial Delhi Gymkhana Club') much later in 1913. There were also gymkhana clubs in smaller cities such as Poona.

Royal Turf Clubs

The turf clubs with racecourses were popular in the Presidencies and many are still flourishing. For example, the Royal Turf Club of Calcutta at Russell Street in the Chowringhee area remains well preserved. The main building of the club once belonged to the Apcar family of shipping magnates. It is a two-storey Palladian-style white building which has not changed much since it was built. It is standing majestically surrounded by green vegetation and apartment blocks. The club 'organized all the major racing events on the banks of the Hooghly River, besides offering its members the finest of European cuisine' (Morris and Winchester, 1983:56). It has now been moved to the Maidan (Parade Ground) near Victoria Memorial.

The Madras Race Club, established in 1777, is probably the oldest club in India. The Mahaluxmee race course at the Bombay Turf Club, established in 1880, is world famous. Originally, the Byculla Club held races in Bombay. In 1883, horse races were shifted to Mahaluxmee, which was created out of the marshy land. The Mahalaxumee race course is located at the Turf Club.

Race courses were not the exclusive preserve of the three Presidencies. They were also found in other parts of India, in Karachi, Lahore and Delhi in the north and Bangalore and Ootacamund in the south. A horse track was found in almost every station in India and 'the grand-stand with its attendant buildings was one of the most characteristic structures of British India' (ibid.:151). The grandstand and racecourses ranged from the simplest to the most lavish. The turf clubs in the Presidencies were the most modern where the British and Indian aristocracy rubbed shoulders. With their grandstands, restaurants, bars and large official residences, they 'seemed to be as important as any High Court or Secretariat' (ibid.).

The young Englishmen or Scotsmen who went out to India as Company officers were fond of horse racing. Apart from the British love of the sport, the fact that cavalry was the backbone of the British army in the eighteenth and nineteenth centuries may also explain the popularity of horse breeding and racing. Each cantonment, the seat of the British army, had a race course. Other equestrian sports such as fox hunting, polo and steeple chasing were also popular.

Calcutta being the early centre of the British power became the leading centre for horse racing. In 1856, the Viceroy's Cup was introduced at the Hastings Race Course.

Cavalry horses were imported from Britain in the early days of horse racing in India. Horse racing received further boost when the Aga Khan and Sir Victor Sassoon extended their patronage as did the Maharajas of Baroda (now part of Gujarat), Burdwan (part of West Bengal), Cooch-Behar (part of West Bengal), and Mysore (Karnataka). Maharajas from the princely states were among the first Indians to adopt horse racing as a sport. Apart from the British, at that time they were the only ones who could afford to indulge in such an expensive sport. The departure of the British and a temporary ban on betting in independent India witnessed a decline in the fortunes of the sport. But now a thriving middle class and rich Indian community with Western pretensions has revived horse racing throughout India.

6

Imperial Splendour of the Presidencies

They (the houses in Madras) are like Pictures of Italian palaces with flat roofs or balustratdes . . . The walls of rooms are sometimes painted as stucco rooms in England of pale green blue.

(Lady Gwillim,[1] 1802)

Viewed from the Hooghly, Calcutta has the appearance of a city with palaces. A row of large superb buildings extend from the princely residence of the Governor-General, along the Esplanade and produce a remarkably striking effect.

(Leopold von Orlich, 1845)

The Presidencies, owned and managed by the Company, boast lavish government houses, palatial churches, statues and forts. The following three forts were built in 1689 as their seats of power in those Presidencies: Fort St George in Madras; Fort William in Calcutta and the Castle in Bombay. Victoria Memorial in Calcutta, the capital of British India until 1912, is likened to the Taj Mahal by some observers. Such pretensions are not well-founded but they do suggest attempts by the British rulers to emulate the House of Timur.

A presidency refers to an administrative unit governed by a president. It is, therefore, strange that the three British East India territories were called presidencies when they were headed by a governor, not a president. Perhaps they were termed 'presidencies' because they were headed by a president of the Governing Council. However, in Madras and

Bombay that head was called a Governor and in Calcutta, Governor-General. It would have, therefore, been more logical to call them 'governorates'. In 1858, when Queen Victoria was proclaimed sovereign of India, the Governor-General acquired the new title of Viceroy, meaning a representative of the Crown.

In the Presidencies, which were the main trading posts of the Company, a lavish programme of public and private buildings was initiated. Their two most important symbols of British pomp and power were a fort, practically a seat of the Company Raj, and a Government House, a residence of the Governor. The magnificent forts and palaces built during the Raj suggest that the British rulers sought to emulate the royal grandeur of the Mughals and their predecessors.

The palatial private residences in the Madras and Calcutta Presidencies built by Clive, Wellesley and Hastings (Hastings House is still standing) at a high cost in a poor country raised eyebrows at the Company headquarters in London. So much so that the Company directors in London wrote to Lord Clive (Edward, son of Robert Clive and Governor of Madras from 1799 to 1803):

> It by no means appears to us essential to the well-being of our Government in India that the pomp, magnificence and ostentation of the Native Governments should be adopted by the former; the expense to which such a system would naturally lead must prove highly injurious to our commercial interests. (cited in Nilsson, 1968:109–10)

Lord Clive defended his decision to build the lavish Government House in Madras in 1802. Referring to the magnificent residence of the Nawab of Arcot next door, he suggested that the Company's Governor could not live in anything less grand. Lord Valentia expressed a similar view: he defended the construction of grand buildings by the Company on the grounds that he 'wished India to be ruled from a palace, not from a counting-house' (see Chapter 10).

The Company's governors in India shared this haughty attitude. It is clear that the commercial interests of the Company were only one among other reasons for which its representatives were based in the Presidencies. To them, political and subsequent, military expansion, were equally paramount. The notions of creating symbols of an imperial presence gained ground as the representatives became increasingly envious of the wealth and ostentation of the Mughal emperor and the Indian princes.

Madras

Madras is a shortened version of the name, Madraspatnam, where the Company built a factory in the seventeenth century. By 1801, all the local rulers were overpowered by the British who controlled southern India with Madras as their administrative and commercial capital. At the beginning, the British lived inside the fort. Later, when trade expanded, they spread out to garden houses in what was known as White Town. The native Indians lived in Black Town now known as George Town. The two were worlds apart: the former full of beautiful white bungalows with verandas and terraces and the latter replete with poor, dusty and filthy huts (Chapter 9, Fig. 9.4).

It is in Madras where the early plans of the Company to gain territorial power in India were hatched and executed. The Company was in competition with the French Company in Pondicherry for gaining control of the Carnatic (Anglicization of Karnataka) coast. The British Company defeated the French forces in the battle of Arcot thus ending the French territorial ambitions in the region (Wild, 1999).

Some of the major imperial landmarks of the Madras Presidency are described below.

Forts and fortresses had represented symbols of power, conquest and security since the days of the Delhi sultans and the Mughal emperors who lived inside the forts. The British followed this age-old tradition and continued building forts not only in the three Presidencies but also in other strategic towns.

Fort St George on the Coromandel coast, the first fortified British settlement in India, was re-designed by Benjamin Robins and expanded in 1750 to accommodate additional personnel and offices (Plate 9). It served as a residential township, and as a centre of the Company's trade and later, its administration. It included warehouses, an arsenal, barracks, the Governor's residence and a church. Although built 100 years earlier, Fort St George had features similar to those of Fort George of Scotland such as a governor's residence inside the fort besides barracks and a church. The earlier Mughal palace fortresses also had barracks, mosques and residences. But the British fortresses had no halls of public and private audiences to meet their subjects and listen to their grievances, which were the distinguishing features of the Mughal fortresses.

Company officers lived inside the fort for security reasons. However, Lord Clive ventured to live outside in a palace overlooking the sea built especially for him. A two-storey building with verandas and balustraded terraces, it was one of the many examples of pomp and lavishness of the British in India, exemplified by a huge banqueting hall decorated with trophies, helmets and shields (Morris and Winchester, 1983:69). British houses and those of other Europeans in the Madras Presidency generally had 'flat-top' roofs, Venetian shutters, Greek and Roman columns and large gardens.

Government House in Madras was separated from Fort St George by the Cooum River. In 1802, Lord Clive inaugurated the banquet hall of the house with much fanfare, including a grand ball to celebrate the Peace of Amiens. A plan was prepared for the construction of a bridge over the river and a huge bridge gate, but this was rejected by the Directors of the Company in London who did not approve of what they considered to be lavish and unnecessary spending.

The High Court of Madras, built in 1889 to 1992 (and designed by J.W. Brassington and H. Irwin) is a remarkable example of Indo-Saracenic architecture. It looks more like a maharaja's palace than a judicial court. One wonders whether justice could not be served in a more modest and less pretentious edifice. Although the building was perhaps inspired by the Gothic Law Courts built in London 20 years earlier, its large arches, domes and minarets are unmistakably Islamic. The arches are so large that they extend from floor to ceiling, serving the practical purpose of providing ventilation apart from their aesthetic aspect. Metcalf (1989:83) claims that they were similar to and were borrowed from the earlier Pathan architecture. He does not specify the sultanate but it would seem he was referring to the Khaljis and Lodis.

Originally, the High Court was located at Marina Yard opposite the Beach Railway Station. It was the seat of the Supreme Court of Madras from 1817 to 1862 and of the High Court from 1862 to 1892. This High Court building was demolished and a new one was built on the same site.

Other notable public monuments in Madras include (1) Madras Railway Station, representing a mixture of the Indo-Saracenic and Dravidian styles of architecture, (2) the general post office inspired more by Byzantine, Saracenic and Travancore architecture than European, and (3) Memorial hall, built with public donations in the wake of the 1857 uprising, to commemorate deliverance from the traumatic events which spared the Madras Presidency but caused much devastation in the Calcutta Presidency and elsewhere.

Apart from palaces and memorial halls, the British left a legacy in the form of statues of emperors and viceroys at strategic locations in the Presidency towns and other major cities such as New Delhi, the last capital of the British Raj. The earlier emperors (Ashoka, for example) left their legacy in the form of pillars and rock edicts (Plate 1), whereas the Mughal equivalents were the portraits of the emperors and royal miniatures (such as Plate 3) as symbols of imperial power.

There are two noteworthy statues in Madras. The first is the statue of Sir Thomas Munro, Governor of Madras from 1820 to 1827. A Scotsman, Munro had a brilliant military career: he overthrew Tipu Sultan and administered Baramahal surrendered by Tipu. In 1817, he was appointed Brigadier-General to command a division charged with control of the southern territories of the Peshwa. He is known to have been an able administrator who reformed the district revenue system and the judicial system of Madras.

Munro's statue is unique in that it shows him riding bareback without a saddle and stirrups. Despite his popularity in Madras, among villagers as well as administrators, there are discussions to remove the statue. Nationalism and anti-imperialist Tamil sentiments seem to be growing. In an article in the *Hindu* newspaper, Sriram (2010) writes: 'Rather than removing Munro, the state administration could think of translating his statements into Tamil and placing them around his statue. Successive generations can then know the requisites of good administration and also realize that all colonial masters were not evil.'

A statue of King George V is located opposite Island grounds near the War Memorial.

A monument to Lord Cornwallis (1786–93), India's third Governor-General, was located inside Fort St George. Erected in 1800 and designed by Thomas Banks, the statue is inside an Ionic rotunda in the Fort Square.

Recent visitors to Chennai (formerly Madras) have found the statues described here still intact despite an ongoing debate to remove them. By contrast, in Kolkata (formerly Calcutta) and Mumbai (formerly Bombay) most of the statues that are reminders of the British Raj have been removed from public places.

While the earlier Mughal rulers built mosques inside and outside forts, the British built Anglican churches. In Madras, three churches of note are St Mary's Church, St George's Cathedral and St Andrew's Scottish Church.

Built in 1680, St Mary's was the first Anglican church in India and perhaps the oldest to be built in the East. In 1795, its original spire, which had been destroyed by the French artillery, was replaced by an obelisk spire. The church is still in use. Located inside the Fort, it is a small church surrounded by much larger buildings. William Dixon, the Master Gunner of the Fort, may have been its architect. Elihu Yale (Governor of Madras and founder of Yale University) was one of its sponsors. The church was entirely rebuilt in 1759.

St George's Cathedral, a much more massive building of white *chunam* (white polished stucco), was consecrated in 1816. Designed by Colonel James Caldwell of Madras Engineers, it has a clock tower and is located near another church, St Andrew's, built by Thomas de Havilland and consecrated in the same year. It was a favourite meeting place for the English community in Madras.

Churches mushroomed after 1813 when the Company succumbed to Evangelical pressure to accept missionaries who were not allowed into India prior to this date.

Calcutta

Calcutta became the capital of British India in 1772 when Warren Hastings, the then Governor-General, moved from Murshidabad, the provincial Mughal capital. In 1773, Bombay and Madras became subordinate to the government at Fort William in Calcutta. Unlike Madras, Calcutta does not have any Indo-Saracenic buildings. Its architecture is primarily English Classical and Gothic (such as Victoria Memorial).

Initially, Calcutta was a trading post of the Company, set up in 1690 (by Job Charnock, a Company agent) about 50 years after the one in Madras. Why was a malarial swamp chosen for a trading post? This site may have been chosen for a trading post because of its natural topography; on its eastern flank, the Hooghly River provided a natural defence with English battleships permanently moored there; on the western side, there was a jungle and large swamps, the Sunderbans, replete with tigers and alligators. The geographical location of Calcutta was better than that of Madras and so were its port facilities. There were Dutch and French settlements (hostile to the British) located nearby in Bengal (for example, the Dutch at Rajshahi and Murshidabad and the French at Chandernagore). Therefore it is not surprising that the British chose to settle in Calcutta.

Calcutta boasts several important landmarks. The construction of Fort William for the Company was started by Sir Charles Eyre near the banks of the Hooghly River. Sir Charles built the south-east bastion and the adjacent walls and John Beard, his successor, added the north-east bastion in 1701.

In 1756, Siraj-ud-Daula, the then Nawab of Bengal, attacked the Fort and took over the city which he briefly renamed Alinagar. Lord Robert Clive ordered the construction of a new Fort in the Maidan after the Battle of Plassey in 1758 when the Nawab was defeated. It was designed by Captain John Brohier and built by bricklayers and carpenters brought especially from England (perhaps the British mistrusted Indians after their battle with the Bengal nawab). In 1766, the old fort was repaired and was used as a customs house.

The new Fort built of bricks and mortar is still used by the Indian Army as its Eastern Command headquarters. It is an octagonal building with three sides opening towards the Hooghly River. The garrison church known as St Peter's, is still standing inside the fort as are many army barracks and houses of commanders.

Fort William was different from Fort St George in Madras in one respect. The public buildings belonging to it were located outside its walls whereas they were located within the ramparts of St George. European settlements in Calcutta were more dispersed, which suggests an increasing sense of security and rapid growth of the city, with constant building activity commensurate with the growing wealth of the European merchants and traders.

Government House is based on the designs of Kedleston Hall in Derbyshire[2] (Fig. 6.1). Lord Wellesley (formerly, the Earl of Mornington), the Governor-General of Calcutta, commissioned Charles Wyatt of the

Fig. 6.1. Government House, Calcutta (Author's Private Collection)

Engineers to design a new Government House on the site of the old on Esplanade Row. It has an arcade of Ionic columns. The north portico has a large staircase under which horse carriages could drive up to the entrance. The south side of the house has a circular colonnade with a dome.

Sprawling Government House was built in the Georgian style of architecture in India which surpassed the splendour of Lord Clive's new house in the Madras Presidency. Lord Wellesley was an aristocrat who did not appreciate his predecessors' modest style of living and working! It is rather puzzling that the Union Jack is not flying on top of the Government House as on the Residency Lucknow (Fig. 1.0, Introduction) and on Fort St George (Fig. 6.1). The House had a chandeliered banquet hall and numerous imposing rooms and staircases. In 1873, James Ferguson, the architect historian, noted that 'there are few modern palaces of its class either more appropriate in design, or more effective in their architectural arrangement and play of light and shade, than this residence (cited in Davies, 1985:69).

Wellesley had a grandiose plan to connect his Calcutta palace with his country house in Barrackpore by means of a 14-mile long avenue.

Fig. 6.2. Belvedere (Hastings) House (Author's Private Collection)

The plan did not materialize because he was called back to London on charges of extravagance!

No less luxurious was Belvedere House, once the private home of Lord Warren Hastings, the first Governor of West Bengal (Fig. 6.2). In 1854, the Company acquired the house which became the official residence of the Lieutenant-Governor of Bengal. It was the scene of many social events such as the Christmas Ball.

Calcutta High Court has a different architectural style from that of the Madras High Court. Its Indo-Gothic style is more akin to that of the Bombay High Court (Fig. 6.3). Designed by Walter Granville, a government architect, it is said to be a replica of the Cloth Hall in Ypres, Belgium. It is not clear why he would favour a Belgian-style building over an English-style one. A fire caused by German shelling during World War I destroyed the building in Belgium which was later rebuilt according to the blueprints of the Calcutta High Court.

Victoria Memorial was conceived by Lord Curzon, the Indian Viceroy (1898–1905), to commemorate the British Empire in India at its peak. Its construction began in 1904 and was completed in 1921 (Fig. 6.4). Designed by Sir William Emerson, it combines a mixture of Italian statues and Mughal domes with open colonnades on its sides. The Memorial contains a museum with British colonial paintings, other mementoes of

Fig. 6.3. Calcutta High Court (Author's Private Collection)

the Raj, French guns captured at the Battle of Plassey, and a black marble throne of a nawab, who was defeated by Clive. Today, it also includes leaders of the Indian Independence Movement and other luminaries of that time as well as various dignitaries of Calcutta. The Memorial

Fig. 6.4. Victoria Memorial (Author's Private Collection)

Fig. 6.5. King Edward VII Arch at the Memorial (Author's Private Collection)

complex contains the King Edward VII Arch (Fig. 6.5) and a large statue of Queen Victoria.

Lord Curzon wanted the Memorial to be entirely European, as something that represented British sovereignty over India. However, it is made of Makrana marble (also used in the Taj) and while largely European, it does contain some Mughal (corner domes) and some Hindu (window arches and filigree work) elements. A revolving statue in bronze of the winged Goddess of Victory (Nike in the Greek mythology) stands at the top of the central dome. Allegorical sculptures personifying Art, Architecture, Justice and Charity surround the dome.

That the Memorial was intended to be a testimony to the great British Empire in India cannot be in any doubt. Lord Curzon had lamented that there was no single important monument of the Empire apart from a few statues of queens, kings and governors. He noted that there was nothing 'to show that the Indian scroll of history had been one on which immortal characters had been inscribed, or that the Victorian Era in particular had witnessed the growth of India from a scattered complex of heterogeneous states and territories into a powerful and consolidated Empire' (Curzon of Kedleston, 1925, vol. I:178–9). However, it is rather ironical that as a memorial of British imperialism it was built at the very time when the imperial forces of the British Crown began a drawdown in India.

Some observers, rather inappropriately, compare the Memorial to the Taj Mahal (Morris and Winchester, 1983:115–6). True, it was dedicated to a queen as was the Taj. It is also true that it is made of white marble as is the Taj. However, in its grandeur it hardly matches the Taj which many consider to be a modern wonder of the world. The two monuments are similar only in one respect: both were attempted to be symbols of two major empires in India. This is evident in the following statement in a speech made by Lord Curzon in 1901:

> Let us have a building, stately and spacious, monumental and grand, to which every newcomer in Calcutta will turn, to which all the resident population, European and Native, will flock, where all classes will learn the lesson of history, and see, revived before their eyes, the marvels of the past. (Speech at Public Meeting, Calcutta, 6 February 1901)

The Town Hall of Calcutta, very close to the Governor's palace in Esplanade and overlooking the Maidan, was completed in 1813. Town halls in the Presidencies and other major towns were important public buildings which served many functions besides being the seat of municipal corporations. According to a ruling of the Governor-General, the town hall was reserved 'for authorized general meetings of the inhabitants of Calcutta, or for meetings of merchants or other classes of society [. . .] and for public entertainments on great occasions' (cited in Nilsson, 1968:116).

There were quite a few statues in Calcutta honouring the following Governors-General: Warren Hastings Cornwallis, Wellesley, Dalhousie in Victoria Memorial Hall; Bentinck opposite the Town Hall; Curzon, Hardinge, Lawrence and Mayo in the Maidan; and Dufferin and Lansdowne at Red Road. However, not all the Governors-General were honoured with statues.[3]

Over the years, the Indian authorities, including those in Calcutta (West Bengal), have relegated most of the statues and monuments of the British Raj to some dingy basements of museums and store rooms. Other monuments from the British period have either been demolished or renamed (for example, the Ochterlony Monument which is now called Shahid Minar). Holwell's monument has also disappeared as have the statues of Lord Curzon and Lord Hardinge (Fig. 6.6).

To their credit, the Indian authorities have made one exception, namely the statue of Queen Victoria who ruled from 1837 till 1901. It is still standing in the Victoria Memorial complex. Its pedestal is lined with a bronze panel and friezes on the sides. Queen Victoria never visited India, but statues of her appeared in different cities throughout India (Bangalore, Bombay, Calcutta, Karachi and Lahore). A sense of history has prevailed instead of pure nationalism. Different West Bengal governments of independent India decided to maintain this important symbol of the British Raj.

The Ochterlony Monument, a tall tower in the Maidan, commemorates the life of Major-General Ochterlony and his victory in the Gurkha Nepal War of 1816. It was designed by Charles Knowles Robinson and financed through public donations. Its style represents a combination of Egyptian, Syrian and Turkish architecture. The column has survived unlike many other Calcutta statues of the Raj.

Other Calcutta landmarks included Holwell's Monument, an octagonal obelisk which stood at the western end of Writers' Buildings.[4] It

Fig. 6.6. Lord Hardinge's Statue and Ochterlony Monument (Author's Private Collection)

is dedicated to the victims of Black Hole, the name given to a small chamber in the old Fort William which was used as a military prison. During the Battle of Plassey between the Bengal Nawab and the British, the former's forces threw nearly 150 British inhabitants into the chamber on the night of 20 June 1756. Only 23 survived, the others dying of suffocation. Holwell himself was also captured but later released when Clive retook the fort.

Calcutta boasted a large number of churches and cathedrals built during the Raj. The cathedral has been in existence since 1814. St Paul's Cathedral was built later (1847) by Bishop Daniel Wilson as an Anglo-Indian Church. Located in a corner of the Maidan, its interior contains mosaics illustrating major events in St Paul's life. The church tower and spire were modelled on Norwich Cathedral. The original tower was destroyed in an earthquake and was later rebuilt. St John's Church in Calcutta was consecrated in 1787, St Andrews in 1815, and St Peter's inside Fort William was consecrated as a garrison church in 1822.

The number of churches built in Calcutta is disproportionate to the small size of the English population of barely 3,000 in 1837 (Wild, 1999:58). Even counting the population of Anglo-Indians, the total number of churchgoers was still rather small. So why were so many churches

Fig. 6.7. Bombay Harbour from Apollo Bunder (Author's Private Collection)

built? Were the English missionaries expecting to convert the entire Hindu and Muslim population of Calcutta to Christianity?!

Bombay

Bombay has abundant landmarks dating back to the Raj. Near the Taj Hotel at Apollo Bunder, the turreted square and the Gateway of India were reminders of Liverpool or Edinburgh (Beaton, 1991:36). The Town Hall of Bombay, a classical building, was similar to many in different parts of England.

Although the Madras and Calcutta Presidencies were the most important, ships bound for these two destinations would first call at Bombay which had much better port facilities. Fig. 6.7 shows the Bombay harbour at Appollo Bunder with two memsahibs on a stroll.

Like Madras and Calcutta, Bombay also had a fort known as the Castle where the army of the Bombay Presidency was stationed. However, it was not such an important landmark as the Bombay Marine, the Bombay naval force which was later renamed Her Majesty's Indian Navy. Bombay also had its share of palatial buildings such as the Governor's House and the Brigadier-General's Bungalow. An English officer in white uniform

Fig. 6.8. Brigadier-General's Bungalow (Author's Private Collection)

in front of the bungalow wearing a Pith helmet (or *sola topi*) crossing a half-clad Indian native is a typical colonial scene of the time (Fig. 6.8).

Governor's House was originally a Portuguese Franciscan friary at Parel (Bombay) built in 1673. In 1719, it was taken over by the Company as a country residence for Bombay Governors. It became the new Government House in place of the earlier building inside the Fort.

Parel grew into an industrial town, which even in those days raised levels of pollution and congestion. To get away from this, the Governor's residence was again shifted to a new Government House at Malabar Point, but it too was abandoned when a governor's wife died there of cholera (Bence-Jones, 1973:78). At least its exterior, it does not match the architectural distinction of the Houses in Madras and Calcutta. This may be partly because it was built piecemeal over a period of time (ibid.:78). However, despite its rather simple and unpretentious exterior, it had a grand banquet hall, meeting rooms and living quarters.

The Bombay Secretariat completed in 1874, was designed by Captain Henry St Clair Wilkins in the Venetian Gothic style. It has arcaded verandas and a huge gable over the west facade. The Clock Tower close to the Secretariat is one of the landmarks of Bombay inspired by Big Ben in London and the Campanile in Florence.

Fig. 6.9. Victoria (Shivaji) Terminus (Author's Private Collection)

The Victoria Terminus, built in 1887 or 1894, was designed by Fred-erick William Stevens, an architect known for the Victorian style of architecture during the British Raj. It is an impressive building originally built in Italian-Gothic style. Some later modifications to it incorporated the Oriental style (Indo-Saracenic) reflected in its domes (Fig. 6.9). It is the largest nineteenth-century building in Asia. The headquarters of the Central Railways and those of the Great Indian Peninsular Railway (GIPR) were located in it. Lady Dufferin, wife of the Viceroy (Lord Duf-ferin), who presided over its inauguration, declared rather haughtily that 'it was too good for the natives'.

His Majesty's High Court Building was built in a Venetian Gothic style, combining elements of Venetian and early English architecture. Statues of Justice and Mercy decorate the top of the building. The design and lay-out of the colossal building were influenced by the British Law Courts in the Strand in London. This is not surprising considering that the English engineers based in Bombay had easy access to designs from their mother country.

A marble statue of Queen Victoria, commissioned by His Highness the Gaekwad of Baroda, was unveiled at Victoria Gardens on 29 April 1872 (Fig. 6.10). Sculpted out of Carrara marble by Matthew Noble

Fig. 6.10. Queen Victoria Statue (Author's Private Collection)

of London, the statue shows the Queen seated in the House of Lords in her robes of state. Inscriptions on the sides and back of the canopy under which the Queen is seated are written in English as well as in three Indian languages (*Illustrated London News*, 1872).

A second important statue in Bombay is that of King Edward VII, Queen Victoria's son. In 1965, it was moved to the Victoria and Albert Museum, from where it was again moved to its final resting place in Byculla, Bombay.

There were many more statues which have disappeared. Douglas (1900) devotes a whole section to 'Some Bombay Statues and Portraits'. Apparently, the new Town Hall was intended, among other purposes, for displaying the statues of Marquis Cornwallis, William Pitt and any future British monuments donated to Bombay (ibid.:81). He quotes the Bombay Government Letter of 22 February 1817 published in the *Bombay Gazetteer*, vol. XXVI:

> They (the statues of Marquis Cornwallis, Mr. Pitt and the Marquis of Wellesley) [...] are likely to remain in an obscure warehouse, unless we can rear a suitable edifice for the reception of such splendid and exemplary testimonies of public respect and gratitude to the services and to the virtues of the most eminent statesmen of our country.

The Gateway of India was perhaps the last British memorial to be built in Bombay in 1911. It was opened in 1924 to commemorate the visit of King George V and Queen Mary. The last British troops to leave India passed through this gateway. It was designed by George Wittet in an Indo-Saracenic style reflected in a 26-metre high archway, four turrets and intricate lattice work carved in stone.

As in the other two Presidencies, Bombay had its share of churches: The Byculla Church, St Thomas's Cathedral and St John's Church, to name only a few. St Thomas's Cathedral has the oldest history. It started as a garrison church which later became a cathedral. Its construction began in 1676 by Governor Gerald Aungier (1672–6) in charge of Surat and Bombay. However, the project was abandoned after his death in 1676, and the church remained incomplete for 40 years. Richard Cobbe, a chaplain of the Company, completed it between 1715 and 1718.

In 1858, St John's Church, also known as the Afghan Memorial Church, was built in Colaba in memory of army officers and soldiers of the British expeditionary army which perished in Afghanistan in 1842. During the Company Raj, the British Army consisted of the three Presidency armies (of Bengal, Madras and Bombay) besides that of the Crown. John Harding, the Anglican Bishop of Bombay, consecrated the Church in January 1858. Its architect, Henry Conybeare, built it in the early English Gothic style which later became popular in Bombay under Governor Bartle Frere. Gothic architecture was accepted as the only style suitable for church architecture, in the belief that 'Gothic alone authentically represented a Christian society' (Metcalf, 1989:98).

Finally, the Byculla Church in Byculla, an extension of Mazegaon (one of the seven islands that formed the city of Bombay) is worth noting. Still intact, it is decorated with Doric columns shipped from England. The columns were intended for the town hall but were found to be too large (Morris and Winchester, 1983:110).

Conclusion

This chapter has described three types of imperial monuments of the Raj:

(1) Those which have been removed (that is, most of the statues except that of Queen Victoria in the grounds of Victoria Memorial in Calcutta).

Table 6.1. The Current Status of the Monuments of the Raj in the Three Presidencies

Category	Madras	Calcutta	Bombay
Removed/ demolished		The following statues: Auckland, Bentinck, Canning, Curzon, Dufferin, Hardinge, Lansdowne, Lawrence, Mayo, Minto, Northbrook; Holwell's monument.	Byculla Club; statues of Cornwallis, Pitt, King Edward VII and Queen Victoria.
Renamed		Ochterlony monument.	Elphinstone Circle; Victoria Gardens; Victoria Terminus; the Town Hall; the Clock Tower.
Preserved	Law Courts (Madras High Court) ; Fort St George; University Senate House; Egmore Railway Station; statue of Munro; Madras Club.	Victoria Memorial and Queen Victoria statue; Hastings House; Fort William; Bengal Club; Writers' Buildings.	Bombay Gymkhana club; High Court, Crawford Market; Gateway of India; Victoria Terminus; the Secretariat; the Clock Tower.

(2) Those which have been renamed (Ochterlony Monument in Calcutta).

(3) Those that are still intact (Victoria Memorial and Hastings House in Calcutta and the Central Secretariat and the Viceregal Lodge in New Delhi).

The current state of the monuments is described in Table 6.1. Most statues in Calcutta and Bombay have now been removed from public places. In Calcutta, the only exception is the statue of Queen Victoria as a reminder of the British imperial presence in India. Some buildings have also disappeared or are being used for different purposes (for example, the Byculla Club in Bombay). Quite a few (especially the street names) have been renamed. However, Madras is an exception, where most statues, monuments and other buildings of the Raj remain preserved for everyone to see.

The gigantic and splendid monuments built in the Presidencies during the Raj are redolent of the earlier Mughal building spree. The British rulers continued to follow the tradition of the pomp and glory of Akbar and Shah Jahan regardless of the cost to the exchequer and the taxpayer. Victoria Memorial had pretensions of rivalling Shah Jahan's Taj Mahal. While these two Mughal emperors built two entirely new cities, Fatehpur Sikri and Shahjahanabad, the British rulers built new summer capitals (Chapter 7) and the new capital of the Raj, New Delhi (Chapter 9).

7

Summer Capitals and Cantonments

> Migration to Simla became a rule of Government, justified not so much by
> the need of a cooler and healthier climate during the great heat of summer,
> as by the Westerly expansion of the territories and responsibilities of the
> Government of India, and the necessity for a more central position than
> the Bay of Bengal.
>
> (Lord Curzon, 1925)

The British summer capitals in the hill stations in India extended the
glamour and splendour of the Raj beyond the three Presidencies. Although Mughal emperors such as Jahangir and Shah Jahan established
gardens in Kashmir, they never shifted their seats of government there.
However, it is true that they used Kashmir as their summer hideout to
escape the heat of the plains.[1]

During a visit to Simla in 1876, Val Prinsep,[2] a writer born in India,
observed that 'everything is so English and unpicturesque here that
except the people one meets are those who rule and make history – a
fact one can hardly realize – one would fancy oneself at Margate' (cited
in Morris and Winchester, 1983:202). Miss Eden noted: 'The sharp
clean air is perfectly exhilarating. I have felt nothing like it – I mean
nothing so English since I was on the terrace at Eastcombe' (Barr and
Desmond, 1982:11).

While the summer capitals were British civil headquarters, cantonments and garrison towns were the seats of its military power and defence
establishment. The military headquarters were established by the Company long before the Crown took over responsibility for its Indian colony.

Each year in summer (from March to October, from 1865 to 1939), the Viceroy, the Commander-in-Chief and other senior officers of the Raj, moved from Calcutta and Delhi to Simla. When Simla became the summer capital, the construction of many grand public buildings and private residences followed to provide accommodation for the Governor-General, the Commander-in-Chief, Private Secretary to the Viceroy, the Lieutenant-Governor of the Punjab and other high officials as well as for rich residents. Commercial buildings also mushroomed: for example, hotels to accommodate tourists and official visitors.

Civil servants were not the only inhabitants of Simla during the Raj. In fact, there were two main groups there: the official and the social. According to Davies (1985:116–17), Simla 'was no longer just a resort; physically it changed into an eccentric suburb of Calcutta, 700 miles away, adding further incongruity to its already idiosyncratic appearance.' By the time of the 1857 uprising, it became known for 'bright ladies and gay gentlemen'. There were 'some wild spirits around, some high living and high gambling and a great deal of not-so-harmless flirting' (Edwardes, 1988:126).

It seems odd that Simla was chosen as the summer capital when the British capital, Calcutta, was located so far away. Would it not have been more appropriate to choose Darjeeling, another hill station in Bengal, which is much closer to Calcutta? Was Darjeeling more suitable only for tea plantations but not for vast constructions for a summer capital? Simla may have been chosen because it was closer to trouble spots in north India (Cawnpore, Delhi, Lucknow and Meerut) where the 1857 uprising had started. Darjeeling may have been rejected because it was a disputed territory between Bhutan, Nepal and Sikkim.[3] Perhaps Darjeeling was not considered a central enough location for a summer capital (Curzon of Kedleston, 1925, vol. 1:232). But in that case, it would seem that Mussoorie supported by Dehra Dun would be a more obvious choice than Simla.

Summer Capitals in the Hills

Over 80 hill stations in different parts of India were developed during the British Raj, including:

North: In the foot of Himalayas, Dalhousie, Kasauli, Kulu/Manali, Murree, Mussoorie, Naini Tal and Simla.

North-east: Darjeeling, Shillong.

West: Poona, Mahabaleshwar.

South: Conoor, Ootacamund, Kodaikanal.

These hill stations were established to provide relief and recuperation for military personnel from the heat, as well as diseases such as cholera, malaria and typhoid which killed thousands of Britons (Wright, 1998:15). Dalrymple (2009:281) notes: 'On 5 July 1857 cholera claimed its second British General: having killed General Anson in Kurnal in May, it now removed his successor, General Barnard as well.' In those days, with unsatisfactory medical treatment, life could be short: a person could be healthy at breakfast but dead by the afternoon (Allen, 1975:174).

The hot temperatures in the plains, combined with the dust and squalor caused many diseases among soldiers and army officers, not to mention debilitating 'tropical fatigue'. The incidence of diseases was considerably lower in the hills. During the cholera epidemics of 1817–19, the transfer of ailing soldiers to the hills led to the virtual disappearance of the disease. Ms Emily Eden, sister of Lord Auckland, the Governor-General, once remarked in Simla that 'Like meat, we keep better here' (Wild, 2001:180).

Hill stations later became more popular as summer retreats for all, especially the memsahibs who outnumbered men. In 1931, Amy Baker noted: 'Up in the hills young men are rare, down in the plains young women are rare. Young men are spoilt in the hills and lost in the plains' (cited in Hyam, 1990:118). Women would retire to Simla to become 'grass widows' when their men-folk had to stay back in Delhi for work. An imbalance in the sex ratio may have been one of the causes of the many scandals that occurred during the Raj.

Another observer (George Carroll of the Indian Police Service and Tutor to the prince of Jodhpur) believed that white women were apt to 'let us down in prestige by going off to the Hills every Hot Weather and leaving one down below. The general understanding was that they went up there to lead a life of immorality, and in many cases, it was true' (cited in Allen, 1975:177).

Hill stations such as Simla, Poona and Murree became the summer capitals of various British administrations. In fact, each of the three

Fig. 7.1. Viceregal Lodge, Simla (Author's Private Collection)

Presidencies had its own summer capital: Ootacamund for Madras (nicknamed 'snooty Ooty'), Poona for Bombay and Simla for Calcutta. Murree (Pakistan) became a summer retreat for officers from the Punjab province.

Simla

Simla became a mountain retreat when Lieutenant Robert Ross, Assistant Political Agent for the Hill States [4] 'built a temporary wooden home there in 1819, followed by Captain Charles Kennedy's (his successor) more permanent log cabin in 1822. Kennedy was appointed Superintendent of the Hill States based in Simla which soon became known as 'a viceregal sanatorium' in view of its pleasant climate' (Lord Amherst, 1827). The early Governors-General (for example, Earl of Auckland, Earl of Ellenborough and Viscount Hardinge) stayed at the Auckland House. Later ones including Viceroys stayed at Peterhof (such as Elgin, Lawrence, Northbrook) or the Viceregal Lodge (Chelmsford, Curzon, Minto) (Fig. 7.1).

This major building activity in Simla cost a substantial amount of money (Table 7.1). In addition to the nearly Rs 6.5 crores (or Rs 65 million), the annual cost of the central government's exodus from Delhi to Simla is estimated at £24,000.

Table 7.1. The Cost of Building Simla

Buildings, Infrastructure and Services	Cost (Rs lakh)
I. *Central government*	
Viceregal Lodge & estate	*c.*35.0
Commander-in-Chief's residence	4.5
Civil Offices of the 'Supreme Government'	56.0
Military Offices	22.0
Legislative Chambers	13.0
Post and Telegraph Offices	13.0
Official residential buildings and and departmental establishments	97.0
Other houses for government employees	175.0
Simla bazaar	106.0
Water supply	54.0
Electricity	24.0
Communications (including roads)	2.0
Sanitation	2.0
Total	603.5
II. *Punjab government*	
Barnes Court (Governor's residence)	6.0
Government offices and residential quarters	22.0
Total	28.0
Grand Total	**631.5**

Source: Buck (1925:280).

The summer retreat of the Viceroy, the Viceregal Lodge, was built in 1888 by Lord Dufferin in the English Renaissance style. The main rooms of the Lodge are built around a great entrance hall decorated with thick teak panelling and a gallery. It looks like many Victorian country houses in England of that period. Lord Curzon made several alterations to it (raising the external tower, for example) at considerable expense to satisfy his whims and fancy.[5]

Originally, the Governor-General rented 'Peterhof', a two-storey tin-roofed chalet, until the Lodge was built. In 1881, Lady Lytton who lived there found it 'the smallest house she had ever lived in, while her husband

Fig. 7.2. Christchurch Cathedral (Author's Private Collection)

called it a pig-sty...' (Morris and Winchester, 1983:54). Peterhof was destroyed by a fire in 1981.

A second prominent building of the Raj was Snowdon Residence where the Commander-in-Chief of the Indian Army lived from 1885 onwards. In the early 1900s, Lord Kitchener got the Snowdon (especially the interior) enlarged and modified to suit his taste and requirements.

Christchurch Cathedral on the Ridge was another magnificent building in Simla (Fig. 7.2). It was designed by Colonel J.T. Boileau in the Gothic style and John Lockwood Kipling (Rudyard Kipling's father) designed the fresco surrounding the chancel window which has now disappeared. The bells of the Cathedral were cast from a cannon captured by the British during the Sikh wars.

The Mall was the main centre and shopping street of Simla where the Indian natives were not allowed. A strict and formal dress code was enforced for going to the Mall; for instance, open-neck shirts were not allowed.

In the twentieth century, Simla declined in importance with the establishment of Delhi as the new imperial capital. The new capital was not the only reason for Simla's decline. The European population in the north started to decline following improved communications with Europe.The strength of the British Army steadily decreased and the political reforms associated with self-rule meant that a larger number of Indians became involved in the administration.

Ootacamund

The official summer capital of the Madras Presidency in the Nilgiri Hills (or the Blue Mountains), Ootacamund was known for its tea and coffee plantations. The Company gained control of the Nilgiri Hills in 1799, following the defeat and death of Tipu Sultan, the Muslim ruler of Mysore, in the fourth Anglo-Mysore war.

Its stunning beauty and its deep valleys at an altitude of over 7,000 feet has earned it the title of 'Queen of the Hill Stations'. Originally, the land there was occupied by the Todas (a local hill tribe) who earned their living by raising water buffaloes. John Sullivan, one of the Governors of Coimbatore, acquired the land from the Todas and developed it into a hill resort planting teak, fruit trees, tea bushes and English varieties of trees and flowers for which the climate was well-suited.

Ootacamund may have developed rapidly partly because its beauty and pleasant climate attracted many private British citizens who decided to settle there. An artificial lake, churches and stone houses were built 'that wouldn't have looked out of place in Surrey or the Scottish Highlands (Abram et al., 2001:1283). Several governors of the Madras Presidency, for example, Stephen Lushington (1827–32), promoted Ooty's development including the construction of St Stephen's Church (Fig. 7.3). Built in the Gothic style, it is one of the earliest buildings of the Raj in Ooty. Unlike other English churches of the period, it has a stucco exterior and simplified buttresses. Timber recovered from Tipu Sultan's palace in Srirangapatnam was used for its construction.

Like other major British towns, Ooty had a Government House built in 1877 when the Duke of Buckingham was the Governor of Madras. The House had a pillared portico copied from the Duke's Summer Palace at Stowe, Buckinghamshire, which today is an English public school.

The Ooty Club, another institution dating back to the Raj, is known for being the place where the rules for snooker were first laid down. The house where the Club was originally (1831) located belonged to Sir William Rumbold, a well-known usurer of Hyderabad. It became a club in 1843.

Fig. 7.3. St Stephen's Church, Ootacamund (© The British Library Board, London)

The 'Ooty Hunt', founded in 184<, was known to be the only hunt between Italy and Australia. The first pack of hounds was transported there in 1844. The hunt appears to have been discontinued for a while before the Commissioner of Nilgris restarted it. In 1859, the 60th Rifles hunted here with a "bobbery pack" of four and a half couples of cross-bred hounds' (Wright, 1998:236).

The Ooty Botanical Gardens, now a public park, were laid out in 1847. Originally, they were intended to promote the study of flora and fauna in and around the Nilgiri hills. Besides having a variety of rare trees and flowers, one of their main attractions was an Italian-style garden bordering a pool.

There were also a few outstanding non-British buildings such as the Fernhill Palace. Built in the style of a Swiss chalet, it is the former summer residence of the Maharaja of Mysore. During the British Raj, army officers staying at the hotel would wear full-dress uniform. An indoor badminton court is a special feature of the palace. Following its construction in 1842, additional ball rooms and private suites were added.

Poona

One of the hill stations for the Bombay Presidency, Poona soon became a popular resort and attracted rich Parsi businessmen who built country houses there. It is rather odd that the Presidency would choose Poona as a hill station, considering that it is less than 600 metres above sea level. It was made the summer headquarters of the Presidency presumably because of its proximity to Panchgani, which is over 1,300 metres above sea level and Mahabaleshwar that is even higher at nearly 1,400 metres. Poona was also the western military capital of the Deccan. The last Peshwa ruler saw his troops being defeated by the British forces from Parvati hill, Poona's highest peak.

Ganesh Khind was the summer palace of the governors of Bombay. It was built by Sir Bartle Frere, Governor of Bombay from 1862 to 1876. It is a rather odd building which suggests that it was built in stages. A shortage of funds might have interrupted its construction. The design of the building was inspired by Queen Victoria's country house (Osborne) on the Isle of Wight.[6] Its tall tower in the middle and Romanesque arches suggest an Italianate style.

Murree

From the very first days of British rule in Peshawar, the British troops began looking for a suitable location in the hills to escape the heat, disease and dangers of the Frontier capital. Nearly 150 miles from Peshawar, Murree seemed to be the perfect choice. It was founded by Sir Henry Lawrence, the Governor of Punjab in 1851.

Originally, it was designed as a sanatorium for British troops stationed in Peshawar near the Afghan border. Apparently, the name Murree

Fig. 7.4. Mall and Holy Trinity Church, Murree (1852) (©Victoria and Albert Museum, London)

comes from the word '*marhi*' which in a local dialect means a place at a high altitude. It is rumoured that the Company bought the land to build Murree from a local raja for only Rs 60. The raja, incensed by the cheek of the British officer concerned, returned half the money to the officer so that his wife (who was wearing a skirt) could buy enough cloth to cover her face and legs!

Murree's layout is similar to that of Simla. Like Christchurch in Simla, Murree's Anglican Holy Trinity Church dominates the centre of the hill station (Fig. 7.4). It is situated close to the Mall Road (now Jinnah Road), a main shopping centre with shops owned by Europeans and Parsis. Until 1947, non-Europeans and natives were not allowed access to the Mall.

Murree became the summer headquarters of the Punjab Government in Lahore for five months each year and remained so until 1876. Like Simla, it had bands, a theatre and sports for its local residents.

The timber-framed Post Office (Fig. 7.5) at Pindi Point as it looked in the nineteenth century resembled that of Simla on the Ridge at the end

Fig. 7.5. Murree Post Office in the Early Nineteenth Century (Courtesy of K. Khalid)

of the Mall. It also bears a striking resemblance to Godfrey Thomas's (a friend of the author) private bungalow, Holme Craig, in Dorset (Fig. 7.6).[7] Built around the same time, the building confirms the widely-held view that the British rulers in India tried to recreate the British physical environment in India.

English army officers and bureaucrats built rambling Victorian mansions on hillsides. By 1850, more than 50 bungalows (for example, Fairfield and Holme) were built near Kashmir Point, Pindi Point and Kuldana Road. On the Mall, which stretches up to Kashmir Point, is a building called the Durdens, the home of Francis Younghusbands. an army officer and an explorer. Behind the Durdens, in the distance, Pinnacle Hill was the residence of the Lieutenant-Governor. Also called Government House, it is now the summer retreat of the President of Pakistan.

Murree was the site of one of the four Lawrence asylums which were intended for the children of army officers and other serving soldiers. The Asylum is still functioning in Murree as a private school for boys.

Fig. 7.6. Holme Craig, Lyme Regis (Dorset, UK) (Courtesy of G. Thomas)

All these summer capitals of the Raj have a British colonial look about them: all have a Mall, a cathedral at the end of it, a typical post-office building, a government house, a Club, and lovely country bungalows, wooden chalets or stone houses as in Ootacamund. Murree is somewhat similar to Simla in its layout and the style of buildings. So is Ootacamund except for its more relaxed and serene appearance. It is reminiscent of England; Stephen Lushington, the then Governor of Madras, described it as 'Malvern at the fairest season' (cited in Davies, 1985:125). Davies (ibid.:124) notes: 'If Simla is like some fading insubstantial dream, far to the south in the Nilgiri Hills, Ootacamund [. . .] evokes an altogether different response. It is a pastiche of rural England preserved in aspic, a window on a forgotten world.'

Cantonments and Garrison Towns

The British rulers created a number of cantonments and garrison towns. These were permanent military camps outside the cities intended mainly for the security of the British population in India. Threats to the British came from two sources: the local rulers and maharajas and the competing trading powers such as the Dutch, the French and the Portuguese. In the Presidencies and the satellite (princely) states of the British Raj, garrison troops were required to maintain peace and administrative unity.

The Company's rule has often been referred to as 'a garrison state' in which its army relied heavily on Indian soldiers. This is understandable since there were no more than 125,000 Europeans, including children, in a population of 250 million inhabitants at that time. The Indian regiments were kept outside the cantonments which were reserved for the British.[8] Segregation was the hallmark of all cantonments, as is colourfully described below:

> Officers were separated from other ranks, of course, married quarters from barrack-blocks, British troops from natives, artillery from cavalry, elephants and camels from oxen and horses: the general had a fine big house in the middle of the camp, and at the end of each barrack-block there was a house for the sergeant-major. (ibid.:90)

Initially, the three Presidency forts were practically like garrison towns housing armies and ammunition. As territories under the Company's control expanded, so did the need for more garrison towns and cantonments. The forts could no longer guard and protect large areas under British control. Therefore, a new type of military strategy was required for rapid troop movements and deployment. The functions of the fort were moved to new cantonments and garrison towns throughout the British-occupied territory. This is how new military urban centres called 'cantonments' were developed.

They enabled the British rulers to keep their distance from what they considered to be the 'inferior natives'. By the 1860s, there were 175 cantonments generally located about five to six miles away from the native towns and cities (Morris and Winchester, 1983:89).

A typical cantonment, an exclusively English township, consisted of a row of uniform bungalows for soldiers, army barracks, separate houses for army officers, a military hospital, a cantonment market and a soldiers' club. Its tidiness and well-organized urban planning contrasted sharply with the native cities and towns where traffic was unregulated and chaotic, and hygiene and sanitation facilities were virtually absent.

In garrison towns such as Barrackpore, Peshawar, Quetta and Rawalpindi, troops were stationed in forts and fortresses to defend the interests of the Company and the Crown. Not surprisingly, the early military stations (rudimentary forms of cantonments and garrison towns) were established near Calcutta, the British capital. In 1783, Dum Dum became the headquarters of the Bengal artillery, and Barrackpore, a cantonment, had a country residence for the Governor-General.

Important cantonments and garrison towns that survive today such as Quetta, Rawalpindi, Peshawar and Cawnpore, are lasting symbols of the British Empire. The first three are now in Pakistan.

Quetta

Accounts of Quetta date back to the eleventh century when Mahmud of Ghazni from Afghanistan captured it. The Mughals were in control of Quetta throughout the sixteenth century. The British briefly occupied it in 1839 during the first Afghan War, but it was not until 1876 that Quetta became part of British India as the capital of British Baluchistan. Its strategic location in the northwestern frontier led the British to station troops there. They developed it as a garrison town by building roads and other infrastructure. Soon, important government buildings mushroomed: the railway station, post and telegraph office, government market, the library and other public buildings. However, since it was

Fig. 7.7. Staff College, Quetta (Author's Private Collection)

developed as an important cantonment, the most significant of Quetta's buildings to survive are the Staff College (Fig. 7.7) the army barracks, some soldiers' homes and the soldiers' club.

The British established a Staff College in 1905 first in Deolali near Nasik in Maharashtra. In 1907, Lord Kitchener, the Commander-in-Chief in India, moved it to Quetta with the name, Quetta Cadet College. The college is headed by a commandant and is divided into two wings: the Headquarters Wing and the Instructional Wing. It prepares students for meeting the challenges of the increasingly complex modes and methods of warfare.

Fig. 7.8 shows a line of English policemen with *sola topis* and sniffer dogs on Bruce Road, one of the main arteries of Quetta cantonment, a typical scene witnessed in most cantonments to keep the natives under control.

A powerful earthquake (7.7 on the Richter scale) on 31 May, 1935 completely destroyed Quetta including one-quarter of the British cantonment area. The remaining three-quarters were damaged but remained habitable.

Bruce Road, Quetta. Summer.

Fig. 7.8. Colonial Policemen in Sola Topis (Author's Private Collection)

Rawalpindi

Rawalpindi, another important garrison town, is located a few miles away from ancient Taxila, the Gandharan capital of India. In 1818, Ranjit Singh, the Sikh ruler of Punjab conquered it. In 1849, the British occupied it after defeating the Sikhs, and it became a permanent garrison town of the British Army. In 1851, under Lord Dalhousie, it became the headquarters of that army's Northern Command and an arsenal was established there. Soon it grew into the largest military garrison of British India (*Imperial Gazetteer of India*, 1883:272).

It had a population of about 75,000 in the 1880s. It was known as the cleanest town in northern British India. Cleanliness made it a favourite first stop for troops arriving fresh from England. The town was adapted to meet the needs of the British army which had about 5,000 troops stationed there. Its growth was also spurred by the construction of the railways. Famines in Kashmir, which drove migrant labour to Rawalpindi in search of work, also contributed to its rapid expansions.

Peshawar

A garrison town in the North-West Frontier Province (NWFP), Peshawar occupied a strategic location near the Khyber Pass along the major trade route to Afghanistan and Central Asia. The NWFP consisted of an administered territory and an unadministered area. The latter suffered from blood feuds, raids for cattle and guns (Allen, 1975:165). In 1849, the Peshawar Division came under British control and remained so until 1947. It consists of Mardan, Hazara and Kohat. Today Mardan is the headquarters of the Pakistan Army.

It was once the capital of the ancient kingdom of Gandhara. Later the Mughals occupied it. In fact, the name Peshawar (meaning border town) is attributed to Akbar. During the sixteenth century, it was under the control of the Afghans. In 1818, the Sikh Maharaja Ranjit Singh conquered Peshawar and controlled the territory until the British annexed it following the Second Sikh War of 1849. A Sikh fort in Bala Hissar on the outskirts of the city is still standing.

The British soldiers' quarters in Peshawar included double-storey bungalows which were superior to the houses of the average local citizens.

At the Peshawar Club, the bar was 'able to sell liquor to foreigners provided that they sign on as a registered alcoholic' (Wild, 2001:196). It is 'the only function that the splendid bar, redolent with the ghosts of hard-drinking officers and respectably tipsy memsahibs, is still able to carry out'.

Cawnpore (Anglicized Spelling of Kanpur)

It was a British cantonment where the sepoy uprising of 1857 started. Many sepoys led by Nana Sahib, the leader of the sepoy revolt, encircled the British garrison trapping British civilians, women and children. The British General (John Stanley Gough) was forced to surrender to the sepoys. Apparently, Nana Sahib promised him and the British civilians safe passage to sail to Calcutta if he surrendered. But the situation changed suddenly when he heard of the imminent arrival of British reinforcements under General Havelock. Nana Sahib decided to fire upon the British as they gathered to board the boats. Many British civilians were killed and their bodies were thrown into the Memorial Well.

The British commissioned a marble statue to be placed on the well as a memorial to the victims. It is decorated with a carved angel (designed and carved by Baron Carlo Marochetti) with crossed arms and holding palms. A Gothic screen surrounded the well. In 1948, this memorial was relocated to the churchyard.

8

Palaces of Learning

Since these educational institutions were intended for the elite, the illiterate millions of India remained illiterate to the end: nevertheless the stones of empire did include here and there, educational stones, stones of Academe, erected for the most part in the full flush of imperial self-esteem.

(Morris and Winchester, 1983)

Parallel to the government palaces built in the Presidencies, the British rulers built palaces of learning such as Mayo College in Ajmer and Aitchison College in Lahore, to provide English education exclusively for the sons of Englishmen and Europeans in India as well as for Indian princes. These educational institutions are so grand and palatial that they cannot be ignored in any study on the pomp and power of the British Empire.

Some schools such as Lawrence Asylum (later School) were originally built for the sons of army officers. Special schools were also built for the sons of princes in the princely states, including Rajkumar College (Rajkot), Mayo College (Ajmer) and Aitchison College (Lahore). St Paul's School in Calcutta (later moved to Darjeeling), was founded for the children of Anglo-Indian families. Besides the schools, three universities were established in the nineteenth century followed by others.

Why would the British Government be keen to provide an English education to the native Indians? There may be several reasons. Thomas Macaulay (member of the Governor-General's Council in the early 1830s) argued that Western education imparted to Indians would create a class of persons who would act as interlocutors between the British and the Indian masses. But it may also have been simply a reflection of dislike by the British for the local culture, languages (Arabic, Sanskrit and Persian) and religions.

Special schools were built for the sons of Indian princes not simply as a benevolent act and a noble gesture to the princely states. These schools were intended to educate sons of confirmed loyalists who sided with the Raj before, during and after the uprising of 1857. Apparently, the names of these loyalists were listed. Invariably, the loyalists belonged to the families of ruling princes, landlords and prominent and wealthy citizens. Education was provided to groom the sons to look up to the British as their superiors and become the future guardians of the Raj. The British authorities believed that Western education would promote a better understanding and trust between the upper classes of Indian natives and their rulers.[1]

While many Indians favoured a British education, others opposed it as an attack on India's local educational and other institutions. For the same reason, many Indians were hostile to the work of missionaries and Evangelical Christians. Up to 1813, the Company continued to patronize the Indian system of education in Persian, Arabic and Sanskrit, as did the Mughals. Vernacular schools were financed by wealthy landowners. However, in the 1830s a decision was taken by Bentinck and Macaulay to launch English education in India, as they believed in its superiority and in the benefits of western science and literature. English replaced Persian as the court language and medium of instruction.

Some schools and colleges, established to impart an English education, were built by the government, while others were built by individual philanthropists such as Sir Henry Lawrence.[2] Some observers (for example, Nehru, 2004:341) have argued that the British government was afraid of the spread of modern education in India, and so it was individual enlightened Englishmen who pioneered the introduction of Western education in India. Moreover, their action inspired Indian philanthropists to found schools along Western lines such as Doon School, Dehra Dun. Although not a direct British legacy, Doon school was built by a Bengali gentleman, Satish Ranjan Das, as an elitist school and in India. Indeed, its first Headmaster (Arthur Foot) was a former science master at Eton College in Windsor.

Western liberal education had the intended consequence of providing good communication between the British rulers and upper-class Indians who alone had access to such education. But it also had the unintended consequence of exposing Indians to Independence movements elsewhere, for example in Ireland and the United States. Indeed, it was the Irish movement that inspired the Indian educated elite. When Nehru visited Dublin, he found 'Sinn Fein' an interesting movement 'since their policy was not to beg for favours but to wrest them'. B.G. Tilak, another freedom fighter and others, adopted the Irish tactics of boycott in their protests against the partition of Bengal (Ferguson, 2003:328).

Another unintended consequence of Western education was the growth of elitism. The promotion of higher education among princes and the upper classes and the neglect of basic and primary education led to widespread educational disparities. The English education system produced 'Anglicized Brown British' in India who looked down upon ordinary Indians.

The English education, 'though limited and perverted', opened the minds of Indians to new ideas (Nehru, 1946:263). It also prepared them for the Colonial Service which may have also been facilitated by Bentinck's policy of Indianization. A few Indians received an English (Western) education not only in India but also in the UK, where Indian students formed the largest proportion of overseas students in the nineteenth and early twentieth centuries. Most of the leaders of India's independence movement, notably Gandhi, Jinnah and Nehru, studied in England and joined the independence movement on their return to India.

A few examples of elitist schools and universities built by the British in India (including what is Pakistan today), are discussed below.

Schools

Sir Henry Lawrence, Resident in Lahore and leader of the Siege of Lucknow, built Lawrence Asylum (later School) in Sanawar (near Kasauli) with a grant by the Maharajah of Jammu and Kashmir.[3] The Asylum was established in 1847 when Lawrence was Commissioner and Agent in the Punjab. Other educational institutions founded by him were established in Mt Abu in Rajasthan (1856), Lovedale in Ootacamund (1858), and Ghora Gali in Murree (1860). Lawrence School Mt Abu is the only one of these that has not survived. The absence of any public or government support and its precarious financial situation may have led to its closure in 1951. Today, it is a Police Training Academy of the Central Reserve Police Force.

Lawrence School, Sanawar in the Simla Hills (Himachal Pradesh) is a co-educational boarding school, perhaps the oldest school for mixed education in India. Its different stone buildings – Birdwood Academic Block, Headmaster's House, Science Labs, dormitories for boys and girls and a library-cum-museum and a chapel – are spread over an area of 139 acres of pine and deodar forests.

Sir Henry Lawrence looked for a suitable location for the school around the cantonments of Sabhathoo, Dagshai, Kasauli, Jutog (Simla). He selected the Hill of Sanawar, which combined different features of an asylum, namely, an isolated place at an altitude with plenty of space. It was also close to where the British troops were stationed.

World War I (1914–8) was the biggest armed conflict in recorded history to which, as a Military School, Sanawar made a significant contribution, perhaps the single largest contribution of all similar institutions in the whole of the British Empire. A group of 14 plus pupils were chosen with two masters for training in signalling.

Lawrence School, Lovedale (Fig. 8.1) is located in the Nilgiri Hills about six kilometres from Ootacamund. In 1922, it received Royal patronage and in 1925 its name was changed to Lawrence Memorial Royal Military School. Its building was inspired by Queen Victoria's summer residence, Osborne House, on the Isle of Wight, and designed by Robert Chisholm in an Italianate style.

Lawrence School (later College) Murree consists of a junior school, a preparatory school and a senior school. In 1860 at the time of its foundation, the School enrolled both boys and girls. However, in 1947 with the creation of Pakistan the girls section of the school was closed. In this respect, Lawrence Murree is different from Lawrence Sanawar and Lawrence Lovedale both of which have remained co-educational institutions.

Chiefs colleges were established for the sons of princes and chiefs of different princely states. One of the objectives of this friendly gesture to the princely class was to ensure its loyalty, not only for the immediate future but also for the long term. Initially, these colleges did not

Fig. 8.1. Lawrence School, Lovedale, Ootacamund (Courtesy of S. Siraj)

concentrate on a formal educational curriculum. Instead, they were intended to make royal pupils 'large-minded, humane and good' (Aijazuddin, 1986:21). There were five such colleges: Rajkumar, Rajkot; Rajkumar, Raipur; Mayo, Ajmer; Daly, Indore, and Aitchison, Lahore. Rajkumar, Mayo and Aitchison are briefly described below.

Rajkumar College (Rajkot, Gujarat) was the first of the Chiefs colleges to be built in India during the British Raj. It was founded in 1868 and formally opened in 1870. Colonel Keatinge built it to provide British education to the princes of western India, particularly Kathiawad.

In 1869, Col. Walter proposed the idea that an Indian Eton was needed for the education of India's young rulers and nobles. As a result, Mayo College was established in 1875. It became the second Chiefs College founded by Richard Southwell Bourke, the sixth Earl of Mayo and Viceroy of India from 1869 to 1872. The College is one of the oldest private schools in India.

The main building of the College (Fig. 8.2) was designed in the Saracenic style which was chosen by the then Viceroy from several entries which also included Grecian and Kolhapur styles. The first student of Mayo was H.H. Maharaja Mangal Singh of Alwar who arrived at the school gates on the back of an elephant. He was accompanied by an entourage of 300 retainers as well as tigers, camels and horses, and a fanfare of trumpets and drums! He came to school daily on an elephant. In the College's heyday, many of the princely pupils lived an exclusive and luxurious life in mini palaces staffed with huge retinues of servants. A far cry from the austerity of the English dormitory!

Most boys had a horse and two or three servants each. A special village had to be built for the servants near Gulab Bari on the east side of Mayo. Servants cooked and looked after their master's belongings including valuables. Generally, a poor relation of a pupil was appointed chief of the retinue of servants whose task was to ensure security against court enemies, and to taste the food to make sure that court intriguers did not poison an heir.

Given the leisurely future for which the pupils were destined, subjects like shooting and riding inevitably loomed larger in the curriculum than more conventional academic subjects. Sports included Athletics, Polo, Riding, Cricket, Hockey, Football and Target Shooting. Jackal hunts on

Fig. 8.2. Main Building of Mayo College, Ajmer (Author's Private Collection)

horseback were also organized on the premises from time to time. Local village games did not get much support from the English staff and soon died out.

However, this emphasis on sports began to change after India's Independence in 1947 when many members of the aristocracy were forced to look for gainful employment. Indeed, the intake began to change as well: the college began to admit pupils from the Brahmin and business classes alongside the Rajput core as long as their parents could afford the fees.

Discipline was never a problem: the students and staff were kept on their toes with the British staff marching around the campus! The first two principals were British army officers who gave top priority to discipline!

Distinguished Chief guests such as viceroys, who were also the official Presidents of the General Council of Mayo College, often attended its annual prize giving function. Their speeches make interesting reading since they were a mix of encouraging loyalty to the Crown and some sound advice. Prizes were given more for physical and moral conduct and less for mental abilities!

Maharaja Hanwant Singh of Jodhpur was 13 when he was sent off to Ajmer to attend Mayo College, much to the grief of his mother who could not bear to be parted from her first-born. In 1936, in spite of the changes then sweeping through India, Mayo College remained very much a Princes' College. Rao Raja (then Kanwar) Nahar Singh, Rao Raja Narpat's younger son, who was then leaving for school in England, remembers being asked by this young prince, 'And what are you taking to school?' 'Two very large trunks', replied Tiger Nahar Singh proudly, but felt compelled, when Hanwant expressed disbelief, to ask, 'Why what are *you* taking?' 'Well,' said the heir to the Gadi of Marwar, 'a couple of cars, a few horses, some guns and, of course, my servants, including a barber and a tailor.' (www.maharajajodhpur.com)

Aitchison College (Lahore) (Fig. 8.3) was the third Chiefs College the foundation stone of which was laid in November 1886 by the Viceroy, the Earl of Dufferin and his wife Ava, the Duchess of Connaught. Named after Lt-General Sir Charles Aitchison, it was built for the education of the relatives of ruling chiefs and noble families of the Punjab in the tradition of Mayo College. Among pupils at the School were: the Maharaja of Patiala (Mohinder Singh) his son Bhupinder Singh and grandson, Yadvindra Singh, and the Rajas of Mandi and Kulu Hill States. Pupils also included Muslim nawabs such as Sadiq Mohammad Khan and his sons. Rich Sikh landlords who studied at the School included Sir Buta Singh of Amritsar.[4]

Unlike Mayo, not all the students at Aitchison were princes or chiefs; many were from the landed aristocracy of the Punjab. However, initially agriculture was not taught.

In 1933, one former student (Hetwa Nanad Kashyap, later Principal of Yadvindra Public School, Patiala) noted that they 'lived in privately furnished large suites of rooms each with a cook, an attendant and some with a 'syce' to look after their private horses' (cited in Aijazuddin, 1986:40). Although less luxurious than Mayo, accommodation at Aitchison was nevertheless elitist.

The student princes and landed aristocrats at Aitchison lacked discipline and the atmosphere was known to be 'libertarian'. In summer, a

Fig. 8.3. Aitchison College, Lahore (Author's Private Collection)

large number of students would take 'assumed leave of absence' to join their parents and relatives in the hill stations. Aijazuddin (ibid.) notes that during this period there would be more cows in the college dairy than there were students in attendance!

Separate religious education and residential facilities were provided for the three main communities (Muslims, Hindus and Sikhs) which necessitated the building of a mosque, a Hindu temple (mandir) and a Sikh gurdwara. However, for several years religious teaching remained optional. The college had a policy of being religion-neutral to avoid any accusation of bias towards one community or another. Extracurricular facilities and sports grounds for cricket, polo, field hockey and tennis were also provided.

Rudyard Kipling was very critical of the establishment of the College. He questioned the wisdom of founding such an institution since he believed it was a waste of resources of a 'Pauper Province' (referring to the Punjab)!

Aitchison vs Mayo

Aitchison College differed from Mayo in several respects. First, the conditions of the student princes differed in the two regions. In the Punjab, the composition of the chiefs differed significantly from that in Rajputana. Punjab consisted of a more multi-religious society with Hindus, Sikhs and Muslims living side by side. Unlike the predominantly Rajput princes at Mayo, in the Punjab there were non-hereditary social groups such as the rich landlords apart from the maharajas. Secondly, Aitchison pupils lacked discipline which was not a problem at Mayo where the early headmasters were from the Army which explained good discipline. However, even at Mayo discipline suffered when its headmasters from the Army left. Thirdly, there was no religious teaching at Mayo due perhaps to the absence of pupils from different religions (most pupils were Hindu Rajputs). There were only a few Muslim pupils from the kingdoms of Hyderabad (part of present-day Andhra Pradesh), Junagarh (part of present-day Gujarat) and Oudh (part of present-day U.P.). Missing were religious symbols of a mosque or a gurdwara which were important features at Aitchison. Mayo had a Hindu temple but no formal religious instruction was offered.

Mayo was financially much better endowed than Aitchison thanks to generous support from the princely states of Rajputana. The latter had perpetual problems, including funding. It appears that no princely state, except Patiala, made any substantial financial contribution to Aitchison. And the number of pupils kept falling for several years. Aijazuddin (ibid.:31) notes that during the first decade of its existence 'pupils were joining in less than expected numbers, while teachers left with undesirable rapidity (over a span of eight years the College lost no fewer than 15 teachers)'.

Finally, Aitchison was much more Europeanized than Mayo. Sons of princes at Aitchison went to school in Rolls Royces and Buicks rather than on the backs of elephants. Also they wore Western blazers, not *achkans*, the knee-length coats buttoned down the front (Hill, 2001:2). The Rajput princes at Mayo were much closer to their roots and traditions. Even to this day traditions are maintained there, including the wearing of turbans (*safaa*) and Jodhpurs for all formal occasions. At Aitchison, pupils wore Western shoes whereas at Mayo they were seated barefoot (Figs. 8.4 and 8.5) in the old Hindu tradition of remaining barefoot at temples of learning, as at temples of worship. The shoes would be left outside the classrooms.

Fig. 8.4. A Class of Princes in Traditional Dress at Mayo (1882) (Courtesy of Mayo College and H. Duggal)

Fig. 8.5. Aitchisonians in Ties and Blazers (1913) (Courtesy of F. Aijazuddin)

Elphinstone College and Sassoon Library, Bombay

Fig. 8.6. Elphinstone College, Bombay (Author's Private Collection)

Universities and Colleges

The schools for British education discussed above were matched by the establishment of English-style universities and university colleges in India. The three Presidency colleges, and universities of Bombay, Madras and Calcutta are a few examples.

Elphinstone College in Bombay was named after Mountstuart Elphinstone, one of the Governors of Bombay. Its main building in Romanesque transitional style is one of the landmarks of the Bombay Presidency (Fig. 8.6). The university convocation hall and library still in existence, designed by Sir George Gilbert Scott, are decorated in the early fifteenth-century French style. The spiral staircase of the library in one corner blends the Medieval and the French Renaissance styles. They are far removed from the local style of architecture. The Gilbert Scott building of Bombay University is still standing and resembles the architecture of the colleges in Cambridge and Oxford in the United Kingdom.

Presidency College of Calcutta is the oldest educational institution in India. It was established in June 1855 on the recommendation of the Governor of Bengal. Upon its establishment, 'scholars' were transferred to it from a Hindu College which had been established earlier, in 1817. The Calcutta University buildings of the Raj are unrecognizable today as they have been replaced by a mixture of other, more recent buildings (Morris and Winchester, 1983:105).

In 1821, the Deccan College of Poona was founded to impart a Western education to the Indians. The college was temporarily closed down in 1934 perhaps for lack of adequate funding but was reopened in 1939. Today, it is a post-graduate teaching and research institute.

The architecture of the university buildings matched the exotic nature of the early curricula and British staff. Quite often, despite their generous financial contributions, Indian philanthropists (both Parsis and Hindus) failed to persuade imperial masters to adapt the Western architectural styles and curricula to local conditions and traditions. Metcalf (1989:98) argues that such Parsi philanthropists as Jehangir and Jews such as Sassoon, were minorities who had immigrated to India from abroad, were highly westernized and identified with the British. They themselves may, therefore, have preferred English and European architecture.

However, there were a couple of important exceptions which were not entirely western. For example, Robert Chisholm, who designed the buildings of the Madras University Senate House (1874–9), made a conscious attempt to blend the English Gothic with the local Mughal styles, or the so-called Indo-Saracenic style, characterized by domes, balconies and arches. Many British architects opposed this style. However, Chisholm, a well-known architect of Madras and a defender of this style, noted that the 'principles of Gothic style of architecture become parched and shriveled in this country (India)' (ibid.:62).

The Mayo College building (Fig. 8.2), designed by Charles Mant, is another example of the Indo-Saracenic style. Metcalf notes that even though this style and elements were contested, the design for this structure 'was to mark the coming of age of colonial building in the Indic style' (ibid.:67).[5]

The British architects and administrators may have finally accepted this style because it was associated with the Mughal Empire whose splendour they tried to emulate. Perhaps it was an attempt to maintain continuity or perhaps they came to realize the intrinsic merits of the arch and dome, two features of the Saracenic style. It is quite likely that the British finally opted for a link with India's past which was glorious (at least architecturally) under the Mughal Empire. Furthermore, Mayo was built for Indian princes who were the descendants of the ancient ruling dynasties. Therefore, it was only appropriate to have some reference to their heritage in architecture.

The Mayo building has a clock tower as did many other colleges and buildings of the Raj such as those in Bombay, Delhi, Calcutta, Lahore and Lucknow. Metcalf (ibid.:78) argues that they are symbols of the British conquest (not of time) as was the Qutb Minar several centuries earlier. The open iron dome on top of the Mayo clock tower is symbolic of the British Crown. Brought to India in the nineteenth century, clock towers were an important feature of Victorian Britain.

Two well-known university colleges in Lahore are the Government College and Forman Christian College. Built during the British Raj in the neo-Gothic style, the Government College building designed by W. Purdon, a superintending engineer, also has a clock tower. Work on the College building commenced in 1872 and was completed five years later. The most important component is the Main Hall (now called the Abdus Salam Hall) with a hammer beam roof.

Forman Christian College, one of the oldest in South Asia, was founded by Charles William Forman who arrived in India in 1847 and settled in Lahore. The Reverends Newton and Forman were members of the Board of Foreign Missions of the Presbyterian Church in the United States. Initially, it started as an English school (the Rang Mahal School), the first Anglo-vernacular educational institution in the Punjab. In 1865, a college department was added to it, which later separated from the school to become an independent Forman Christian College. In 1889, the College shifted to new premises but these were demolished in the 1940s, and were replaced by a new building (Aijazuddin, 2004:123).

To conclude, British educational institutions (schools and university colleges) during the Raj were sponsored by public as well as private initiatives and funds. Whereas institutions such as Mayo College and the Chiefs Colleges were directly funded by the British government, those such as the Lawrence Schools and St Paul's School were initially conceived and designed by individual philanthropists. These latter institutions subsequently received supplementary public funding from the government exchequer. Public contributions to some private educational institutions provided a lifeline to many of them, but the lack of such support ruined others such as Lawrence School in Mt Abu. It was forced to close due to the lack of public financial support.

While the British rulers promoted secondary and higher education, they totally neglected basic and primary education. This glaring neglect may partly account for mass poverty at the time of India's independence in 1947.

The educational edifices discussed above represented an important symbol of the power and glory of the British Raj. They cost an enormous amount of taxpayers' money which could have been used more productively elsewhere. In physical appearances these buildings closely resembled the government palaces discussed in Chapter 6.

9

British India and the Mother Country

Even those residences (in Calcutta) intended for families of very moderate incomes cover a large extent of ground and afford architectural displays which would be vainly sought amid habitations belonging to the same class in England.

(Woodruff, 1963)

This chapter compares the British pomp and show in London with that in Bombay, Calcutta, Delhi, Lahore and Madras. Also compared is the situation of Company officers (or 'servants' as they were then called) in the Indian colony with those in the parent Company in London.

In theory, the economic conditions of the Company officers in India may have been expected to be much less attractive than those in the mother country. However, paradoxically, this was not the case. In India, they made money fast and amassed substantial wealth before returning to England. Many prosperous merchants built grand town houses in the three Presidencies which were far more luxurious than those of their counterparts in London. Those of English nabobs in Calcutta and Delhi (Figs 6.2 and 9.6, for example) were also more spacious. Palaces of viceroys in the Presidencies were lavish compared with those of similar rank in London. These 'glistening white houses with a stucco burnt from sea shells' had 'long-carved verandas, odd towers and unexplained cupolas' (Wild, 1999:51–2). They resembled 'the scaled down versions of

Fig. 9.1. Terraced Houses, Clapham Common, London (Author's Private Collection)

English country houses and Palladian mansions rather than the narrow London town house' (White, 2012:35).

London town houses of the period (Fig. 9.1) 'were fairly small in size with simple external designs which relied for impact on their grouping into terraces, squares and crescents' (Davies, 1985:62). Green's mansions in Bombay (Fig. 9.2) also looked more imposing. Even sailors' homes in Bombay built in a Venetian Gothic style, blended with neoclassical and Moorish architecture, looked more impressive (Fig. 9.3).

The uniform quarters and districts with terraced houses of London and other English towns did not exist in Calcutta or other Indian towns. For example, in Calcutta and Madras, there were two towns in one: one for the European elite and the other for the Indians. The former contained luxurious and spacious detached houses for a rather small number of Europeans. The latter were poorer (with few exceptions) and over- crowded. The reason for these stark contrasts was clearly the different social and economic conditions of the British vis-à-vis the native inhabitants.

It was possible to build such enormous houses in Calcutta and other Presidency capitals, surrounded by private gardens because of the much

Fig. 9.2. Green's Mansions, Bombay (Author's Private Collection)

larger open space available. In India, land and labour were cheap, which allowed the construction of spacious houses and bungalows. Maintenance of such buildings and communication between rooms was also facilitated by the ready availability of domestic servants and 'orderlies'.

Fig. 9.3. Sailors' Home, Bombay (Author's Private Collection)

Company officers did not just live in opulent and vast houses; their social life in the Presidencies was also far more luxurious, dazzling and agreeable than that of their counterparts in London. Chapter 5 discussed the pleasures of keeping local concubines and mistresses (bibis) who were always willing to please their white masters for a small price. There is evidence to suggest that the Company officers found native Indian women more interesting than the white memsahibs. In letters written from India during 1828–41, Samuel Brown (1878) of the Bengal Civil Service notes:

> I have observed that those who have lived with a native woman for any length of time never marry a European [. . .] So amusingly playful, so anxious to oblige and please, that a person after being accustomed to their society shrinks from the idea of encountering the whims and yielding to the fancies of an English woman.

Besides the submissive company of the native Indian women, the Company officers in India enjoyed a large retinue of domestic servants and 'orderlies' who were at their beck and call. This kind of easy and relaxed life of the British rulers in India was rare back in London (as portrayed in Fig. 5.2, which shows an Indian servant giving a pedicure to his English master while another is keeping him cool with a native fan).

How were the Company officers in the Presidencies able to enjoy a life of such comfort and luxury? The rapid growth of trade in the East was certainly an important factor. The Company successfully exploited opportunities available to its merchants and traders (Lawson, 1993). Many Company officers had mercantile backgrounds in England and Scotland. The decline of Portuguese power in India, coinciding with a weakening of the Mughal Empire, may have also been fortuitous and favourable to the British. The Mughal rulers granted the Company the right to establish factories and forts and to collect revenue on their behalf. For example, in Bengal and Bihar, the Company enjoyed the right to trade without having to pay customs duties. These privileges enabled it to develop economic clout and later, a political foothold, in the country.

However, there were adverse side-effects of the rapid growth of trade in the East. The Company officers started indulging in corruption, smuggling, illegal trade and gambling (ibid.:71–3). Warren Hastings, the Governor of Bengal from 1772 to 1785, faced corruption charges on returning to England. He was tried before the House of Lords, and, although acquitted in the end, his reputation was ruined (Chapter 10). Lord Robert Clive, Governor of Bengal (1757–60 and 1765–7), who was recalled to England in 1803, also had to pay a price for his extravagance, including the building of a luxurious house for himself.

There was a serious problem of drinking and gambling in Madras in the eighteenth century. The Company, though concerned, failed to put an end to these vices. Gambling was also common in eighteenth-century London following spectacular growth in trade with the Indian sub-continent, North America and West Indies. White (2012:97) notes that this trade expansion led to 'chocolate (and gaming) houses of St James's, the brothels of Covent Garden and Charing Cross . . .' He concludes: 'No nation in Europe is so much addicted to Play as we are (in 1751)' and 'nor any City where there are greater Sums lost than London' (ibid.:335).

London vs Indian Presidencies

As Calcutta prospered more quickly than Madras and Bombay, rivalries grew among the Presidencies. Similar rivalries also increased between the Company servants in India and their counterparts and masters in London.

The old magnificent buildings of the Company Raj in the Presidencies, especially the Government Houses, proudly called the 'palaces' (Bence-Jones, 1973) (Figs. 6.2, 6.8 and 7.1) and the later buildings belonging to the British Crown in New Delhi such as the Viceroy's Palace (Plate 10), Metcalfe House and Ludlow Castle (Fig. 9.6) matched, if not surpassed, those in London. The Government Houses resembled some of the lavish country mansions in Britain.

These grand mansions and other edifices built by the British, was inspired by the Classical, Gothic and Victorian styles of architecture in England. For example, Norwich Cathedral provided the model for St Paul's Cathedral in Calcutta, and the Gothic architecture in Bombay was reminiscent of Victorian London

The Company officers in Calcutta spent lavishly on their houses, which were regarded as 'upstart villas and extravagant creations' (Roberts, 1835:2). By comparison, even rich Londoners did not believe in spending on the facades of their houses, given their puritanical inclinations according to an architect (Rasmussen, 1937:192).

There was another difference between the large and expensive private residences in Calcutta and the country mansions in England. While the latter belonged to the English aristocracy, the private bungalows in Calcutta were built by merchants and Company officers who, while not necessarily enjoying a high social status, were perhaps lucky enough to have made quick fortunes in India.

There were other similarities between London and the Presidencies, such as rampant prostitution, drinking and gambling, and widespread poverty. Chapter 5 noted the existence of brothels in Calcutta and the low morals of young English women living there. As a port town, Calcutta always had its brothels and red light districts. In around 1780, Sobha Bazar was frequented by sailors. Later, brothels spread to Lal Bazaar and Sonagachi areas (Singh, 1990:38). In London also, prostitution was rampant. Travellers from Europe were surprised to find prostitutes everywhere. And 'Frenchmen were among those most shocked by the "extraordinary licentiousness that reigns openly in London"' (White, 2012:347).

As in London, excessive drinking was widespread among the English community in Calcutta in taverns run by Willsons and Spencers. In 1780, in London metropolis, the number of ale houses licensed to sell drinks was estimated at 330 inns, 550 taverns, 656 coffee houses and 6,786 ale houses, or a total of 8,322 drinking establishments (ibid.:326). Both working class people and aristocrats indulged in drinking. Ben Franklin, a teetotaller working at Watts's printing house noted: 'My companion at the press drank every day a pint before breakfast, a pint at breakfast with his bread and cheese, a pint between breakfast and dinner, a pint at dinner, a pint in the afternoon about six'o clock, and another when he had done his day's work' (ibid.:328).

Cheap production of Hollands (a spirit introduced on the accession of a Dutch king in 1689) and Geneva (English gin) must have further contributed to excessive drinking by the labouring classes. In their case, poverty often drove them to excessive drinking.

In seventeenth-century England, a quarter of the population was 'permanently in the state of poverty and underemployment, if not of total

Fig. 9.4. Black (George) Town, Madras (1851) (© The British Library Board, London, 248/20)

unemployment (Wilson, 1965:231). The Poor Laws and workhouses of Tudor England were a response to the miserable living conditions of those times. Charles Dickens's *Oliver Twist* (1837–8), Disraeli's *Sybil (or The Two Nations)* (1845), and Mayhew's *London Labour and the London Poor* (1861), highlighted the division of Victorian society into rich and poor.

In London, 'the poor seemed to pose the greatest danger to the wealthy and to the very institutions of the state The poor threatened most acutely when they congregated in large numbers in ill-drained tight-clustered, crumbling districts' (White, 2007:30). Poverty was particularly acute among the Irish and Arab immigrants. Dickens wrote a letter to Angela Burdett-Coutts (a philanthropist) that the area around Victoria Street 'is a maze of filth and squalor, so dense and deserted by all decency . . . '

Poverty in the Presidency towns of Madras and Calcutta was even more appalling than in London. The conditions prevailing in the Black Town area of Madras in 1851 (Fig. 9.4) illustrate the abject poverty and squalor there. The majority of the poor Indians lived in thatched huts in shanty towns, and walked barefoot as illustrated in the figure. Madras 'province was in the lowest depth of misery and wretchedness' due in part to wars between the British and Haidar Ali, the ruler of Mysore. Poverty situation became worse in the wake of the Madras famine of 1873 (Dutt, 1902:111–12).

Similarly, in Calcutta the poor earned little and were malnourished. The poverty situation in Calcutta is best summed up by the Report of the Famine Inquiry Commission (1945) headed by Sir John Woodhead:

> A considerable section of the population was living on the margin of sub-sistence and was incapable of standing any severe economic stress [...] very bad health conditions and low standards of nutrition, and the absence of "a margin of safety" as regards either health or wealth. (cited in Nehru, 1946:428fn)

Delhi and Lahore vs London

Delhi was different from the Presidency towns of Calcutta, Madras and Bombay in one important respect. There the British lived side by side with the Indians at least until Metcalfe and Ludlow started building their own palaces in the Civil Lines.[1] Unlike Madras, there were no separate 'black' and 'white' towns. Social apartheid between the whites and Indians was less prevalent in Delhi than in the Presidency towns. For example, the English and the Indians (nawabs and other rich Indians) mixed socially at the homes of Colonel Skinner and Raja Hindu Rao (Gupta, 1981:9). But this was before the 1857 uprising. Growing mistrust between the two communities in the post-uprising period prompted the English to create their own Colony in the Civil Lines. Their virtual control over Delhi meant that the British rulers could transform the old Mughal city into one planned on the Western style with plenty of open spaces.

At the Delhi Durbar in 1911, King George V announced the transfer of the capital from Calcutta to New Delhi. This decision was taken despite protests by Lord Curzon who thought Delhi was a 'mass of deserted ruins and graves' and a city of 'dead dynasties'. He contrasted this with Calcutta which he claimed was representative of British India, a modern city built by the British. Curzon believed that building a new capital in Delhi would entail an unnecessary financial burden noting that a project of building the new capital of Delhi 'is still in the course of being carried out, at an inexcusable cost to the finances of India, and without any resultant advantage to a single public interest' (Curzon of Kedleston,1925, vol. I:181).

In the end, Delhi won over Calcutta which was considered geographically too remote (as the British discovered only too well during the 1857 uprising). Traditionally, Delhi was the capital of the earlier Indian empires, which may also have weighed in favour of Delhi. Lord Hardinge, the then Viceroy, wanted Delhi to be worthy of its royal predecessors.

A number of new royal monuments were built in the new capital city. The Viceroy's Residence, the Council House, the Central Secretariat and the All India War Memorial (now India Gate), are surviving testaments to a building spree, which was reminiscent of that of the Mughal Empire.

New Delhi

By 1927, £10 million pounds had already been spent on building the new capital. Another £5 million pounds were spent before the new city was completed (Byron, 1931:14). The British rulers defended such an enormous expenditure by noting that they were simply imitating the Indian taste for lavishness and splendour. They reminded their critics that the Indian princes and the Mughal emperors had also indulged in excessive and reckless ostentation.

An aerial view of New Delhi (Plate 10) with its Memorial Arch at one end and the Secretariat (Fig. 9.5) and Viceregal Lodge at the other, shows a similar layout to the New Admiralty Arch in London leading to the Mall on way to the Queen Victoria Memorial and Buckingham Palace. It also resembles the Champs-Elysées in Paris with the Arc de Triomphe at one end and Place de la Concorde at the other.

The Viceregal Lodge was the residence of the British Viceroy until India's independence in 1947. Now called Rashtrapati Bhawan, it is the official residence of the President of India. It has 340 rooms spread over four floors. A huge dome in the middle of the mansion is one of its main distinguishing features. Lutyens succeeded in building an imperial palace adapted to the local environment. The building was indeed like a

Fig. 9.5. Indian Parliament, Council Chamber and the Secretariat (Author's Private Collection)

palace, complete with a Durbar Room fitted with a throne; a state dining room, and banquet halls.

Lutyens[2] and Baker were the two main architects charged with building the new capital of British India. While the former built the Viceregal Lodge, the latter built the Council Building and the Central Secretariat. Metcalf (1989:227) observes that Baker and Lutyens adopted the notion of 'an architectural style that "grafted" some of the simpler elements of "Eastern" design from such nearby sites as Mandu on to a Western form'. In 1931, Robert Byron wrote about the high dome of the Palace: it was 'like the shout of the imperial suggestion – a slap in the face of the moderate average-man, with his second-hand ideals' (Morris and Winchester, 1983:80).

Did Lutyens aim to establish continuity with the Imperial past? This is unclear. However, one thing seems certain, that the architectural style should be imperial and grand, a symbol of the British Empire, a jewel in its Crown. It was not necessarily meant to be English, Mughal or Hindu in style.

The War Memorial Arch commemorates those who died during World War I. It has a canopy nearby which once contained the statue of King George V (removed when India became independent). Now the statue stands forgotten at Coronation Park as a dusty relic of the British Empire.

There were three different options for the choice of architecture for the new capital: (1) the Classical British, as in Calcutta, (2) the Indo-Saracenic, as in Madras and (3) Indian architecture as reflected in the Mughal buildings in Delhi and Agra. There were critics and defenders of each of these options. For example, Curzon and Lutyens were in favour of (1); William Emerson and Samuel Swinton Jacob were in favour of (2) and Hardinge, the Viceroy, favoured (3). Lutyens was not impressed by the Mughal Indo-Saracenic style; he even believed that the Taj Mahal lacked the basic principles of architecture![3]

No Indian architect was consulted about the plans for a new capital. Was it because the British rulers were convinced that the Empire was there to stay, and that the Indian society would continue to remain traditional and inferior?

The British planners divided up South Delhi's urban space into different localities marked by occupational rank, race and social hierarchy.

Naturally, Indian clerks were close to the bottom of the league table. As for the Anglo-Indians, Davies (1985:225) cites Anthony King who commented that 'the Anglo-Indians [...] looked down upon by both (the British and Indians) were located outside the walls of the indigenous city and on the perimeter of the imperial capital'. While this may well be true, such Anglo-Indians as Skinner and others working for the Indian Railways were socially accepted since they provided very useful services to the British.

The face of the new Imperial capital was similar to that of London, at least, in some respects. The main shopping area of New Delhi, Connaught Place, looked like a poor imitation of Oxford Street or Regent Street in London (Fig. 9.9), and there was little difference between General Post Office of Calcutta, Delhi or London. The Banquet Hall in Madras looked like Buckingham Palace. Government Houses in Madras and Calcutta were symbols of British Imperial power and homes of the representatives of the Crown.

Old Delhi

The British had close associations with Delhi even before it became the new capital. It is here that they overcame the uprising. They launched their last attack on the rebels from the Ridge in Old Delhi. It is also here that they captured the last Mughal emperor, Bahadur Shah II, in the Red Fort which became the headquarters of the British Army. Barracks were built inside the fort, which one observer described as a 'kind of howling desert of barracks, hideous, British and pretentious' (Prinsep, 1879:24). To put their stamp on Red Fort, the British even changed the names of Lahore and Delhi Gates to Victoria and Alexandra Gates. Finally, Delhi was the site of three Royal Durbars, those of 1877, 1903 and 1911.

There are remnants of the Raj even in Old Delhi: the Old Secretariat, Metcalfe House, Ludlow Castle (Fig. 9.6), the Clock Tower and Town Hall in Chandni Chowk, a memorial garden to John Nicholson (a general in the Bengal army of the Company)[4] in Kashmiri Gate and the Mutiny Memorial on the Ridge.

From 1912 to 1926, the Council Chamber (Legislative Council, which formerly met at the Government House, Calcutta) met at the Old

Fig. 9.6. Ludlow Castle, Old Delhi (© Victoria and Albert Museum, London)

Secretariat, but moved to the newly constructed Parliament House in January 1927.

Metcalfe House,[5] Sir Thomas Metcalfe's (1795–1853) residence, was built in a colonial style with stone columns, wide verandas and basement rooms (*tehkhanas*). Sir Thomas was the Governor-General's Agent at the Mughal imperial court. His daughter Emily (Lady Clive Bayley) had vivid memories of the House as one where the 'rooms were so large, so lofty, and there were so many of them, all on one floor, and all twenty-four feet in height' (Davies, 1985:143). It was badly damaged during the 1857 uprising.

Ludlow Castle belonged to Samuel Ludlow, a surgeon with the Company, based in the Delhi Residency from 1813 to 1831. It later became the Commissioner's House and then the Delhi Club in 1857 until it was given to a school in the 1890s.

The Victoria Clock Tower facing the Town Hall was built in the post-uprising period. Positioned axially to the Tower was a statue of Queen Victoria which has now been removed.

The British ruling authorities cleared out a vast area called Chandni Chowk to create an open space and provide better road and rail transportation. Apparently, there was a water tank on the site where the Tower was built. This tank and a canal running through Chandni Chowk (*Nahar-i-Bahisht*) were later covered over.

The Mutiny Memorial Tower located at the Northern Ridge in the Civil Lines is built on the site of a British Camp. Dedicated to all those who gave their lives during the 1857 uprising, it is a rough replica of the Prince Albert Memorial, 'its illegitimate first cousin' (Dalrymple, 1993:149) in Kensington Gardens in London north of the Royal Albert Hall. Gothic in design and octagonal in shape, it stands on a two-tiered base covered with ornamental designs.

Lahore

Lahore was the British capital of Greater Punjab. As in Delhi, in Lahore also the remnants of the splendours of the Mughal Empire (the fort and its palaces, Jahangir's and Nur Jahan's tombs and Shalimar Gardens) have survived side by side with the symbols of the British Empire (notably, Aitchison College and Government College, General Post Office, Montgomery Hall, and the Cathedral).

The General Post Office, built in 1849 near the Lahore Museum, is still standing and is in good condition. It is an attractive building with a big clock tower and four minarets. It is another example of the Indo-Saracenic style of architecture in the class of Mayo College in Ajmer (Fig. 8.2) and the Madras University Senate House.

The two buildings, Lawrence Hall (built in 1861–2) and Montgomery Hall (built in 1866) (Fig. 9.7) are located in the Lawrence Hall Gardens, and were joined together by a covered corridor designed to hold public meetings, grand balls and durbars. The halls were dedicated to the memories of Sir John Lawrence, Chief Commissioner of the Punjab (1853–7) who subsequently became Viceroy of India (1863–9), and Sir Robert Montgomery, the second Lieutenant-Governor.

The Lahore Cathedral, made of fine brick and grey stone, was designed by Oldrid Scott, son of Sir Gilbert Scott. Its foundation stone was laid in 1874 and it was consecrated in January 1887.

Fig. 9.7. Montgomery Hall, Lahore (Author's Private Collection)

London

London was the capital of the British Empire and its colonies. Major policy decisions concerning the colonies were made here rather than in the colonies, as were all acts of Parliament. Its many imperial landmarks inspired imperial buildings in India. Major landmarks of London include Queen Victoria Memorial and Buckingham Palace, the New Admiralty Arch (Fig. 9.8) and Piccadilly Circus and Regent Street (Fig. 9.9). Another major landmark, established in 1825 and named after the Prince Regent (later King George IV), is a trendy shopping street in London's West End, which may have influenced the Connaught Place shopping centre in New Delhi

Queen Victoria (1837–1901) Memorial in front of Buckingham Palace was dedicated by King George V (Queen's grandson) in 1911. It was sculpted by Sir Thomas Brock and completed in 1914 when the bronze statues around it were installed.

The British Houses of Parliament (also known as the Palace of Westminster) are situated on the banks of the River Thames. Originally there was a palace on the site built by King Edward the Confessor in the first half of the eleventh century. In 1834, a fire destroyed the Parliament buildings which were rebuilt between 1840 and 1888 in the neo-Gothic style in

Fig. 9.8. New Admiralty Arch, London (Author's Private Collection)

harmony with the nearby Gothic Westminster Abbey. Sir Charles Barry designed the present buildings including the Clock Tower (or Big Ben) and the Victoria Tower.

Fig. 9.9. Regent Street (Author's Private Collection)

The New Admiralty Arch is named after the Royal Naval Headquarters nearby. It was commissioned by King Edward VII (Queen Victoria's son and successor to the throne), designed by Sir Aston Webb and completed in around 1911 after the King's death. There are five arches leading from Trafalgar Square to the Mall in the direction of Buckingham Palace. The designer may have aimed at separating the subjects crowding the Square and the monarch on the other side of the New Admiralty Arch. Or was it an unintended chance event to perpetuate the class divisions in Britain in mortar and stone?

It was common practice to build commemorative columns in the British Empire. The Muslim rulers in India and elsewhere built towers (*minars*) whereas the British built arches, commemorative columns, clock towers, statues and other memorials. Examples of these are the Ochterlony and the Holwell columns in Calcutta and the Nelson column in London.

Conclusion

The British builders during the Raj felt more comfortable reproducing or imitating Britain's architecture rather than adapting it to the local environment. This was true especially of the buildings in the three Presidencies, but also of other monuments (such as the Mutiny Memorial on the Ridge, Old Delhi and the Chowringhee in Calcutta). Emily Eden, sister of Lord Auckland, Governor-General, likened the Chowringhee to Regents Park in London. Bishop Reginald Heber described his arrival in Calcutta in the following words: 'We saw Calcutta with its white houses glittering through the twilight [. . .] with an effect not unlike that of Connaught Place and its neighbourhood, as seen from a distance across Hyde Park' (cited in Davies, 1985:55).

Lord Curzon who exhorted Indians to take pride in their crafts and architecture preferred to jettison the Indo-Saracenic style when he built the Victoria Memorial in Calcutta. He favoured a classical European style for the memorial because he felt that Calcutta had no truly indigenous style of its own. He argued that no Indian style was suitable for the needs of a museum. Were these reasons really valid? It is more likely that Curzon was keen to build an imperial symbol of the British Empire on Indian soil, unmindful of the fact that it had to be financed by Indian taxpayer. Furthermore, his view that the memorial would do much 'to bind together the two races' (Metcalf, 1989:204) was also somewhat naïve and exaggerated.

It is rather paradoxical that in 1900, Curzon urged the Amritsar municipality to avoid European designs, which are 'commonly base, inartistic and vulgar'. Instead, he suggested, 'adhere to your old Indian and Persian models, which were the product of a race of natural artists, and upon which the modern world will never improve' (Curzon of Kedleston, 1990–6). Yet he chose a British design for Victoria Memorial. To be fair, Curzon admired Indian architecture and did a lot to promote its conservation. He deserves credit for founding the Archaeological Survey of India. The apparent paradox may be explained by his desire to put an imperial stamp on British buildings in India. His love for pomp and ceremony is well known.

There were several debates concerning what the truly imperial British style should be for the buildings of the Raj in India. One school, called 'aesthetic imperialists' à la Davies, recommended imitating Roman monuments. A second school, 'the native revivalists' weighed in favour of indigenous Indian architecture. Finally, the imperialists won the day.

India was seen as an imperial state of Britain which was amply demonstrated by the proclamation of Queen Victoria as the Empress of India. Metcalf (1989:239) notes that Lutyens's 'viceregal palace, together with his beaux-arts layout for New Delhi, embodied on a grand scale an ideal of empire'. The British aloofness in social life was extended to their aloofness of architecture. This was true as much of the palaces and country houses in the Presidency towns as it was of the new capital in Delhi.

Part IV

Conclusion

10

Pomp, Extravaganza and Poverty

The manner of life of the rich (in the Mughal Empire) in their great super-fluity and absolute power, of the common people in their utter subjection and poverty – poverty so extreme and so miserable that the life of the people cannot be adequately depicted or described.

(Francis Pelsaert, 1626)

Cheap labour was another jewel in the crown of the Raj. At the back of the jewel was the squalor, hunger, filth. disease and beggary. Only when I came out of the army did I see what a terrible thing it was that a country had been allowed to exist like this. Such snobbery, so many riches, so much starvation.

(Ed Brown, 1920s)

The introduction to the book discussed the key features of empires, notably: (1) domination and power (2) the pomp and ostentation of emperors, and (3) the poverty and misery of the subjects. This final chapter discusses these aspects of the Hindu, Muslim and British empires and to what extent the legacy of India's imperial rulers was marked by pomp, vainglory and extravagance.

Different empires are compared highlighting their common elements as well as differences. They are summarized on the basis of six different criteria, namely, autocratic or democratic, exploitative or benevolent, ostentatious/ornamental or utilitarian (Table 10.1).

Most empires had a common feature of ostentation and wasteful expenditure. But some, such as the Mauryan Empire of Ashoka and that

Table 10.1. Characteristic Features of the Major Indian Empires

Features\empires	Maurya	Gupta	Mughal	British
Autocratic	x	x	x	x
Democratic				
Exploitative			x	x
Benevolent	x	x	x	
Ostentatious/ornamental			x	x
Utilitarian	x	x		

of the Guptas were more benevolent than the Mughal and British empires that followed. They were less pompous and ostentatious and more utilitarian. Ashoka built rock edicts and pillars throughout his kingdom to spread information about the tenets of the empire, necessitated more for administrative reasons than for vainglory. He and subsequent Gupta emperors responded to the spiritual needs of the people by building stupas and temples. People, who were quite religious at the time, would have considered it a normal duty of the ruler to provide them with proper and adequate places of worship.

However, there are indications of pomp and extravagance by the post-Gupta smaller Hindu kingdoms, for example, that of the Chandelas in central India and Vijayanagar in the south. The Indian princes also indulged in great pomp and extravaganza (Chapter 1). In fact, they were the yardstick for the British governors who justified their own lavish spending by arguing that they had to match the pomp and extravagance of the Indian princes and of the House of Timur (Mughal Empire).

The pomp and vainglory of regional (northern and southern) princely kingdoms was no match for the extravagance of the Mughal and British empires discussed below. There are striking similarities in the approaches of these two major empires. In both cases, reckless extravagance stands in sharp contrast to the prevailing conditions of poverty and squalor of their subjects.

Mughal Extravaganza and Power

The Mughals were extravagant master builders like the British. A large number of their palaces, forts, mausoleums, mosques and pavilions described in Chapter 4 bear testimony to the grandeur, power and extravagance of their Empire.

Most royal monuments cost a fortune, too large perhaps for even rich and wealthy emperors.[1] Although the Mughal emperors spent most of their money on their military establishments, including the salaries of their officers and noblemen (*mansabdars*), a substantial amount was also spent on royal monuments.[2]

Akbar's successors (Jahangir and Shah Jahan) surpassed him in conspicuous expenditure of monumental proportions.[3] The palaces and mausoleum built during Shah Jahan's reign cost much more than those of either Akbar or Jahangir, estimated by Moosvi at nearly Rs 29 million (cited in Richards, 1993:127). The wisdom of such lavish expenditure could be questioned when the existing Agra Fort and palaces would have been adequate. One plausible reason for new construction is that it satisfied the vanity of the emperor who probably wanted to immortalize his name. Shah Jahan found both the Agra and Lahore forts (used as capitals by his predecessors) rather too congested for a monarch. The cities of Agra and Lahore were also overcrowded. Furthermore, both already had Mughal monuments in abundance. Shah Jahan must have wanted to leave his own legacy behind by creating a new capital. Hambly (1982:445) believes that 'he may also have aimed at outshining the lavish building programme initiated by Shah Abbas I (of Persia) at Isfahan . . . '

A colossal amount of money was spent on building Shahjahanabad as the new capital. Mughal sources such as *Amal-i-Salih* (see Salih, 1923, 1927 and 1928) note that Shah Jahan spent Rs 6 million on the palace fortress (Red Fort) and Rs 1 million on the Jama Masjid. The Halls of Special and Public Audience, the Hayat Baksh palace garden and Imtiaz Mahal (or Rang Mahal) inside the fortress cost an additional Rs 7 million.

Shah Jahan inaugurated Shahjahanabad with a spectacular display of wealth, pomp and power. The Hall of Special Audience was decorated with brocaded velvet from Turkey and silk from China. The emperor sat on a specially-built throne enclosed by a golden railing.

The Taj Mahal must have cost a fortune considering that it took nearly 20 years to build employing a workforce of over 20,000.[4] It is believed to have cost Rs 5 million, but this may well be an underestimate as it is not clear whether this amount refers only to on-site expenses or also to the cost of the materials (Table 10.2). The estimated figure may also

Table 10.2. Cost of the Mughal Monuments

Name of building/monument	Cost(Rs million)
Agra	
Congregational marble mosque and fort buildings	6.0
of which: Fort	3.5
Taj Mahal	5.0
Akbar's tomb	1.5
Total	**12.5**
Delhi	
Shahjahanabad (palace fortress)	6.0
Public buildings in the household sector	2.8
Hall of Special Audience	1.4
Hall of Public Audience	0.25
Hayat Baksh garden and the bath	0.60
Imtiaz Mahal and Aramgah	0.55
Bazars, houses, offices, stables, etc.	0.40
Harem buildings	0.70
Jama Masjid	1.0
Total	**13.7**
Lahore	
Buildings and garden	5.0
of which Jahangir's tomb	1.0
Grand Total	**31.2**

Sources: *Amal-i-Salih (Memoirs of Shahjahan) (1923–28); Tuzuk-i-Jahangir (Memoirs of Jahangir)*; Smith (1892).

exclude the cost of the interior decorations such as the screen around the sarcophagus (originally made of gold and precious stones) that took ten years to make, or the gardens, mosques and other trappings. Therefore, it is not surprising that later estimates are much higher, ranging from Rs 18 million to Rs 40 million (Eraly, 2007:378).

Shah Jahan's extravagance is further exemplified by his use of expensive imported building materials, precious stones and personnel (architects, craftsmen and masons) from abroad for the building of Shahjahanabad and the Taj Mahal (see Chapter 4). The Peacock Throne built by him is another example of the display of his wealth and 'immense quantity of precious stones accumulated successively in the treasury from the spoils of war of ancient Rajas and Pathans . . .' (Bernier, 1901:269). It was 'the grandest object of sumptuary art ever devised by man' (ibid:269fn), a symbol of Shah Jahan's vainglory. The best craftsmen of his Empire took seven years to complete at an enormous cost of Rs 30–40 million (ibid.). Such was his vanity and passion for a lavish style of living.

Nobles, princes and amirs were almost as lavish in their spending as the Mughal emperors. Their private mansions were as grand and spacious as those built later by the British rulers. They looked like forts and fortresses. Forbes, an English traveller, notes that 'they were much larger than the palaces in Europe' and cost an enormous amount to build (Forbes, 1813, vol. 4:61–2). Mughal sources (for example, Salih, 1928, vol. 3:45) give varying estimates of the cost of these palaces, ranging from Rs 100 thousand to Rs 2 million. Although the upper range may be a bit exaggerated, there is no denying the fact that these mansions were luxurious and worthy of princes (see Blake, 1991:50 for a detailed description of the Mughal mansions).

During the Mughal period, a large proportion of royal revenue was hoarded. Moosvi (1987:201) states that 'in 1595–6, an amount of Rs 15 to 18 crores (or Rs 150 to Rs 180 million) was probably transferred to the imperial hoard'. Much of this money came in the form of agricultural surplus from the peasantry. Royal income consisted of land revenues, other taxes, and gifts to the emperor by the nobility, land owners and visiting dignitaries, as well as war booty looted after each conquest. Whatever was not hoarded was distributed to the landowners.

Hoarding by the nobles was equally excessive. Shaista Khan, the governor of Bengal, is said to have accumulated Rs 380 million in just 13 years. Other nobles left behind a more modest hoarding of between Rs 3 million and Rs 10 million at the time of their death (Raychaudhuri, 1982a:183).

During Akbar's reign, wealth remained highly concentrated among the royals and nobles, and this continued during the reigns of Jahangir and Shah Jahan. Jahangir is known to have spent the bulk of the royal treasury left behind by Akbar. Qazwini, Shah Jahan's first official historian, notes that Jahangir spent Rs 6 crores out of Rs 7 crores (cited in Moosvi, 1987:198).

The lavish building activity and wars during the reign of Shah Jahan, and the frequent and long wars during Aurangzeb's rule, took a heavy toll on the royal exchequer. Despite external Shah Jahan's facade of splendour and opulence, his 'reign concealed a crumbling interior' (Sarkar, 1975:349). The financial resources at the disposal of the Empire started to dry up. Gradually, its splendour and royal glory faded into near oblivion.

Poverty and Famines

The Mughal extravaganza needs to be assessed in the context of the living conditions of ordinary citizens. Writing about Akbar's reign, for example, Moreland (1920:254) notes that 'the mass of the nobles were steeped in luxury and that the mass of the people were miserably poor, poorer even than they are to-day'. Spear (1990:47) states that 'most European travellers commented on the dire poverty of the countryside'. Yet he also observes that 'taking it all in all Mughal India, with an estimated hundred million inhabitants, had for about a century and a half a standard of life roughly comparable with that of contemporary Europe, though arranged on a different economic and social pattern' (ibid.). Similarly, Bernier, who lived in India from 1656 to 1658, describes poor people as 'deprived of the means of subsistence and their children being taken away as slaves'.

During the Mughal Empire, revenue collection was ruthless. Many contemporary observers believed that the revenue collectors extracted agricultural surplus above the bare subsistence level for the peasants, who were always under pressure to sell the bulk of their crops keeping little for their own consumption. This led to their further impoverishment.

Maddison (2004) estimates that India's gross domestic product (GDP) per capita (a proxy for per capita income) (in 1990 international dollars) was consistently lower than that of the UK from 1500 to 1700, that is, the Mughal period (Chart 10.1). In years 1 to 1000, the period of the Hindu empires, it was slightly higher than that in the UK but it remained constant for 200 years. Later Maddison (2006:46) noted that:

> West European income was at a nadir around the year 1000. Its level was significantly lower than it had been in the first century. *It was below that in China, India and other parts of East and West Asia* (emphasis added).

Chart 10.1. GDP per capita in India and the UK (1–1930). Source: Maddison (2004)

Average per capita income figures hide vast income inequalities and the very high standard of living of the nobles. Although the Mughal rulers and nobility led lavish life styles, the standard of living of the ordinary citizens (who suffered oppression and exploitation by the imperial officers) was lower than that of the European peasants (Maddison, 1971).

The following figures give some indication of the vast income inequalities. During Akbar's reign, the top 25 amirs, princes and officers took 30 per cent of the total assessed revenue of the Empire, with the bulk of the remainder going to the Emperor (Eraly, 2007:166). During Shah Jahan's reign, 36.5 per cent of the total revenue went to 68 princes and amirs and another 25 per cent to 587 officers (ibid.).

During Aurangzeb's reign, peasant revolts by Jats, Marathas and Sikhs were accompanied by a growing assertiveness of provincial governors for greater autonomy. These revolts suggest economic oppression and poverty. However, some scholars (for example, Bose and Jalal, 1998:50) argue that the revolts were masterminded by wealthy landowners in prosperous, not poor areas. It is more likely that both the rich and the poor were equally opposed to making contributions to the Empire's expensive wars.

Four economic classes existed in Mughal India: (1) the peasants and rural workers, (2) the urban poor, (3) the middle class and (4) the upper class. Rural incomes and the wages of the urban poor were generally quite low. But Desai (1972:50) notes that 'the standards of food consumption of both the urban workers and the peasants were probably higher in Akbar's time than in the early sixties'. Chandra (1982:465) states that the 'low-paid worker of Akbar's time was able to help keep the standard of nutrition much higher than now because of cheap meat, *ghi* and milk'. The middle class (which consisted of lower administration officials, shopkeepers, traders and such professionals as physicians), was relatively prosperous. The upper class consisted of senior court officers, nobles, autonomous chiefs, rajas and wealthy merchants. A large proportion of the population (about 26 million) of 100 million depended for their livelihood on the armed forces and their associated activities. The bulk 'were maintained at a level of bare subsistence' (Raychaudhuri, 1982a:179).

The Mughal nobles are known to have 'received salaries which were probably the highest in the world at that time' (Chandra, 1982:468). Under Akbar, a noble or amir of the highest rank enjoyed a net monthly income of Rs 18,000, the equivalent of about Rs 1.3 million in modern currency (Eraly, 2007:81). Under Shah Jahan, these salaries and incomes were even higher. Eraly (ibid) notes that the 'average income of the top 655 members of the ruling class was over 200,000 rupees, the equivalent of about fourteen million rupees in the currency of the mid-1990s'. Although the officers/amirs had to pay for some military obligations, their net incomes were substantial enough for them to enjoy a luxurious life style.

Bernier (1901:252) remarked that 'in Delhi there was no middle state. A man must either be of the highest rank or live miserably' He writes about 'these wretched mud and thatch houses in Delhi', which led him to label the city as 'a collection of many villages' or a 'military encampment' (ibid:246). He describes the tyranny of governors and revenue collectors over the ordinary citizens often 'so excessive as to deprive the peasant and artisan of the necessaries of life, and leave them to die of misery and exhaustion' (ibid:226). Many royal buildings were financed through special taxes on the poor peasantry which further added to its financial burden. Some observers (for example, Eraly, 2007) claim that the tax rates during the Mughal period were much higher than they had been during the pre-Mughal period.

Famines occurred during the Mughal period rather frequently as they did during the British Raj later (see below): in 1614–5 and 1618–9 during Jahangir's reign, and in 1630, 1640–1, 1645–6 and 1659–60 during Shah Jahan's (Moreland, 1923:205–19). Drought and the failure of rains resulted in a lack of adequate food supply and its distribution. This was

exacerbated by poor transportation facilities, which prevented the movement of surplus food in the north to scarcity areas in the south and west
of the country. Food imports from Persia did not provide adequate relief
due to time constraints. The famines resulted in the disruption of normal economic activity, human misery and starvation. Historical accounts
of the effects of starvation and hunger are horrendous. For example,
Johan van Twist, a Dutch merchant, narrated stories of cannibalism and
the sale of children during the famine of 1630–1 (cited in Moreland,
1923:212–13).

Although famine relief measures such as free public kitchens, tax
remittance and cheap loans were put in place, they could not overcome the overall food deficiency. However, 'the measures actually taken
were not only inadequate but tardy . . . ' (ibid.:214). Too little was spent
on famine relief relative to the royal family's personal expenses. Eraly
(2007:169) notes that 'the 100,000 rupees disbursed by Shah Jahan
for famine relief was a mere one-tenth of the annual pin-money of
Mumtaz Mahal'.

Extravaganza and Power of the Raj

The extravagance of the British Raj that followed the Mughal Empire
was no less shocking. In the earlier Mughal tradition, the British also
expressed the power and glory through lavish monuments on which vast
amounts of taxpayers' money were spent.

Victoria Memorial in Calcutta rivals the Mughal monuments in its
imposing appearance and the high price tag of Rs 1 crore and five lakhs
(or £1.2 million). In its construction, Makrana marble from Rajasthan
was used, similar to what Shah Jahan had used for the Taj Mahal. The
marble had to be transported all the way from Rajasthan to Calcutta,
which would have required a 17-mile long goods train.

Government House in Calcutta built by Lord Wellesley, the Governor-
General, was known to be one of the finest buildings anywhere. In 1902,
Curzon entertained German and Austrian army officers in that House
who admired it for its scale and grandeur. They believed 'it transcended
the palaces of many kings'. Sixty years earlier, 'the famous Dost Mo-
hammed [. . .] expressed similar sentiments when he asked if there was
really in Europe a larger house than Government House' (Curzon of
Kedleston, 1925, vol. I:74).

The lavish Government Houses and forts were built at a high cost to Indian taxpayers. For example, the Government House in Calcutta is estimated to have cost £63,291, a sum considered excessive by the Company's directors in London (Bence-Jones,1973:41–2). The Viceregal Lodge in Simla cost even more, well over £100,000 (ibid:141), and the Viceregal Lodge in New Delhi, 'cost more than a million sterling' (ibid:197). Lutyens's palace (the Lodge) has been likened to Versailles (France), Schonbrunn (Austria) and other palaces in Europe.

Travellers to Madras in the eighteenth century have recorded in admiration the magnificent buildings they saw on arrival. Writing on Madras in 1781, William Hodges writes that 'the buildings offer to the eye an appearance similar to that what we may conceive of a Grecian city in the age of Alexander (Hodges, 1793). In 1780, Eliza Fay remarked: 'I could have fancied myself transported to Italy, so magnificently are they (Madras houses) decorated, yet with the utmost taste' (Fay, 1817).

To Robert Byron, an architectural critic, Lutyens's Delhi (not to be confused with Old Delhi which remains a semblance of Mughal India) was 'the Rome of Hindostan'. Dalrymple (1994:83) notes that 'New Delhi was very deliberately built as an expression of unconquerable might of the Raj'. Nehru saw New Delhi 'as the visible symbol of British power, with all its ostentation and wasteful extravagance' (cited in ibid:85). In planning New Delhi as the new capital, the British preserved the social hierarchy and class system of colonial India which the leaders of independent India have maintained despite the charade of an egalitarian society and poverty alleviation. The VIP culture has also survived.

Even the lesser regents at the courts of indigenous rulers enjoyed a lavish style and grand living in palatial buildings. For example, the Residency of Lucknow (Fig. 1.0, Introduction), Bangalore and Hyderabad, were built on the models of the stately mansions back home in Britain.

By all accounts, the Company masters in London were embarrassed by the excessive amount of expenditure on government buildings. They indicted Lord Wellesley (known as the 'Sultanized Englishman') who was responsible for earmarking 'the most colossal sum for building himself a vast new Government House in Calcutta' in order to protect him (in his words) from 'the stupidity and ill-bred familiarity' of Calcutta society (Dalrymple, 2002:345–6). The cost of building and furnishing it was considered excessive. The Directors noted that 'in two years, 1801/2 and

1802/3, the charges of plate and furniture alone exceeded Sirca Rupees 1,60,000 or (as calculated by them) £18,560', implying an exchange rate of Rs 8.6 to the pound sterling at that time (cited in Curzon of Kedleston, 1925:48).

The misuse of funds was not confined only to the construction of palatial buildings. Large sums of money were also squandered on social entertainment and drinking parties. Wellesley gave several parties at Government House 'such as had never before been seen in Calcutta' (ibid.:208). Chronicles of the Raj describe big dinners, balls, dancing and drinking parties even before Wellesley's excesses became public knowledge. Great breakfasts are mentioned to which over a 1,000 guests would be invited!

During Curzon's time, the number of meals served to visitors, guests or residents of Government House rose to 3,500 in one month, from 2,700 a few years earlier (ibid.:233). Bodyguards of the governors, a retinue of other staff, French chefs and others, all cost the Company a minor fortune. Lord Moira is known to have appointed a Chamberlain and other personal assistants 'purely for Show and State at large salaries' (ibid.:214). The Bengal and Agra Guide for 1841 notes that full dress balls, masquerades, crowded dinner parties and military shows were the order of the day during Hastings's time.

Celebrations and entertainments at Government House and elsewhere included illuminations of government buildings and fireworks. Curzon notes that 'enormous sums were spent by Lord Wellesley and his successors, upon this form of rejoicing' (ibid.:236).

However, not everyone shared the view of the Company directors about the Governor's lavish expenses on building the Government and Council Houses. There were a few who defended such lavishness and life of luxury, including Lord Valentia (1809, vol. I:235) who noted that:

> The sums expended upon it have been considered as extravagant by those who carry European ideas and European economy into Asia, but they ought to remember that India is a country of splendour, of extravagance and of outward appearances; [. . .] I wish India to be ruled from a palace, not from a counting-house.

Company governors sought to emulate the Indian maharajas and their palaces. Their regular contacts with Indian princes had fully exposed them to the latter's ostentatious life style. The reaction of the Company directors that ostentation by the Company servants in India would be injurious to their commercial interests was understandable. The contrast between the life styles of the Company servants and that of the man in the street was clearly astounding.

Keeping up with the Joneses was at its best during the British Raj. The durbars and coronations were the Empire's show of pomp and ostentation to match that and Indian princes. Royal visits to various colonies including India were organized meticulously with great pomp and ceremony. For example, the Prince of Wales visited India in 1876 when festivities included receptions and durbars in Calcutta and Bombay attended by Indian princes and other dignitaries. Three durbars took place in India in 1877, 1903 and 1911. Presided over by the Viceroy representing the British Crown, they 'served to nationalize a local ceremonial idiom by bringing together princely India and British India in week-long festivals of chivalric unity, feudal hierarchy and imperial subordination' (Cannadine, 2001:109). As the British King's representative, the Duke of Connaught attended the 1903 durbar. He visited India again in 1921 for the opening of new legislatures in Madras, Calcutta, Bombay and New Delhi.

In 1911, King George V attended the Delhi Durbar and proclaimed himself Emperor of India in the midst of unprecedented pomp and show. This rich display was matched by a pageant of Indian princes on the backs of elephants and in golden attire. Elaborate planning was undertaken by the mandarins in Calcutta and London through viceregal correspondence which might 'suggest that the British Raj depended less on justice and good administration than on precedence, honours and minute distinctions of dress' (ibid.:51).

The British rulers in India justified the high cost of such extravaganza as well as their scale, duration and lavishness on the grounds that these festivities appealed to their Indian subjects (ibid.:138). But nothing could be further from the truth. As one observer has noted, 'few Indians were stirred by the pomp of Empire' (Woodruff, 1963, vol. 2:307). Whatever the logic of pomp and splendour, it was clearly out of place in a poor country.

Observing that in the 1930s the Raj continued to be no less 'ostentatiously ornamental', Cannadine (2001:56) had this to say:

In the hands of such prestige-conscious viceroys as Lords Willingdon and Linlithgow, New Delhi was the setting for the grandest living on earth, with bowing and curtseying, more precedence and protocol, than anywhere else in the empire, London included. At its peak in the 1930s, Viceroy's House employed a staff of six thousand servants, and they were as carefully graded and ranked below stairs as the officialdom and princes of the Raj were above. And this ordered and ornamented regime was still mimicked (and competed with) throughout both princely and official India. The future King Edward VIII remarked that he had never known what authentic regal pomp really meant until he had stayed with Lord Lloyd. And Lloyd was not the viceroy but merely the governor of Bombay.

The British extravaganza was matched by that of the Indian princes who were wooed by the British as the 'natural rulers of Indian society'. The princes spent lavishly on palaces, jewellery and, in a few rare cases, also on such beneficial projects as hospitals and universities. They attended royal coronations in London in style and extravagance. For example, the Maharaja of Jaipur attended King Edward VII's coronation when he was accompanied by 125 officers and attendants. A whole ship was chartered for his journey to London (ibid.:112).

At the royal durbar of 1911, King George V acknowledged the ruling princes as those 'whose existence and security is so closely bound up with that of the British Empire' (ibid:54). The loyalty of the Indian princes and their military and financial contributions were essential for British military expeditions. Ferguson (2003 53) notes that in 1773 'Hastings accepted the offer of 40 million rupees from the Nawab of Oudh to fight the Rohillas, an Afghan people . . .'

Personal Fortune-Making

Many governors, governors-general and viceroys were excessively greedy and accumulated huge amounts of wealth in India within a short time span. Indian Civil Service emoluments during the Company Raj 'were very considerable' and Governors, Members of Council, and High Court Judges 'did make in a few years what would now be regarded as ample fortunes' (Curzon of Kedleston, 1925, vol. II:97).

Hastings, sent to India to curb corruption, made a fortune through illegal activities. His impeachment in the British House of Commons included accusations that he received money 'against the orders of the Company, the Act of Parliament and his own sacred engagements; and that he applied 'the money to purposes totally improper and unauthorized (and with) enormous extravagances and bribery in various contracts with a view to enrich his dependants and favourites' (Ferguson, 2003:55).

It is well known that Robert Clive made an immense fortune of over £400,000 a year in India and displayed it on his return to England in July 1767 (Paxman, 2011:79). Many titles and honours were bestowed upon him. However, it is ironical that the House of Commons turned upon him soon after his return to London. Members of the House such as 'Gentleman Johnny' Burgoyne claimed that all land seized by British subjects in India belonged to the Crown, and that, therefore, Clive had no right to receive massive personal payments. Clive who was called upon to explain himself before the House remained unrepentant and arrogant till the bitter end. His hubris and haughtiness is reflected in his following statement before the House:

> An opulent city lay at my mercy; its richest bankers bid against each other for my smiles; I walked through vaults which were thrown open to me alone, piled on either hand with gold and jewels [. . .] at this moment I stand astonished at my own moderation. (ibid.:79)

Clive was exonerated for a lack of adequate number of votes in the House of Commons. It would not be surprising if he had bribed quite a few Members of Parliament to vote in his favour! He could certainly have afforded it.

Richard Barwell made so much money in India that he was nicknamed Nabob Barwell. He returned to England with a fortune estimated at £800,000 with which 'he could easily afford to buy Lord Halifax's estate and house of Stanstead' (Curzon of Kedleston, 1925, vol. II:98). All the senior members of the British administration in India enjoyed handsome salaries as well as generous allowances for gardens, country houses and family houses. When some of these allowances disappeared, others such as the Durbar and Furniture Funds were added. And of course, the fortunes made in India were sometimes supplemented by bribery, gambling and illicit trading.

Curzon (ibid.:96) describes three periods of the British fortune-making in India:

(1) Before the second Administration of Clive 'when the pagoda tree was shaken recklessly into the lap of every Civil Servant from the head of the Government downwards, and when the immense fortunes secured by illicit trading, bribery and the like rendered the so-called Indian Nabob an object of well-merited loathing and scorn in this country' (UK) (p. 96). Clive was known as the biggest nabob;

(2) The second period of Cornwallis when illicit activities were curbed; and

(3) The last period of the Crown Raj when the Indian service was no longer considered a means of making fortunes. An increase in the cost of living and a fall in the exchange value of the rupee eroded its glamour.

Poverty and Famines

The extravaganza described above contrasts sharply with the poverty and misery suffered by the Indians in the Presidency town of Madras (see Fig. 9.4). In the 1860s, the local economic and social conditions in Delhi were appalling. Gupta (1981:81) notes: 'Eight thousand people queued for meals daily at the Idgah asylum.' At Delhi Gate, four thousand women were given ration (*Mofussilite*, 26 February 1861). And some English visitors to Delhi in 1869 found that 'everybody in Delhi seems very poor'. In the late nineteenth century (1896–1900), the situation became much worse with the influx of famine victims from Rajasthan. Old Delhi in 1908 must have been even further impoverished after the construction of Lutyens's glittering new capital a few kilometres away (Fig. 10.1).

Penderel Moon, an ICS officer, remarked that 'the British Raj could not tackle the main problems of India, which were economic [. . .] foreign power could not achieve the revolutionary steps that would be necessary to change the Indian peasant life' (cited in Allen, 1975:218). However, it seems that it was not so much the inability of the foreign power to

Fig. 10.1. An Old Delhi Street, Chandni Chowk (1908) (Author's Private Collection)

tackle India's economic problems as its lack of interest in improving the lot of the local people. Instead, it was more concerned with private gain and the public good of the mother country.

British rule was marked by several famines, notably, the famine of 1783–4, which is estimated to have killed more than fifth of the Indian population, and the Bengal famine of 1942 and 1943, which may have killed between 1.5 million and 3 million. In 1791, 1801 and 1805, food shortages were often severe and distribution of food to areas of scarcity inadequate. This scarcity led to poverty, destitution and death. One observer (Gholan Hossein Khan) noted that the poor natives in India had no recourse left other than 'begging and thieving'. Another found that many people 'have already quitted their homes and countries; and numbers unwilling to leave their abodes, have made covenant with hunger and distress and ended their lives in the corner of their cottages' (Ferguson, 2003:53).

The British government in London remained indifferent during the Bengal famines. It refused to allow more food imports into India. In a letter of 24 October 1944 to Winston Churchill, Lord Wavell, the then Viceroy of India, noted that 'the vital problems of India are being treated by His Majesty's Government with neglect, even sometimes with hostility and contempt' (Wavell,1973:95). This attitude was not peculiar to problems in India. When famine struck in Ireland in the 1840s, the British government's response was also negligent and 'in some measure positively culpable' (Ferguson, 2003:xxi).

In the case of the Bengal famine of 1942 and 1943, matters were made worse by the fact that it coincided with sharply rising imperial expenditure on the Indian Army, which was borne by the Indian taxpayer, not by the British Exchequer.

To conclude, British colonial rule may have brought peace to India, but it did not bring prosperity. Some observers (such as Nehru, 1946) contest the validity of the generally-held view that the British brought peace. Nehru argues that India had a far more uninterrupted peaceful existence for prolonged periods than Europe has had, and that the notion that the Pax Britannica brought peace and order to India is 'one of the most extraordinary of delusions'.

Pauperization and Exploitation

The pauperization of the Indian population occurred also in other ways. Resources were drained from the Indian periphery and repatriated to the metropolitan centre (London).[5] The British in India spent money on imported British goods rather than Indian. When the USA protected its industries behind tariff walls in the nineteenth century, India was not allowed to impose similar tariffs. The British could freely export their goods to the Indian market, including cheap English textiles, which was a major blow to the Indian textile industry.[6] India became a major market for British goods and an important source of raw materials for British industry (Maddison, 1971).

Furthermore, the establishment of British rule in India reduced the number of local rulers and their royal courts as well as rich landlords. This led to a decline in domestic demand for luxury handicrafts. Maddison (ibid.) notes that 'between 1757 and 1857, the British wiped out the Mughal court, and eliminated three-quarters of the warlord aristocracy...' A large number of local chiefs (zamindars) were also eliminated. In their place a British and Indian bureaucracy, with European consumption patterns, was established, which led to a decline in the

Table 10.3. De-Industrialization of India (1750 to 1900)

Region/Country	1750	1800	1830	1860	1880	1900
Relative shares of world manufacturing output (%)						
Europe as a whole	23.2	28.1	34.2	53.2	61.3	62.0
UK	1.9	4.3	9.5	19.9	22.9	18.5
France	4.0	4.2	5.2	7.9	7.8	6.8
Russia	5.0	5.6	5.6	7.0	7.6	8.8
India	24.5	19.7	17.6	8.6	2.8	1.7
Per capita levels of industrialization (relative to UK in 1900=100)						
Europe as a whole	8	8	11	16	24	35
UK	10	16	25	64	87	100
France	9	9	12	20	28	39
Russia	6	6	7	8	10	15
India	7	6	6	3	2	1

Source: Bairoch (1982).

demand for Indian manufactures. Strong competition from European imports exacerbated this decline, leading to de-industrialization in India. In 1750, at the virtual end of Mughal rule, India's share of world manufacturing output (24.5 per cent) had been higher than that of Europe (23.2 per cent). But by 1900, that share fell to less than 2 per cent, whereas that of Europe rose to 62 per cent (Table 10.3).

The decline of the Indian handicraft industry was not compensated for by the growth of modern industry. Raw materials from the Indian periphery fed industries in Great Britain rather than being processed in India. De-industrialization and the resulting unemployment of artisans and craftsmen were the main causes of poverty in India at that time. Ferguson (2003:216) admits that 'the average Indian had not got much richer under British rule. Between 1757 and 1947 British per capita GDP increased in real terms by 347 per cent, Indian by a mere 14 per cent.' Chart 10.1 shows that Indian GDP per capita during the British Raj (1820 onwards) remained almost constant. The wide gap between the British and Indian GDPs per capita is explained by the opening of the Indian market for British goods and the repatriation of profits back to Great Britain.

Nehru (1946:247) suggests a close and positive connection between the length of British rule and growth of poverty so that 'those parts of India which have been longest under British rule are the poorest today'. These parts were Bengal and Bihar, ruled by the British for nearly 200 years. Yet Bengal was a prosperous and rich province before the arrival of the British.

The British rulers did little to promote mass education or technical and vocational training, focusing instead on introducing English higher education to the elite in order to create docile and loyal Indian princes and civil servants. Basic and primary education was largely ignored and was financed mainly by poor local authorities. Since majority of the population had no access to education, at India's independence in 1947, illiteracy was extremely high.

Eurocentric explanations for Indian poverty generally refer to lack of knowledge, education and technical advance. Yet Indian historians (for example, Parthasarathi, 2011) provide evidence of the existence of modern industry and technological development during the pre-British period. Apart from technology and industry, Indian trade flourished in such goods as textiles. Gujarati cloth merchants were known to be superior to their British and Portuguese counterparts (ibid.:239–40). On the basis of a study of the businesses of Jamsetjee Jejeebhoy, Siddiqi (1995) concludes that entrepreneurial skills and financial resources were not lacking in nineteenth-century western India. During the earlier Mughal period, structures of such extraordinary architectural beauty as the Taj and Humayun's tomb could not have been built without the existence in the country of technical manpower and skilled workers. Babur admired the skill of Indian craftsmen and many Islamic sources mention the existence of skilled masons and craftsmen in India during the Mughal and pre-Mughal periods. Referring to these sources, Ashraf (2000:145) notes that Firoz Shah Tughluq 'assigned 4,000 of his slaves to be trained' as skilled masons to raise the stock of local skilled manpower in India.

The British colonial rulers, unlike the Mughals, are often credited with investments in irrigation and railways, which led to the growth of agricultural and industrial output. But these investments may have benefited the British masters much more than their Indian subjects. The former extracted huge amounts of taxes from the agricultural incomes of those who benefited from canal irrigation. Improved communications through railways also enabled the British rulers to exercise greater administrative control over the local population.

Lord Hastings's impeachment in the British House of Commons in London (reproduced below) further confirms the exploitation of Indian subjects by the British rulers (Ferguson, 2003:54–5).

With gross injustice and treachery against the faith of nations, in hiring British soldiers for the purpose of extirpating the innocent and helpless people [. . .] the Rohillas . . .

With various instances of extortions and other deeds of maladministration against the Rajah of Benares . . .

(With) the numerous and insupportable hardships to which the Royal Family of Oude (Oudh) has been reduced . . .

With impoverishing and depopulating the whole country of Oude (Oudh), rendering that country, which was once a garden, an inhabited desert . . .

With a wanton and unjust, and pernicious exercise of his powers, and the grave situation of trust which he occupied in India, in overturning the ancient establishments of the country and extending an undue influence by conniving extravagant contracts, and appointing inordinate salaries . . .

Conclusion

The scale of lavish expenditure on the symbols of imperial power discussed above was comparable during the Mughal and British empires. So was the extent and depth of poverty. The lavish spending on monuments often occurred at the expense of the poor citizens.

It is difficult to compare the respective costs of building the Mughal and British monuments for lack of a suitable *nominal* exchange rate between the rupee and the pound during the Mughal and British periods. Another problem is that of converting the *real* worth of the rupee in pound equivalent. Nevertheless, some rough approximation is possible.

There is enough evidence to show that the buildings of the British Empire were not designed as modest and functional museums or memorials, but rather as symbols of British power to remind its subjects of the Empire where the sun never set. English travellers to such Presidency towns as Madras and Calcutta confirmed the grandeur and spaciousness of the palatial buildings they saw. Calcutta was known as the city of palaces.

The total cost of the Mughal extravaganza, estimated at Rs 31 million (Table 10.2) may be roughly calculated as the equivalent of £3.6 million at the rate of Rs 8.6 to the pound (that is, the exchange rate used by the Company Directors in London). This figure is much lower than the £15 million spent by the British on creating the new capital in Delhi, not counting the Viceregal Lodge, Simla (£100,000), Victoria Memorial Calcutta (£1.2 million) and Government House, Calcutta (£63,291). A lower rupee/pound exchange rate may narrow the gap but it is unlikely to eliminate it. However, to the extent that the rupee's real worth during the Mughal period would probably have been much higher, it might be safe to assume that both the Mughals and the British were equally extravagant!

In contrast, living standards of the rural and urban poor were quite low during both the Mughal and British empires. Thanks to the detailed statistics on the wages of urban workers during Akbar's reign given in *Ain-i-Akbari*, Moosvi (1973) was able to estimate the purchasing power of the lowest urban wages in Agra in Akbar's time (1595) and in 1886–95 (the British period) for such basic goods as food and clothing. She concludes that the purchasing power of urban workers for different items of basic food was much lower during the British times than during Akbar's. However, reverse was the case for clothing: cotton textiles were much more abundant and cheaper during the British Raj. On the basis of his estimates, Moreland (1920:192) concludes: 'urban real wages in the north of India stood at somewhere about the same level in Akbar's time as in 1911, and that there has been no pronounced change in the standard of remuneration of these classes of the population'.

It is no exaggeration to say that the greatness of most empires – the Greek, Roman, Mughal and British – lay in their grandiose buildings and architecture in general. This is true of the Mughal Empire in India as much as that of the British. Each successive ruler tried to outdo his predecessor. Did the British rulers try to outdo the Mughals? There is some evidence to suggest that they did even if they may not have fully succeeded. The Victoria Memorial in Calcutta is an example of such an attempt. So is Lutyens's Delhi and the Viceregal Lodge (Palace), the Secretariats and the War Memorial there. Although architecturally different, the British monuments sought some continuity with the earlier Mughal splendour. Some elements of Mughal architecture were blended with the European to create a hybrid style.

The glimpses of different empires presented in the book show that they are not similar when judged by the different criteria noted above. In pomp, extravagance and poverty, the Mughal and the British empires were alike. The earlier Hindu empires of the Mauryas (especially Ashoka's) and the Guptas stand apart as a separate group. They were less pretentious than pompous, and more benevolent than autocratic. Ordinary people during those empires were prosperous, not poor and wretched. Nevertheless, in the end all the empires collapsed perhaps under their own weight. To find out why they did so is not our concern here. That is the subject matter of another book.

Notes

Introduction

1. Lord Valentia (or George Annesley), the second earl of Mountnorris (1770–1844), belonged to an influential Anglo-Irish family from Newport Pagnell in the county of Buckinghamshire, UK. As a member of Parliament for Yarmouth, Isle of Wright, he travelled extensively in Asia and wrote an account of his travels (Viscount Valentia, *Voyages and Travels to India, Ceylon, . . . in the years 1802, 1803 and 1806*, London, 1809). Valentia is often addressed as either Viscount or Lord. A 'viscount' is above a 'baron' in the ranks of the English nobility. Earls and viscounts are generally addressed as 'Lords'.

2. Francois Bernier was a French traveller and physician who lived in India for several years. He was a personal physician of Aurangzeb, the Mughal emperor. His book, *Travels in the Mughal Empire* (London, 1901), is mainly about Aurangzeb's court.

3. The earliest Indian Hindu kingdoms can be traced back to around 600 BC (Romila Thapar, *A History of India*, New Delhi, 1990). Independent tribal republics may have existed prior to this period.

4. Of course, the Delhi sultans dreamt of expanding their rule to the rest of India in order to establish an empire. They attempted to conquer the Deccan and areas further south by military means, but failed. Ala-ud-din Khalji also launched campaigns in Gujarat and Malwa, and captured the Rajput forts of Rathambore and Chittor. However, eventually, intrigues in the northern kingdoms led to the breakaway of these annexed territories from the Delhi Sultanate. Thus the dream of the Delhi sultans to establish an all-India empire was never fulfilled.

5. There are many books on Mughal India but only a few draw extensively on the Persian and Urdu primary sources. These are, namely, William Dalrymple (*The Last Mughal*, London, 2009) and Abraham Eraly (*Emperors of the Peacock Throne*, New Delhi, 1997, and *The Mughal World*, New Delhi, 2007).

6. The British Raj appears to have been administered by very few people, as indicated by the following figures: in 1805 there were only 31,000 British in India out of which 22,000 were employed by the army and 2,000 in civil government. Even in 1931, there were only 168,000 British in India, of which 60,000 were employed by the army. The British formed a very small proportion of the total population, no more than 0.05 per cent. (See Angus Maddison, *Contours of the World Economy 1–2030 AD*, Oxford, 2007, p. 119).

7. In 1857, at the time of the uprising, the British Indian armies of Bengal, Bombay and Madras had only 45,000 soldiers compared to 240,000 Indian troops. By 1863, the number of the British soldiers had increased to 65,000 and that of Indian soldiers fell to 140,000 (*The New Encyclopaedia Britannica*, London, 1981, vol. 9, p. 409).

8. Residents were agents of the Governor-General who acted as guardians of the territories not directly under British control. They practically ran the government machinery and kept a watchful eye on any anti-British activity.

9. Lord Canning, Governor-General, who later became the first viceroy of the Crown, abolished the 'Doctrine of Lapse' which had been opposed by the Indian princes and the general population.

Chapter 1 Maurya and Gupta Empires and Later Kingdoms

1. Ashoka believed in Buddha, dharma and sangha (the Buddhist order) and strove to promote discipline in the sangha. Historical records show that the Third Buddhist Council was held in the 17th year of Ashoka's reign. At this Council, Ashoka expelled a large number of dissidents.

2. Some historians tend to equate the concept of *dharma* with Buddhism. However, the historian Romila Thapar argues that it is wrong to treat *dharma* and Buddhism as synonymous. According to Thapar (*A History*, 1990, p. 85), one historian (which she does not name) maintained that Ashoka 'was both a monk and a monarch at the same time'. Thapar argues that it is wrong to treat dharma and Buddhism as synonymous.

3. The political situation from the fall of the Guptas to the rise of King Harsha in the seventh century is unclear for lack of documented information. It can be assumed that any decline of a major empire involves large-scale

uncertainty, displacement of people as well as the emergence of small and weak kingdoms. Of the four kingdoms, the Maitrakas, believed to be of Iranian origin, lasted the longest. They continued to rule until the middle of the eighth century when the Arab attacks on India started (Romila Thapar, *A History*, 1990, pp. 142–4).

4. Abd-ur-Razzaq was an emissary of the King of Persia who was received by the King of Vijayanagar, Deva Raya II, at his royal palace in 1443.

5. The accounts of Domingo Paes provide first-hand and graphic details about the Vijayanagar empire and its capital, the city of Vijayanagar. He visited the capital during the reign of its most powerful king, Krishna Deva Raya. He writes not only about the immense wealth of the king but also about the Battle of Raichur fought between Deva Raya and Adil Shah of Bijapur.

6. Duarte Barbosa was a Portuguese writer and traveller. Born in Lisbon in around 1480, he worked for the Portuguese government in India for several years between 1500 and 1516–17. His historical account, presented in the *Book of Duarte Barbosa* (1516), is one of the first examples of Portuguese travel literature.

Chapter 2 The Pre-Mughal Muslim Kingdoms

1. The Omayyad or Umayyad dynasty was the first Islamic empire based in Damascus, which lasted from AD 660 to AD 750. It was founded by Umayya ibn Abd Shams, the great-grandfather of the first Umayyad caliph.

2. Internal frictions and intrigues among the local Rajput rajas weakened their power and attracted Muslim invaders from abroad.

3. A typical bell and chain motif of Hindu architecture suggesting the sounding of the bell to invoke a Hindu deity is found in almost all Hindu temples.

4. Deogiri (or Daulatabad) had a chequered history. Before Mubarak Shah Khalji laid claims to it, Malik Kafur mounted two campaigns against the Yadava vassal of Deogiri, in 1306–7 and 1312 respectively.

5. Ibn Batuta (or Abu Abdullah Muhammad) (1304–70) was an Arab traveller and jurist from Morocco. He travelled extensively around the world including South Asia and Southeast Asia. He was a legal expert (*qazi*) at Mohammad Tughluq's court in Delhi. His written accounts, at times fanciful, are the main sources of information about the early Islamic rulers in north India.

6. Fortifications in the form of thick walls around the mausoleum of Ghiyas-ud-din Tughluq may have been built to protect it from the Mongol invasions during his reign. The Mongol threats continued until 1306 when troubles started in Transaxonia in Central Asia (corresponding approximately

to present-day Uzbekistan, Tajikistan, southern Kyrgyzstan, and southwest Kazakhstan) which forced them to return there.

7. Mulla Abdul Qadir Badaoni (c.1540–1615) was an Indo-Persian historian who lived in India during the Mughal Empire. Zia-ud-din Barani (1285–1357) was born into an aristocratic family of Meerut and Bulandshehr in Uttar Pradesh. He was a historian and political thinker who lived during the reigns of Mohammad Tughluq and Firoz Shah Tughluq of the Delhi Sultanate. His two well-known works are: *Tarikh-i-Firoz Shahi*, an account of Firoz Shah's rule, and *Fatwa-i-Jahandari*, a treatise on the Muslim caste system in India.

Chapter 3 The Deccan Muslim Kingdoms

1. Colonel Philip Meadows Taylor was an adviser to the ruler of Hyderabad. He is describing Bijapur in an introduction to a photographic album.

2. As many as 14 sultans governed the Bahmani kingdom before its break-up. Zafar Khan, the founder of this kingdom, had been the governor of Mohammad Tughluq of the Delhi Sultanate but rebelled and declared independence when the Sultan's kingdom was weakening. In 1347, Zafar Khan ascended the throne in Daulatabad with the title of Sultan Bahman Shah but soon shifted his capital to Gulbarga. Most of his reign was spent consolidating his territory formerly controlled by the Delhi Sultanate's government in Daulatabad. Many Muslim nobles, who had been loyal to the Tughluq ruler in the north, shifted their allegiance to him.

3. These five independent kingdoms seem to have been weakened by internal divisions and constant warfare with the Hindu kingdom of Vijaynagar, which may have attracted the Mughals to the Deccan. In 1615, the Mughals defeated the combined forces of Ahmadnagar, Bijapur and Golconda. Intrigues and quarrels among the Nizam Shahis encouraged the Mughals to conquer the sultanate. In 1600, Akbar's commander, Abul Fazl, conquered Ahmadnagar and had Chand Bibi, the then Nizam Shahi ruler, murdered. In 1636, Murtaza III, the last Nizam Shahi ruler, was imprisoned when Aurangzeb annexed the sultanate to the Mughal Empire.

4. The founder of the kingdom, Malik Ahmed Shah Bahri, was originally a Hindu who converted to Islam. He was governor of Junnar (during the Bahmani rule) who defeated the Bahmani army in 1490, declared independence and established the Nizam Shahi dynasty. The territory of this sultanate extended from Gujarat to Bijapur to the northwestern part of the Deccan.

5. Chand Bibi, Sultan Ibrahim's sister was known for her gallantry in defending the Ahmadnagar fort against the Mughal attacks. She appealed to Muhammad Quli, the Qutb Shahi ruler to join forces against the enemy but failed to win his support (George Michell and Mark Zebrowski, *Architecture and Art of the Deccan Sultanates*, Cambridge, 1999, p. 17).

6. The fort remained in the hands of the Mughals until 1759, when Kavi Jang, the fort commandant, was bribed. He sold it to the cousin of the third Peshwa. In August 1803, the fort was surrendered to General Wellesley, who later became the Duke of Wellington.

7. The Qutb Shahi dynasty was the third to emerge from the breakdown of the Bahmani Kingdom. Its sultans chose Golconda as their capital, but this was later shifted to Hyderabad by Muhammad Quli Qutb Shah. Golconda was an important centre of a flourishing diamond trade. Sultan Quli Qutbul Mulk (1518–43), the founder of the dynasty, was a governor in the Bahmani kingdom who declared independence after the death of his Master, Mahmood Shah Bahmani. Mulk was fond of architecture and founded the Qutb Shahi style which is a fusion of the Hindu, Pathan and Persian styles.

8. Muses, the Greek goddesses, who inspired poets, philosophers and musicians, included:

Calliope ('the beautiful of speech'), muse of poetry.
Erato ('the amorous one'), muse of love.
Euterpe ('the well-pleasing'), muse of music and lyric poetry.
Melpomene ('the chanting one'), muse of tragedy.
Polymnia ('the singer of many hymns'), muse of sacred singing.
Terpiscore ('the one who delights in dance'), muse of choral song and dance.
Thalia (the blossoming one'), muse of comedy.
Urania ('the celestial one'), muse of astronomy.
Clio ('the glorious one'), muse of history.

As Clio was broken, only eight are standing (see http://www.iaac.us/dakshina darshanam/hyderabad falaknuma.htm).

9. It is believed that the Nizam smoked cheap cigarettes and wore the same cap for 30 years. He rarely entertained. Visitors invited for tea were 'supposedly rationed to one biscuit each' (Maharaja of Baroda, *The Palaces of India*, London, 1980, p. 136).

10. Jean-Baptiste Tavernier (1605–89) was a French traveller and gem merchant who undertook six voyages to Persia and India at his own expense. At the behest of Louis XIV, his patron, he published '*Les Six Voyages de Jean-Baptiste Tavernier*' (Six Travels of Jean-Baptiste Tavernier), which included extensive descriptions of the Mughal court.

Chapter 4 The Mughal Empire and Beyond

1. With the defeat of Humayun, the fort was taken over by Sher Shah Suri who renamed it Shergarh.

2. Stephen Blake (*Shahjahanabad*, Cambridge, 1991) notes that the Iranian architects of Shahjahanabad built it on the basis cf cosmological principles, an analogy between the microcosm (man) and the macrocosm (the universe). The fortress palace represented the microcosm and the city of Shahjahanabad, the macrocosm.

3. For example, the Shahjahanabad fort was designed by Ahmed Lahwari who was also the chief architect of the Taj Mahal in Agra. Its construction was supervised by architects Ustad Hamid, Ghayarat Khan and Makramat Khan who also supervised the construction of the Taj (Sheila Blair and Jonathan Bloom, *The Art and Architecture of Islam*, New Haven, 1994).

4. Nadir Shah looted the Peacock Throne and brought it back to Persia in 1739–40. He also brought several other thrones, but they were all broken to pieces after his death. It is said that Nadir Shah had a duplicate made of the Peacock throne. The throne in the Gulistan Palace (Teheran) could well be this duplicate (Central Bank of Iran, *The Crown Jewels of Iran*, Teheran, 1964).

5. In fact, there were two Delhi Gates: the Delhi Gate of Red Fort (used by people working inside the fort) faces the Delhi Gate of the city.

6. Some historians believe that Haji Begum supervised the construction of Humayun's tomb after his death. But she was mostly in Mecca during the nine-year period of the tomb's construction. Therefore, it is doubtful that she was in charge of the day-to-day supervision of its construction (Ajit Bhalla, *Royal Tombs of India*, Ahmedabad, 2009).

7. Jean-Baptiste Tavernier, who visited India between 1640 and 1667 selling diamonds, believed that Shah Jahan had intended to build his own tomb of black marble (so-called Black Taj Mahal) opposite the Taj Mahal. However, many scholars do not share this view, as they have not found any mention of this in any historical records.

8. The Mughals also built other gardens in Lahore from the sixteenth to the eighteenth century. So did the later Sikh rulers, an outstanding example being Badami Bagh created by Maharaja Ranjit Singh (see Muhammad Latif, *Lahore*, Lahore, 1892, pp. 250–50b).

9. According to one estimate, Akbar's treasures amounted to 522.4 million florins (John de Laet, *The Empire of the Great Mughal*, Bombay, 1928). Francis Pelsaert and Ferishta (Muhammad Qasim Hindu Shah) estimate a figure of around Rs 10 crores (or Rs 100 million), besides seven million

gold *muhrs* and a vast amount of other treasures. Pelsaert was a Dutch merchant (*c.*1595–1630) who worked for the Dutch East India Company. He commanded a ship – the Batavia – which ran aground off the coast of Western Australia in June 1629. Ferishta was a Persian historian (1560–1620) who was appointed Captain of the guards of Sultan Murtaza Nizam Shah of Ahmadnagar in 1587. When Prince Miram overthrew his father, Nizam Shah, Ferishta moved to Bijapur in 1589, where he worked for Sultan Ibrahim Adil.

10. However, Akbar's dress was simpler and less ostentatious. He was rarely seen wearing any diamonds, only a necklace of pearls.

11. Niccolao Manucci worked at the Mughal court during Shah Jahan's reign as Dara Shekoh's (Shah Jahan's son) artilleryman. He wrote a detailed account of Mughal history, *Storia de Mogor* or *Mughal India* (London, 1907), but many historians consider it to be unreliable.

12. The Resident at the Mughal Court wielded powerful control over the emperor. At one time, his responsibilities were so great that a Commissioner was appointed to share them.

13. In a memorandum in 1948, Thomas Metcalfe proposed that the Emperor be moved to the Qutb. However, Lord Napier thought it would be better to send him to Fatehpur Sikri (Charles Napier, *Defects, Civil and Military in Indian Government*, London, 1853, p. 270).

14. The tongue of the son of a raja was cut off on the orders of Jahangir as punishment for keeping a Muslim concubine (Abraham Eraly, *The Mughal World*, New Delhi, 2007, p. 26).

15. The British colonial rulers used horses for transportation, sporting events and military manoeuvres. For example, the Bengal Lancer Regiment used them for tent pegging, using the lance to unearth tent pegs of the enemy. On Sunday afternoons, the British cavalry in India (and other parts of the empire in Southeast Asia and Africa) would compete in games on horseback to improve their readiness for war. In this respect, the British followed the Persians and Central Asians who used polo as a means of training their cavalry for warfare.

Chapter 5 Social Glimpses of the Raj

1. The Company men were very different from the Empire men. The former were considered to be 'sensuous and emotional and passionately devoted to [. . .] friends'. On the other hand, 'the Empire man was essentially boyish, inspired by team games and team spirit, whilst at the same time hating

physical contact and rampantly homophobic' (Antony Wild, *The East India Company*, London, 1999, p. 106).

2. Sir David Ochterlony (1758–1825), a Scotsman, was twice Resident in Delhi (1803–6 and 1818–22), but was better known for his conquest of Nepal in 1816.

3. In 1901, the first car in Madras was owned by Mr. A.J. Yorke, a director of Parry and Co., who used to drive daily from Ben's Garden in Adyar to Parry's in Black Town.

4. Indian guests were described by an English woman as 'a perfect bevy of princes, suave, watchful, ready at the slightest encouragement to crowd round the Resident, or the Commissioner, or the Brigadier, with noiseless white-stockinged feet. Equally ready to relapse into indifference when unnoticed' (cited in Denis Judd, *The British Raj*, Hove, 1964, p. 42).

5. Privy purses were allowances granted to the Indian princes from public revenue for their private expenses.

6. These were not British sports and were quite popular during the Mughal period, for example (Gail Simmons, POLO: Game of Kings, *Saudi Aramco World*, 2013). Babur was a polo player who established the game as a royal pastime.

7. Lord Moira, the Governor-General of Fort William from 1813 to 1823 (and Marquess of Hastings from 1816 onwards), visited Ghazi-al-din Haidar, the King of Oudh, to have dinner at his palace just after his accession in 1814 (See *The Private Journal of the Marquess of Hastings*, London, 1858.)

8. The Anglo-Indians are defined narrowly as those whose paternal (but not maternal) lineage can be traced back to England. Their origin is attributed to intermarriages between Company servants and native Indian women. They were openly discriminated against, barred from holding any civil or military office with the Company (Ronald Hyam, *Empire and Sexuality*, Manchester, 1990, p. 116). Later, they were banned from any Government House entertainment, and by 1835, all interracial marriages had been forbidden (see Antony Wild, *The East India Company*, London, 1999, p. 105). There were 300,000 to 500,000 Anglo-Indians at the time of India's independence.

9. James Skinner was an Anglo-Indian with a Scottish father and an Indian Rajput mother. As an Anglo-Indian of mixed blood, he was initially denied a commission by the Company. Peeved at this, he joined the forces of the Maratha Maharaja Scindia. When the British defeated the Marathas, 800 men on horses offered their services to the British on the condition that they would be led by James Skinner.

10. Willingdon Sports Club in Bombay established in the 1920s, was the only club which admitted Britons and Indians from the start (see Jan Morris and Simon Winchester, *Stones of Empire*, Oxford, 1983, p. 55).

11. The other noteworthy clubs were Madras Club (1831), the Byculla Club, Bombay (1833), and the Western India Turf Club, Bombay (1837).

12. Philip Davies (*Splendours of the Raj*, London, 1985, p. 36), remarks that 'Madras lacked a proper focus for informal social activities.' Although the project was a private initiative, it was endorsed by the then Governor, Stephen Lushington. Several buildings were acquired and extensions made to provide additional sports and residential facilities. Initially, a house and garden belonging to Thomas Webster was purchased for the Club, and in the following year (1832), an octagonal building of Italian marble was built. Gradually sports facilities were added as were the residential quarters.

13. The Bengal Club once had on display many beautiful portraits of eminent personalities of the Raj and other memorabilia, but these have now been removed.

14. In 1845, the Club moved from its original location on Tank Square to its present premises, which were at one time the residence of Lord Macaulay (Thomas Babington), Legal Member of the Governor-General's Council (1834–8).

15. Personal communication with Sandhya Sondhi, resident of Mumbai, January 2011. Sandhya was born and brought up in Bombay.

16. In the 1870s and 1880s, the Club was located in the Town Hall. In 1890, it moved to Ludlow Castle, an old Residency, and subsequently, it was moved out of the city (Narayani Gupta, *Delhi between Two Empires* 1803–1931, Delhi, 1981).

17. The word 'gymkhana' was first used by the British in Rurki (India) in 1861, and is attributed to Major John Trotter (*The Encyclopaedia Britannica*, Cambridge, 1910).

18. Jan Morris and Simon Winchester (*Stones of Empire*, Oxford, 1983, p. 61), believe that the gymkhana club provided lighter relief as it was an 'easier-going sort of place, where women and families were welcome, and it had tennis, badminton and racquet courts, skating-rinks sometimes, cricket-pitches, golf-links in later years, and a generally cheerful ambience'.

Chapter 6 Imperial Splendour of the Presidencies

1. Lady Gwillim was the wife of the Chief Justice of Madras. She wrote these lines in a letter to her mother and sister.

2. Kedleston Hall, built in a neoclassical style, belonged to the family of Lord Curzon. The family lived on an estate in Kedleston from the thirteenth century onwards. The Hall, run by the National Trust, contains a museum displaying various objects obtained by Lord Curzon during his tenure as Viceroy of India from 1899 to 1905.

3. Those who were denied recognition through statues included 'Sir John McPherson, Sir John Shore, Sir George Barlow, the first Lord Minto, Lord Amherst, Lord Ellenborough, the first and second Lords Elgin, Lord Lytton and Lord Ripon' (Curzon of Kedleston, *British Government in India*, London, 1925, vol. II, pp. 138–9).

4. Built in 1780, the Writers' Building was a hostel and training centre for the Company's young clerks or writers. It was replaced in the nineteenth century perhaps because it looked like barracks.

Chapter 7 Summer Capitals and Cantonments

1. The Mughal love for gardens dates back to Babur, the first Mughal emperor of India.

2. Val (Valentine) Cameron Prinsep was a writer and painter, and the son of Henry Thoby Prinsep, a wealthy Indian civil servant. He was born in India in 1836 and died in London in November 1904.

3. We owe this point to Krishnan Srinivasan, former Foreign Secretary, Government of India.

4. In 1815, Major-General Sir David Ochterlony put Lieutenant Robert Ross in charge of the Nasiri Batallion, an early Gurkha force. Later Lieutenant Ross was appointed assistant to Sir David Ochterlony in the latter's role as Superintendent of Political Affairs and Agent of the Governor-General in the territories of the Hill chiefs between Jamuna and the Sutlej rivers (Coleman, 1999).

5. The Lodge is now the Indian Institute of Advanced Study.

6. Osborne House was Queen Victoria's sprawling family home where she spent summers with her consort, Prince Albert, and her nine children. Designed by Prince Albert himself, it was built between 1845 and 1851 in the Italian Renaissance style. 'It is impossible to imagine a prettier spot', remarked the Queen on her first visit to the House. Queen Victoria died at the House in 1901.

7. I am grateful to Linda Staines of 'Clathymore', Tibbermore, Perthshire, Scotland, for drawing my attention to the Holme Craig.

8. Speaking about Bangalore, Winston Churchill notes: 'The British lines or cantonments are in accordance with invariable practice placed five or six

miles from the populous cities which they guard; and in the intervening space lie the lines of the Indian regiments' (Winston Churchill, *My Early Life*, London, 1930, p. 118fn).

Chapter 8 Palaces of Learning

1. Several boys from these schools (for example, Lawrence School, Sanawar) served in the British Army during World War I. A school chapel at Lawrence School was built in 1934 to honour them.

2. Lawrence was addressed as 'Sir' but not as 'Lord' or 'Viscount' because he was a 'baronet' and therefore, not a 'peer'. A 'baronetcy' is the only hereditary title that is not a 'peerage'. A baronet should not be confused with a baron who is entitled to be addressed as a lord. For more details, see *Burke's Peerage*, or a website, hereditarytitles.com.

3. Antony Wild (*Remains of the Raj*, London, 2001, p. 229), notes that Lawrence School Sanawar was built 'on a hill top near Kasauli donated to him (John Lawrence) by the Maharaja of Patiala'. In fact, the Maharaja of Patiala had no connection with the School. He had associations with Aitchison College, Lahore which may have led to this error.

4. Information supplied by Syed Babar Ali of Lahore, Pakistan, in a personal communication. Babar Ali is a member of the School's Governing Body. The history of the College can be traced to the Wards' School in Ambala, which in 1868 was intended as a school for the young Sikh wards (Sardars) of the District. However, later the scope of the school was broadened to admit all government wards living in other parts of the Punjab.

5. The choice of an appropriate architecture for Mayo school was not easy. Four different architects submitted seven different designs to three viceroys out of which Mant's Saracenic design was finally chosen (see Thomas Metcalf, *An Imperial Vision*, London, 1989, pp. 68–9).

Chapter 9 British India and the Mother Country

1. In the 1830s, Thomas Metcalfe built his house (named as the Metcalfe House) which is still standing. Metcalfe was the British Resident who, along with his brother, Lord Metcalfe, settled in Delhi.

2. Edward Lutyens did not know India and had never visited it.

3. Thomas Metcalf (*An Imperial Vision*, London, 1989) presents a detailed account of the conflicting views regarding the kind of architecture that would be most suitable for a new Imperial capital.

4. John Nicholson was a victim of the siege of Delhi during the 1857 uprising. Earlier, he had fought in the first Afghan war and the First and Second Sikh Wars. He is buried in a small overgrown cemetery outside Kashmiri Gate.

5. Metcalfe House now belongs to the Indian Ministry of Defence and houses the Defence Science Research Laboratory, and Ludlow Castle (which underwent many modifications) houses two state schools. The original castle has been replaced by a new red-brick building.

Chapter 10 Pomp, Extravaganza and Poverty

1. For example, Jahangir notes that it took 15–16 years to build the Agra Fort at a cost of Rs 3.5 million (Henry Beveridge, *Tuzuk-i-Jahangiri*, London, 1909). During his reign Akbar built 500 masonry buildings inside the fort besides Humayun's tomb (Abul Fazl, *Ain-i-Akbari*, Calcutta, 1894, vol. II).

2. John Richards (*The Mughal Empire*, Cambridge, 1993, p. 76), estimates that expenditure on the imperial household (including the harem and building construction) during Akbar's reign amounted to Rs 4.7 million. He continues: 'Akbar drew upon vast revenue to build up his treasure and to support his lavish expenditures on luxurious display' (p. 77).

3. William Moreland (*From Akbar to Aurangzeb*, London, 1923, p. 196), observes that Jahangir spent large sums of money on ornamental buildings in Agra and Lahore. Francis Pelsaert observes that 'numerous sarais and palaces were built by the Empress Nur Jahan [...] as an expression of her desire for lasting fame...' (cited in ibid., London, 1923, p. 197).

4. According to Mughal sources, Rs 50 lakhs (Rs 5 million) were spent on building activities (cited in Giles Tillotson, *Taj Mahal*, London, 2008, p. 81); Muhammad Salih, *Amal-i-Salih*, 1927, vol. 2, pp. 556–8), which was equivalent to the annual household budget.

5. According to Angus Maddison's estimates, from 1868 to the 1930s India's export surplus amounted to about 1 per cent of India's national income. In other words, about one-fifth of India's net savings 'which might otherwise have been used to import capital goods', were transferred to the United Kingdom. Furthermore, British personnel in India accounted for 5 per cent of India's national income (see Angus Maddison, *Contours of the World Economy*, Oxford, 2007, p. 121).

6. As noted by Angus Maddison (ibid.), p. 118, 'After 1757, when the EIC (East India Company) took over the governance of Bengal, the British relationship with India became exploitative.'

Bibliography

Abram, David, Devdan Sen, Nick Edwards, Mike Ford and Beth Wooldridge, *The Rough Guide to India* (London, Penguin Group, 2001).

Aijazuddin, F.S., *Aitchison College Lahore 1886–1986* (Lahore, Aitchison College, 1986).

———— *Lahore Recollected-An Album* (Lahore, Sang-e-Meel Publications, 2004).

Alam, Muzafar, 'Trade, State Policy and Regional Change: Aspects of Mughal-Uzbeck Commercial Relations c.1550–1750', *Journal of the Economic and Social History of the Orient*, vol. 37, no. 3, 1994.

Alfieri, Bianca Maria, *Islamic Architecture of the Indian Sub-continent* (London, Laurence King, 2000).

Allen, Charles (ed.), *Plain Tales of the Raj* (London, Century in association with Deutsch and the British Broadcasting Corporation, 1985).

Ansari, Muhammad Azhar, *Social Life of the Mughal Emperors* (Allahabad, Shanti Prakashan, 1974).

Appodorai, A., *Economic Conditions in Southern India* (1000–1500 AD) (Madras, University of Madras, 1936).

Ara, Matsuo, 'The Lodhi Rulers and the Construction of Tomb-Buildings in Delhi', *Acta Asiatica*, vol. 43, 1982.

Asher, Catherine B., *Architecture of Mughal India*, vol. I.4, The New Cambridge History of India (Cambridge, Cambridge University Press, 1992).

Ashraf, K.M., *Life and Conditions of the People of Hindustan (1200–1550 AD)* (New Delhi, Gyan Publishing House, 2000).

Badaoni, Abdul Qadir, *Muntakhab-ut-Tawarikh*, 3 vols, translated by G.S.A. Ranking, W.H. Lowe and T.W. Haig (Calcutta, Asiatic Society, 1884–1925).

Bairoch, P.,'International Industirlization Levels from 1750 to 1980', *Journal of European Economic History*, vol. 11, 1982.

Baker, Robert S. and James Sexton (eds), *Aldous Huxley Complete Essays*, vol. II, 1926–1929 (Chicago, Ivan R. Dee, 2000).

Ballhatchet, K., *Race, Sex and Class under the Raj: Imperial Attitudes and Policies and their Critics*, 1793–1905 (London, Weidenfeld and Nicolson, 1980).

Barani, Zia-ud-din, *Tarikh-i-Firoz Shahi* (Calcutta, Royal Asiatic Society of Bengal, 1862).

_____ *Fatwa-i-Jahandari* (Lahore, Idarah-i-Taqiqat-i-Pakistan, Danishgah-i-Punjab, 1972).

Barbosa, Duarte, *The Book of Duarte Barbosa: An Account of the Countries Bordering on the Indian Ocean and their Inhabitants*, 2 vols, translated by Mansel Longworth Dames (London, Hakluyt Society, 1918, 1921).

Barr, Pat, *The Memsahibs: The Women of Victorian India* (London, Secker and Warburg, 1976).

Barr, Pat and Ray Desmond, *Simla* (London, Scolar Press, 1982).

Bawa, Vasant Kumar, 'The Politics of Architecture in Qutb Shahi Hyderabad: A Preliminary Analysis', in M.A. Nayeem, Anirudhha Ray and K.S. Mathew (eds), *Studies in the History of the Deccan: Medieval and Modern* (Delhi, Pragati Publications, 2002).

Beaton, Cecil, *Indian Diary and Album* (Delhi, Oxford University Press, 1991).

Begley, W.E., The Myth of the Taj Mahal and a New Theory of its Symbolic Meaning,' *Art Bulletin*, March 1979.

Bence-Jones, Mark, *Palaces of the Raj: Magnificence and Misery of the Lord Sahibs* (London, Allen and Unwin, 1973).

Bernier, Francois, *Travels in Mogul Empire* AD *1656–1668* (London, Constable & Co., 1901).

Beveridge, H., *Tuzuk-i-Jahangiri (Memoirs of Jahangir)* 2 vols. Translated by A. Rogers (London, Royal Asiatic Society, 1909 and 1914).

Bhalla, A.S., *Royal Tombs of India* (Ahmedabad, Mapin, 2009).

_____ *Buddhist Art in Asia* (London, Austin Macauley, 2014).

'Bijapur,' *Gazetteer of the Bombay Presidency*, vol. XXIII, Bombay, Government Central Press, 1884.

Blair, S. and J. Bloom, *The Art and Architecture of Islam, 1250–1800* (New Haven, Yale University Press, 1994).

Blake, Stephen P., *Shahjahanabad: the Sovereign City in Mughal India 1639–1739* (Cambridge, Cambridge University Press, 1991).

Bose, Sugata and Ayesha Jalal, *Modern South Asia* (London, Routledge, 1998).

Brendon, Piers, *The Decline and Fall of the British Empire 1781–1997* (London, Jonathan Cape, 2007).

Brown, Percy, *Indian Architecture, Islamic Period* (Bombay, Taraporevala, 1956).

Brown, S. Sneade, *Home Letters written from India 1828–41* (London, C.F. Roworth, 1878; Paperback edition, 2011 by the Cambridge University Press).

Buck, Sir Edward J., *Simla, Past and Present* (Bombay, Times Press, 1925; originally published in 1904 by Thacker Spink of London).

Bunce, Frederick W., *Royal Palaces, Residences and Pavilions of India* (New Delhi, D.K. Printworld, 2006).

Bussagli, Mario, *Indian Miniatures* (London, Paul Hamlyn, 1969).

———— 'India of the Mauryas', in Bussagli and Sivaramamurti, *5000 Years of Indian Art* (Bombay, Tulsi Shah Enterprises, 1978).

Bussagli, Mario and C. Sivaramamurti, *5000 Years of the Art of India* (Bombay, Tulsi Shah Enterprises, 1978).

Byron, Robert, 'New Delhi', *Architectural Review*, January 1931.

Cain, P.J. and A.G. Hopkins, *British Imperialism: Innovation and Expansion, 1688–1914* (London, Longman, 1993).

Cannadine, David, *Ornamentalism: How the British Saw their Empire* (London, Allen Lane, The Penguin Press, 2001).

Central Bank of Iran (Bank Markazi Iran), *The Crown Jewels of Iran* (Teheran, 1964).

Chandel, S.L., *Early Medieval State* (New Delhi, Commonwealth Publishers, 1989).

Chandra, Satish, 'Standard of Living: Mughal India', in Tapan Raychaudhuri and Irfan Habib (eds), *The Cambridge Economic History of India, c.1200–1750*, vol. I (Cambridge, Cambridge University Press, 1982).

———— *Mughal Religious Policies, the Rajputs and the Deccan* (Delhi, Vikas Publishing House, 1993).

Chitnis, K.N., *Socio-Economic History of Medieval India* (New Delhi, Atlantic Publishers, 2009).

Chopra, P.N., *Some Aspects of Social Life during the Mughal Age (1526–1707)* (Jaipur, Shiva Lal Agarwala, 1963).

Churchill, Winston S., *My Early Life* (London, T. Butterworth, 1930).

Clarke, Basil F.L., *Anglican Cathedrals Outside the British Isles* (London, S.P.C.K., 1958).

Colas, Alejandro, *Empire* (Cambridge, Polity Press, 2007).

Coleman, A.P., *A Special Corps: The Beginnings of Gorkha Service with the British* (Edinburgh, Pentland Press, 1999).

Collins, Larry and Dominique Lapierre, *Freedom at Midnight* (New Delhi, Vikas Publishing House Pvt. Ltd., 1976).

Cunningham, Alexander, *Mahabodhi or the Great Buddhist Temple under the Bodhi Tree at Buddha-Gaya* (London, W.H. Allen & Co., 1892).

Curzon of Kedleston, 'Speeches by H.E. the Lord Curzon of Kedleston', in *Curzon Papers, India Office Records*, 4 vols. (Mss Eur. FIII/559, 1900–6).

———— *British Government in India: The Story of the Viceroys and Government Houses*, 2 vols. (London, Cassell, 1925).

Dagens, Bruno (ed.), *Mayamatam: Treatise of Housing, Architecture and Iconography*, 2 vols. (New Delhi, Motilal Banarsidass Publishers Pvt. Ltd., 1994).

Dalrymple, William, *City of Djinns* (London, Flamingo, 1994).

———— *White Mughals* (London, HarperCollins, 2002).

———— *The Last Mughal: The Fall of a Dynasty, Delhi, 1857* (London, Bloomsbury, 2009; Paperback edition) (first published 2006).

Davies, C.C., *Warren Hastings and Oudh* (London, Oxford University Press, 1939).

Davies, P., *Splendours of the Raj* (London, J. Murray, 1985).

Davis, L.E. and R.A., Huttenback, *Mammon and the Pursuit of Empire: The Political Economy of British Imperialism 1860–1912* (Cambridge, Cambridge University Press, 1986).

de Courcy, Anne, *The Fishing Fleet: Husband-hunting in the Raj* (London, Weidenfeld and Nicolson, 2012).

de Laet, John, *The Empire of the Great Mughal*, translated from Latin by J.S. Hoyland and S.N. Bannerjee (Bombay, D.B. Taraporevala, 1928).

Desai, A.V., 'Population and Standards of Living in Akbar's Time', *Indian Economic and Social History Review*, vol. 9, no. 1, January 1972.

Dhammika, Ven. S., *The Edicts of King Ashoka* (Berkeley, Dharma Net edition, 1994).

Dickens, Charles, *Oliver Twist* (London, Richard Bentley, 1838).

Digby, Simon, 'Northern India under the Sultanate: Economic Conditions before 1200', in Tapan Raychaudhuri and Irfan Habib (eds), *The Cambridge Economic History of India*, vol. I: c.1200–1750 (Cambridge, Cambridge University Press, 1982).

Disraeli, Benjamin, *Sybil or the Two Nations* (London, Thomas Nelson and Sons Ltd., 1845).

Diver, Maud, *The Englishwoman in India* (London, W. Blackwood, 1909).

Dodwell, H.H. (ed.), *Cambridge History of India, vol. 5 British India* (1497–1858) (Cambridge, Cambridge University Press, 1929).

Douglas, James, *Glimpses of Old Bombay and Western India* (London, Sampson, Low, Marston & Co., 1900).

Doyle, Michael W., *Empires* (Ithaca, Cornell University Press, 1986).

Dutt, R.C., *The Economic History of India Under Early British Rule* (London, Kegan Paul, 1902).

Eaton, Richard, M., *A Social History of the Deccan, 1300–1761, Eight Indian Lives*, The New Cambridge History of India, vol. I.8 (Cambridge, Cambridge University Press, 2005).

Edelstein, M., 'Imperialism: Cost and Benefit', in R. Floud and D. McClosky (eds), *The Economic History of Britain since 1700*, vol. II (Cambridge, Cambridge University Press, 1994).

Edwardes, Michael, *The Sahibs and the Lotus: The British in India* (London, Constable, 1988).

Edwards, S.M. and H.L.O. Garrett, *Mughal Rule in India* (Delhi, S. Chand, 1974).

Eldridge, C.C., *British Imperialism in the Nineteenth Century* (London, Macmillan, 1984).

Elliot, H. and J. Dowson, *The History of India as Told by its Own Historians: The Mohammadan Period*, vol. IV (London, Trübner & Co., 1867).

Eraly, Abraham, *Emperors of the Peacock Throne – The Saga of the Great Mughals* (New Delhi, Penguin Books, 1997).

———— *Gem in the Lotus – The Seeding of Indian Civilization* (London, Phoenix, 2005).

———— *The Mughal World – Life in India's last Golden Age* (New Delhi, Penguin Books, 2007).

———— *The First Spring: The Golden Age of India* (New Delhi, Penguin/Viking, 2011).

———— *The Age of Wrath: A History of the Delhi Sultanate* (New Delhi, Penguin/Viking, 2014).

Fanshawe, H.C., *Delhi: Past and Present* (London, J. Murray, 1902) (New Delhi, Asian Educational Services Reprint, 1998).

Fay, Eliza, *Original Letters from India 1779–1815* (London, 1817) (London, Hogarth Press, 1925 edition).

Fazl, Abul, *Ain-i-Akbari*, translation by H.S. Jarrett (Calcutta, Baptist Mission Press, 1894).

Ferguson, James, *History of Indian and Eastern Architecture* (London, J. Murray, 1910).

Ferguson, Niall, *Empire: How Britain Made the Modern World* (London, Allen Lane, 2003).

Ferishta, *Tarikh-i-Ferishta* (History of the Rise of the Mahomedan Power in India), translated by John Briggs, 2 vols. (Bombay, Government College Press, 1831).

Forbes, J., *Oriental Memoirs*, vol. IV (London, White, Cochrane & Co., 1813).

Foster, Sir W., *Early Travels in India* (London, Oxford University Press, 1921).

Fukuzawa, H., 'A Study of the Local Administration of the Adilshahi Sultanate (A.D. 1489–1686)', *Hitotsubashi Journal of Economics*, vol. III, no. 2, June 1963.

———— 'The State and the Economy: Maharashtra and the Deccan: A Note', in Tapan Raychaudhuri and Irfan Habib (eds), *The Cambridge Economic History of India*, vol. I: c.1200–1750 (Cambridge, Cambridge University Press, 1982a).

———— 'Standard of Living: Maharashtra and the Deccan', in Raychaudhuri and Habib (ibid., 1982b).

Furneaux, J.H. (ed.), *Glimpses of India* (Philadelphia, Historical Publishing Company, 1895).

Ganguli, B.N. (ed.), *Readings in Indian Economic History* (London, Asia Publishing House, 1964).

Garrett, H.L.O. and S.M. Edwardes, *Mughal Rule in India* (London, Oxford University Press, 1930).

Ghoshal, U.S., 'Economic Condition', in R.C Majumdar (ed.), *The Delhi Sultanate* (Bombay, Bharatiya Vidya Bhavan, 1960a).

———— 'Hindu Society' in R.C Majumdar (ed.), *The Delhi Sultanate* (Bombay, Bharatiya Vidya Bhavan, 1960b).

Grewal, J.S., *The Sikhs of the Punjab*, The New Cambridge History of India, vol. II.3 (Cambridge, Cambridge University Press, 1990).

Grover, Satish, *Islamic Architecture in India* (New Delhi, CBS Publishers and Distributors, 2002).

Gupta, Narayani, *Delhi Between Two Empires 1803–1931* (Delhi, Oxford University Press, 1981).

Habib, Irfan, *The Agrarian System of Mughal India* 1556–1707 (Bombay, Asia Publishing House, 1963).

———— 'Northern India under the Sultanate: Agrarian Economy', in Tapan Raychaudhuri and Irfan Habib (eds), *The Cambridge Economic History of India*, vol. I: *c.*1200–1750 (Cambridge, Cambridge University Press, 1982a).

———— 'Northern India under the Sultanate: Non-agricultural Production and Urban Economy', in Raychaudhuri and Habib (ibid., 1982b).

———— (ed.), *Medieval India vol. I* (Delhi, Oxford University Press, 1992).

Habib, Mohammad and Khaliq Ahmad Nizami (eds), *A Comprehensive History of India, The Delhi Sultanate* (AD 1206–1526) (Delhi, People's Publishing House, 1970).

Haidar, Raana, 'The Bengal Club: Club of Clubs', Parts I and II, *HOLIDAY Metropolitan*, 15 and 21 February 2008.

Haig, Wolseley and Richard Burn (eds), *The Cambridge History of India*, vol. IV on the Mughal Period (Cambridge, Cambridge University Press, 1937).

Hambly, G., *Cities of Mughal India* (New York, G.P. Putnam's Sons, 1968).

———— 'Towns and Cities: Mughal India' in Tapan Raychaudhuri and Irfan Habib (eds), *The Cambridge Economic History of India*, vol. I: *c.*1200–1750 (Cambridge, Cambridge University Press, 1982).

Harlow, Barbara and Mia Carter, *Imperialism and Orientalism: A Documentary Sourcebook* (Oxford, Blackwell, 1999).

Hill, John, *Maharajas in the Making: Life at the Eton of India* 1935–40 (Lewes, Book Guild, 2001).

Hobson, John M., *The Eastern Origins of Western Civilisation* (Cambridge, Cambridge University Press, 2004).

Hodges, William, *Travels in India During the Years 1780, 1781, 1782 and 1783* (London, J. Edwards, 1793).

Holman, D., *Sikandar Sahib: the Life of Col. James Skinner, 1778–1841* (London, Heinemann, 1961).

Hutchings, F.G., *The Illusion of Permanence: British Imperialism in India* (New Jersey, Princeton University Press, 1967).

Huxley, Aldous, 'Agra and Fatehpur Sikri', in Jesting Pilate (1926) reprinted in Robert S. Baker and James Sexton (eds), *Aldous Huxley: Complete Essays*, vol. II, 1926–1929 (Chicago, Ivan R. Dee, 1926, 2000).

Hyam, Ronald, *Empire and Sexuality: The British Experience* (Manchester, Manchester University Press, 1990).

Irving, Robert Grant, *Indian Summer: Lutyens, Baker and Imperial Delhi* (New Haven, Yale University Press, 1981).

James, Lawrence, *The Rise and Fall of the British Empire* (London, Macmillan, 1994).

——— *Raj: The Making and Unmaking of British India* (London, Little, Brown and Company, 1997).

Jeffrey, R. (ed.), *People, Princes and Paramount Power: Society and Politics in Indian Princely States* (New Delhi, Oxford University Press, 1978).

Judd, Denis, *The British Raj* (Hove, Wayland Publishers, 1972).

——— *The Lion and the Tiger: The Rise and Fall of the British Raj 1600–1947* (Oxford, Oxford University Press, 2004).

Kaye, M.M. (ed.), *The Golden Calm – An English Lady's Life in Moghul Delhi* (Bayley, Lady Emily Clive) (Exeter, Webb and Bower, 1980).

Keay, John, *The Honourable Company: A History of the East India Company* (London, HarperCollins, 1991).

Keene, H.G., *The Fall of the Moghul Empire* (London, W.H. Allen, 1876).

Khan, Inayat (Shajahan's courtier), *Shahjahan Nama*, translated by W.E. Begley and Z.A. Desai (Delhi, Oxford University Press, 1990).

Khan, Manju and K.J. Parel, *SANAWAR – A Legacy* (Solan, HP, Systems, 2007).

Khan, Omar, *From Kashmir to Kabul* (Ahmedabad, Mapin; Munich, Prestel, 2001).

Kincaid, Dennis, *British Social Life in India 1608–1937* (London, Routledge & Kegan Paul, 1938).

Kumar, Dharma, 'Regional Economy: South India', in Dharma Kumar and Megnad Desai, *The Cambridge Economic History of India*, vol. 2 (Cambridge, Cambridge University Press, 1983).

Kumar, Dharma and Megnad Desai (eds), *The Cambridge Economic History of India*, Vol. 2, *c*.1751–*c*.1970 (Cambridge, Cambridge University Press, 1983).

Labh, Vijay Lakshmi, *Contributions to the Economy of Early Medieval India* (New Delhi, Radha Publications, 1996).

Lal, Deepak, *In Defence of Empires*, Wendt Lecture at the American Enterprise Institute, Washington DC, October 2002.

Lal, K.S., *Twilight of the Sultanate* (London, Asia Publishing House, 1963).

—————— *History of the Khaljis 1290–1320* (Bombay, Asia Publishing House, 1967).

Lallanji, Gopal, *Economic Life of Northern India, 700–1200* (Delhi, Motilal Banarasidass, 1965).

Latif, S.M., *Lahore: Its History, Architectural Remains and Antiquities* (Lahore, New Imperial Press, 1892) (reprinted by Sang-E-Meel Publications, 1994).

Lawson, Philip, *The East India Company: A History* (London, Longman, 1993).

Lee-Warner, W., *The Protected Princes of India* (London. Macmillan, 1894).

Lehmann, J.H., *All Sir Garnet: Life of Field Marshall Lord Wolseley* (London, Jonathan Cape, 1964).

Lloyd, T.O., *The British Empire 1558–1983* (Oxford, Oxford University Press, 1984).

Maddison, Angus, *Class Structure and Economic Growth: India and Pakistan since the Mughals* (London, Allen and Unwin, 1971).

—————— '*World Population, GDP and Per Capita GDP, 1–2000 AD*', http//www.ggdc.net/Maddison/content.shtml, 2004.

—————— *The World Economy* (Paris, OECD Development Centre, 2006).

—————— *Contours of the World Economy 1–2030 AD: Essays in Macroeconomic History* (Oxford, Oxford University Press, 2007).

Maharaja of Baroda, *The Palaces of India* (London, Collins, 1980).

Majumdar, R.C. (ed.), *The Delhi Sultanate* (Bombay, Bharatiya Vidya Bhavan, 1960).

Mangan, J.A., 'Eton in India: The Imperial Diffusion of a Victorian Educational Ethic', *History of Education*, vol. 7, 1978.

Mannuci, Niccolao, *Storia do Mogor* (Mughal India) translated by William Irvine (London, J. Murray, 1907).

Marathé, Kaumudi, *Temples of India: Circles of Stone* (Mumbai, Eshwar, 1998).

Marshall, John, 'The Monuments of Muslim India', in Sir Wolseley Haig (ed.), *The Cambridge History of India*, vol. III on the *Turks and Afghans* (Cambridge, Cambridge University Press, 1928).

Marshall, P.J., 'The Personal Fortune of Warren Hastings', *Economic History Review*, vol. 17, 1964.

——— *East Indian Fortunes: The British in Bengal in the 18th Century* (Oxford, Clarendon Press, 1976).

——— (ed.), *The Cambridge Illustrated History of the British Empire* (Cambridge, Cambridge University Press, 1996).

——— (ed.), *The Oxford History of the British Empire, vol. II, The Eighteenth Century* (Oxford, Oxford University Press, 1998).

Mayhew, A., *The Education of India* (London, Faber and Gwyer, 1926).

Mayhew, Henry, *London Labour and the London Poor*, 4 vols. (London, Griffin, Bohen & Co., 1861).

Metcalf, Barbara and Thomas Metcalf, *A Concise History of India* (Cambridge, Cambridge University Press, 2002).

Metcalf, Thomas, R., *The Aftermath of Revolt: India 1857–1870* (Princeton, Princeton University Press, 1964).

——— *An Imperial Vision: Indian Architecture and British Raj* (Berkeley, California University Press and London, Faber & Faber, 1989).

Meyer, K.E. and S.B. Brysac, *Tournament of Shadows* (London, Abacus, 1999).

Michell, George and Mark Zebrowski, *Architecture and Art of the Deccan Sultanates*, vol. I.7, The New Cambridge History of India (Cambridge, Cambridge University Press, 1999).

Mirza, M.W., 'Muslim Religion and Society', in R.C Majumdar (ed.), *The Delhi Sultanate* (Bombay, Bharatiya Vidya Bhavan, 1960).

Monserrat, Father Anthony, *Journey to the Court of Akbar*, translated by J.S. Hoyland (London, Oxford University Press, H. Milford, 1922).

Moorcroft, W., *Travels in the Himalayan Provinces of Hindustan and the Punjab, from 1819 to 1825*, edited by H.H. Wilson (London, J. Murray, 1841).

Moorhouse, Geoffrey, *Calcutta* (London, Weidenfeld, 1971).

Moosvi, Shireen, 'Production, Consumption and Population in Akbar's Time', *Indian Economic and Social History Review*, vol. 10, no. 2, 1973.

——— *The Economy of the Mughal Empire: c.1595: A Statistical Study* (Delhi, Oxford University Press, 1987).

Moraes, Dom, *Bombay* (Amsterdam, Time-Life, 1979).

Moreland, W.H., *India at the Death of Akbar: An Economic Study* (London, Macmillan, 1920).

——— *From Akbar to Aurangzeb* (London, Macmillan, 1923).

Morison, T., *Imperial Rule in India* (London, A. Constable and Co., 1899).

Morris, Ellen, K., 'Symbols of Empire: Architectural Style and the Government Offices Competition', *Journal of Architectural Education*, vol. 32, 1978.

Morris, James, *Pax Britannica: The Climax of an Empire* (London, Faber, 1980).

Morris, Jan and Robert Fermor-Hesketh (eds), *Architecture of the British Empire* (London, Wiedenfeld and Nicolson, 1986).

Morris, Jan and Simon Winchester, *Stones of Empire: The Buildings of British India* (Oxford, Oxford University Press, 1983).

Moxham, Roy, *The Great Hedge of India* (New York, Carroll and Graf Publishers, Inc., 2001).

Mukherjee, Sumita, *Nationalism, Education and Migrant Identities – The England-returned* (Abingdon, Routledge, 2009).

Napier, C.J., *Defects, Civil and Military in Indian Government* (London, Charles Westerton, 1853).

Naqvi, Hamida Khatoon, *Agricultural, Industrial and Urban Dynamism under the Sultans of Delhi 1206–1555* (New Delhi, Munshiram Manoharlal Publishers, 1986).

Naqvi, S.A.A., *Humayun's Tomb and Adjacent Buildings* (New Delhi, Archaeological Survey of India, 2002).

Nehru, Jawahar Lal, *The Discovery of India* (London, Meridian Books, 1946).

Nilsson, Sten, *European Architecture in India* 1750–1850 (London, Faber, 1968).

Nizami, Khaliq Ahmed, *Royalty in Medieval India* (Delhi, Munshiram Manoharlal, 1997).

Nurullah, Syed and J.P. Naik, *A History of Education in India (During the British Period)* (Bombay, Macmillan, 1951).

O'Brien, Patrick, 'The Costs and Benefits of British Imperialism 1846–1914', *Past and Present*, vol. 120, 1988.

Orlich, Leopold von, *Travels in India* translated from the German by H.E. Lloyd (London, Longman, 1845).

Pandey, S.N., *Economic History of Modern India* (1757 to 1947) (New Delhi, Readworthy, 2008).

Panikkar, K.M., *A Survey of Indian History* (New Delhi, Asia Publishing House, 1947).

Panter-Downes, Molly, *Ooty Preserved* (London, Century, 1967).

Parthasarathi, P., *Why Europe Grew Rich and Asia Did Not* (Cambridge, Cambridge University Press, 2011).

Paxman, Jeremy, *Empire: What Ruling the World Did to the British* (London, Penguin Books, 2011).

Peck, Lucy, *Delhi – A Thousand Years of Building* (New Delhi, Roli Books Pvt. Ltd., 2005).

Pelsaert, F., *Jahangir's India* (translated by W.H. Moreland and P. Geyl) (Cambridge, Cambridge University Press, 1925).

Porter, Bernard, *Critics of Empire: British Radicals and the Imperial Challenge* (London, Macmillan, 1968).

Prasad, Beni, *History of Jahangir* (London. Oxford University Press, H. Milford, 1922).

Prinsep, Val C., *Imperial India* (London, Chapman and Hall, 1879).

'Quetta', *First Queen's Regimental Journal*, November 1935.

Rahim, M.A, *History of the Afghans in India* AD *1545–1631* (Karachi, Pakistan Publishing House, 1961).

Ramusack, B.N., *The Princes of India in the Twilight of Empire* (Columbus, Ohio State University Press, 1978).

Ransom, James, 'European Architecture in India', *Journal of the Royal Institute of British Architects*, 3rd ser., vol. 12, 1905.

Rasmussen, S.E., *London: the Unique City* (London, Jonathan Cape, 1937).

'Rawalpindi Town', *The Imperial Gazetteer of India*, vol. 20, 1883.

Raychaudhuri, T., 'A Reinterpretation of Nineteenth Century Indian Economic History', *Indian Economic and Social History Review*, March 1968.

_____ *Bengal under Akbar and Jahangir* (Delhi, Munshiram Manoharlal, 1969).

_____ 'The State and the Economy: The Mughal Empire', in Tapan Raychaudhuri and Irfan Habib (eds), *The Cambridge Economic History of India*, vol. I: *c.*1200–1750 (Cambridge, Cambridge University Press, 1982a).

_____ 'Non-agricultural Production: Mughal India', Raychaudhuri and Habib (ibid., 1982b).

_____ 'The Mid-Eighteenth Century Background', in Dharma Kumar and Megnad Desai (eds), *The Cambridge Economic History of India*, vol. 2, *c.*1751-*c.*1970 (Cambridge, Cambridge University Press, 1983).

Richards, John F., *The Mughal Empire*, vol. I.5, New Cambridge History of India (Cambridge, Cambridge University Press, 1993).

Ridge, Mian, 'Remnants of a Colonial Past in India', *International Herald Tribune*, 14–15 August 2010.

Roberts, Emma, *Scenes and Characteristics of Hindoustan*, 3 vols. (London, W.H. Allen & Co., 1835).

Roy, Tirthankar, *An Economic History of Early Modern India* (Abingdon, Routledge, 2013).

Ruggles, D. Fairchild, *Islamic Gardens and Landscapes* (Philadelphia, University of Pennsylvania Press, 2008).

Rushbrook-Williams, L.F., *An Empire Builder of the Sixteenth Century* (London, Longmans, Green & Co., 1918).

Rutherford, Alex, *Empire of the Mughal: Raiders from the North* (London, Headline Review, 2009).

_____ *Empire of the Mughal: Brothers at War* (London, Headline Review, 2010).

——— *Empire of the Mughal: Ruler of the World* (London, Headline Review, (2011).

——— *Empire of the Mughal: The Tainted Throne* (London, Headline Review, 2012).

Said, Edward, *Orientalism* (London, Routledge & Kegan Paul, 1978).

Salih, Muhammad, *Amal-i-Salih*, vol. 1 (1923), vol. 2 (1927), vol. 3 (1928) (Calcutta, Royal Asiatic Society of Bengal, 1923–39).

Santen, Han Walther Van, 'Trade between Mughal India and the Middle East, and Mughal Monetary Policy c.1600–1660', in Karl Haellquist (ed.), *Asian Trade Routes* (London, Curzon Press, 1991).

Sarkar, Jadunath, *History of Aurangzeb*, 5 vols. (Calcutta, M.C. Sarkar & Sons, 1912–25).

——— *Shivaji and his Times* (Calcutta, M.C. Sarkar & Sons, 1919).

——— *Fall of the Mughal Empire*, 4 vols. (Calcutta, M.C Sarkar & Sons, 1932).

Sarkar, Jagdish Narain, *Studies in Economic Life in Mughal India* (Delhi, Oriental Publishers, 1975).

Sastri, N. and K.A. Aiyar, *A History of South India* (Madras, Oxford University Press, 1966).

Schneer, J., *London 1900: The Imperial Metropolis* (New Haven, Yale University Press, 1999).

Sewell, Robert, *A Forgotten Empire: Vijayanagar* (London, S. Schonnenchein & Co. Ltd., 1900) (translation of the Chronicle of Fernao Nuniz).

Sharp, H., *DELHI: Its Story and Buildings* (London, Oxford University Press, 1921).

Shepperd, Samuel T., *The Byculla Club 1833–1916* (Bombay, Bennett & Coleman, 1916).

Siddiqi, Asiya (ed.), *Trade and Finance in Colonial India*, 1750–1860 (Delhi, Oxford University Press, 1995).

Simmons, Gail, 'POLO: Game of Kings', *Saudi Armaco World*, July–August 2013.

Singh, Hemani, *Recovering Delhi's Red Fort: Presence of Past in the Present*, MA Thesis, Technological University of Eindhoven, the Netherlands, 2010.

Singh, Khushwant, *Kalighat to Calcutta 1690–1990* (New Delhi, Lustre Press, 1990).

Singh, Vidyotma, *Indian Society* (Delhi, Vista International, 2006).

Sivaramamurti, C., 'The Art of Medieval Hindu India' in Bussagli and Sivaramamurti, *5000 Years of Indian Art* (London, Paul Hamlyn. 1978).

Smith, Vincent A., 'A Greco-Roman Influence on the Civilisation of Ancient India', *Journal of the Asiatic Society of Bengal*, vol. 58, 1889.

——— *AKBAR: The Great Mughal 1542–1605* (Oxford, Clarendon Press, 1892).

Spear, Percival, *Twilight of the Mughals* (Cambridge, Cambridge University Press, 1951).

———— *The Nabobs; A Study of the Social Life of the English in Eighteenth Century India* (London, Oxford University Press, 1963).

———— *A History of India*, vol. 2 (London. Penguin Books, 1990).

———— *Delhi – Its Monuments and History* (Delhi, Oxford University Press, 1994).

Sriram, V., 'Unsung Hero of Madras', *The Hindu Magazine* (Sunday), 25 July 2010.

Stamp, Gavin, 'Victorian Bombay: Urbs Prima in Indis', *Art and Archaeology Papers*, no. 11, June 1977.

———— 'British Architecture in India', 1857–1947, *Journal of the Royal Society of Arts*, no. 129, 1981.

'Statue of the Queen at Bombay', *Illustrated London News*, 8 June 1872.

Stein, Burton, 'Vijayanagara c.1350–1564', in Tapan Raychaudhuri and Irfan Habib (eds), *The Cambridge Economic History of India*, vol. I: c.1200–1750 (Cambridge, Cambridge University Press, 1982).

———— *Vijayanagara*, The New Cambridge History of India, vol. I.2 (Cambridge, Cambridge University Press, 1989).

Stockwell, Sarah (ed.), *The British Empire: Themes and Perspectives* (Oxford, Oxford University Press, 2008).

Tadjell, Christopher, *The History of Architecture in India* (London, Architecture Design and Technology Press, 1990).

Tavernier, Jean-Baptiste, *Travels in India*, translated by VD Ball, 2 vols. (London, Macmillan, 1889).

Thapar, Romila, *A History of India*, vol. 1 (New Delhi, Penguin Books, 1990).

The Encyclopaedia Britannica, 'Gymkhana', 11th Edition (Cambridge, at the University Press, 1910).

The Marchioness of Bute (ed.), *The Private Journal of the Marquess of Hastings* (London, Saunders & Otley, 1858).

The New Encyclopaedia Britannica, 'History of the Indian Subcontinent', vol. 9, 1981.

Thompson, E., *The Making of the Indian Princes* (London, Oxford University Press, H. Milford, 1943).

Thompson, E. and G.T. Garratt, *The Rise and Fulfilment of British Rule in India* (London, Macmillan & Co., 1934).

Tillotson, Giles, *Taj Mahal* (London, Profile Books, 2008).

Tindall, Gillian, *City of Gold: The Biography of Bombay* (London, Temple Smith, 1982).

Tomlinson, B.R., *The Economy of Modern India 1860–1970* (Cambridge, Cambridge University Press, 1989).

Tripathi, R.P., *Some Aspects of Muslim Administration* (Allahabad, Indian Press, 1936).

Useem, John and Ruth Hill Useem, *The Western Educated Man in India: A Study of his Social Roles and Influence* (New York, Drysden Press, 1955).

Valentia, Viscount, *Voyages and Travels to India, Ceylon . . . in the Years 1802, 1803, 1804, 1805 and 1806*, vol. I (London, William Miller, 1809).

Vernède, R.V., *British Life in India* (Delhi, Oxford University Press, 1997).

Victoria and Albert Museum, *The Indian Heritage: Court Life and Arts under Mughal Rule* (London, V&A Museum, 1982).

Watson, Francis, *A Concise History of India* (London, Thames and Hudson, 1979).

Wavell, Archibald, *The Viceroy's Journal* edited by P. Moon (Oxford, Oxford University Press, 1973).

Wells, H.G., *The Outline of History* (London, Cassell and Company Ltd., 1920).

Werner, Louis and David Wells, 'Bijapur: Gem of the Deccan', *Saudi Aramco World*, vol. 64, no. 2, 2013.

White, Jerry, *London in the Nineteenth Century: A Human Awful Wonder of God* (London, Jonathan Cape, 2007).

———— *London in the 18th Century: A Great and Monstrous Thing* (London, Vintage, 2012).

Wild, Antony, *The East India Company: Trade and Conquest from 1600* (London, HarperCollins, 1999).

———— *Remains of the Raj: The British Legacy in India* (London, HarperCollins, 2001).

Wilson, C., *England's Apprenticeship 1603–1763* (London, Longmans, 1965).

Winks, R.W., *The Oxford History of the British Empire* (Oxford, Oxford University Press, 1999).

Woodruff, Philip, *The Men Who Ruled India*, vol. 1 *The Founders*, and vol. 2, *The Guardians* (London, Jonathan Cape, 1963).

Wright, Gillian, *Hill Stations of India* (New Delhi, Penguin Books, 1998).

Yazdani, G. (ed.), *The Early History of the Deccan* (London, Oxford University Press, 1960).

Yule, Col. H. and A.C. Burnell (eds), *Hobson-Jobson: A Glossary of Anglo-Indian Colloquial Words and Kindred Terms, Etymological, Historical, Geographical and Discursive* (London, J. Murray, 1886).

Index

Plate 1 Ashoka Pillar, Vaishali (Courtesy of Wikimedia Commons)

Plate 2 Qutb Minar, New Delhi (Author's Private Collection)

Plate 3 Shah Jahan, the Master Builder (© Victoria and Albert Museum, London)

Interior of Dewan-Khas, Fort Delhi.
Built by the Emperor Shahjahan between 1638 & 1648 A. D.

Plate 4 Interior Inlay Decorations, Diwan-i-Khas, Red Fort (Author's Private Collection)

Plate 5 Peacock Throne, Red Fort (© Victoria and Albert Museum, London)

Plate 6 Humayun's Tomb through a Pavilion Arch, Delhi (Author's Private Collection)

Plate 7 Interior View of the Shish Mahal, Lahore Fort (Courtesy of A. Zaman)

Plate 8 David Ochterlony with Indian Nautch Girls (© The British Library Board, London)

Plate 9 Fort St George on the Coromandel Coast, Madras (© *The British Library Board, London*)

Plate 10 Aerial View of New Delhi with War Memorial, Viceregal Lodge and Secretariat (Courtesy of R.K. Ahooja)

Lightning Source UK Ltd.
Milton Keynes UK
UKHW021335170320
360484UK00005B/280